Sanctissimo ac Beatissimo
Patri
& D. N. Sixto Quinto
Pontifici Maximo
Cæsar Baronius Congregationis
Oratorij Presbyter sempiternam
felicitatem.

Quod a Beato Apostolo Paulo in re
maximi momenti aliquando dictum
est: Nè qui plantat est aliquid, neque qui rigat, sed qui incrementum
dat, Deus: id ego, Pater Beatissime,
in annalibus meis Ecclesiasticis con-
ficiendis plane sum expertus. Neque
enim deliberate ac consulto tantum
opus, ante annos circiter triginta
aggressus sum; nec meis viribus fre-
tus, quas nullas aut perexiguas
esse intelligebam, ad universam historiam Ecclesiasticam maximis difficul-
tatibus involutam, explicandam
accessi: ~~qui id ab initio ne cogitare quidem
ausus eram, a quo omne
datum optimum descendit~~, ita dispo-
nente, ac paulatim, me propemo-
dum inscio, incrementum dante, ea
paruulo semine non parua arbor
est exorta.

qui id ab initio ne cogitare quidem
ausus eram; sed Deo ipso, a quo omne datum optimum descendit, ita dis-
ponente, ac paulatim, me propemo-
dum inscio, incrementum dante, ea paruulo semine non parua arbor est
exorta.

Ciò che in negotio di grandissima impor-
tanza disse una uolta il Dottor delle Gen-
ti S. Paulo: Nè qui plantat est aliquid ne
que qui rigat, sed qui incrementum dat,
Deus: questo stesso ho esperimentato io
al uiuo, Padre Beatissimo, nella com-
positione delli miei Ecclesiastici Annali. Imperoche che non cominciai delibera-
mente, e con animo risoluto una opera cosi grande trenta anni prima in
circa; ne meno confidato nelle mie forze,
quali esser nulle, o molto picciole co-
nosceuo, diedi principio ad esplicare
tutta l'historia Ecclesiastica inuolta
in grauissime difficultà: il che non ha
uorei hauuto ardire ne meno ci pensa-
re dal principio: ma disponendo con tale
fatte Dio! A quo omne datum optimum
descendet: et a poco a poco dando l'au-
mento, io quasi non sapendo, da un picciol
seme non picciola pianta è risorta.

CAESAR BARONIUS

Cardinal Caesar Baronius, 1538–1607

CAESAR BARONIUS,

Counter-Reformation Historian

Cyriac K. Pullapilly

UNIVERSITY OF NOTRE DAME PRESS

NOTRE DAME   LONDON

End sheets: Draft letter of Cardinal Caesar Baronius
dedicating a volume of the *Annales* to Pope Sixtus V.

Library of Congress Cataloging in Publication Data

Pullapilly, Cyriac K
    Caesar Baronius, Counter-Reformation historian.

    Bibliography: p.
    Includes index.
    1. Baronio, Cesare, Cardinal, 1538–1607. I. Title.
BX4705.B2P8   270'.09 [B]   74–12567
ISBN 0–268–00501–X

TO

MY MOTHER

ANNA PULLAPILLY

Whose countless sacrifices for
my sake are surpassed only by
her faith and piety.

Publication of this volume
was assisted by a grant from
The American Council of Learned Societies
as a result of a grant from the Andrew W. Mellon Foundation

Contents

Preface

Caesar Baronius lived in a period of bitter controversy, perhaps unparalleled, in the history of Western civilization. Confrontations between Catholics and Protestants on the theological front were not only ideological disputes, as they would be today, but were explosive situations in a very literal sense.

Theological arguments not only broke the unity of the Western Church but also led to armed conflicts between groups and nations, and they eventually helped create what sociologists like Max Weber call the Protestant culture, a culture perhaps just as distinct from the medieval culture as the theological foundations of the new churches were distinct from those of the old church. The sixty-nine-year period which covered the life span of Baronius, 1538–1607, saw the irreversible alienation of the dissident groups, a corresponding tendency toward rigidity in the old church, and, of course, the beginnings of the so-called new culture.

Baronius represented, as a person and as a historian, the old church and the old culture. He did not start his public career until after the Council of Trent finally drove a wedge between Catholicism and Protestantism, but he wholeheartedly endorsed the Tridentine definitions and supported the Tridentine spirit.

He could not have done otherwise, because he remained all his life essentially an old-fashioned Catholic, nurtured in the medieval piety which had been characteristic of the hinterland of southern Italy, untouched by the Christian humanist or early evangelical movements. In confronting the Protestants he sought, as most Catholic leaders did in those days, a total victory over them—a complete submission of the Protestants to the papal authority and an acceptance by them not only of the Tridentine theological precepts but also the old ecclesiastical order. The question of concession or conciliation was not to be considered at all—total victory was the goal.

Indeed the Catholics were successful in achieving total victory in many parts of Europe, thanks to the concerted efforts of religious orders and the papacy, and, of course, the help of secular rulers. Theological and historical treatises also entered into the picture, at least as tools in the hands of Catholic educators and preachers.

Not the least of these tools was the *Annales Ecclesiastici* of Baronius. Though originally conceived as a series of informal sermons on the history of the Church to a devout group of Catholics who frequented Philip Neri's oratory in Rome, the *Annales* grew into a work of monumental proportions; it eclipsed the *Magdeburg Centuries*—which had created much consternation among Catholics—and provided definitive historical evidence, at least for believing Catholics, for the validity of the hierarchical order of the Church which had been questioned by the Protestants.

Baronius' lifelong work on the history of the Church resulted not only in the compilation of the *Annales* but also in the collection and codification of an enormous amount of historical data, a feat never before accomplished by one man. He systematically scrutinized and correctly used in the *Annales* at least a major portion of these data, although not in a literary style and analytical form which his humanist predecessors and contemporaries would have employed. Baronius broke new ground in historical investigation, to earn the title of the father of modern church history.

His fame as a scholar was only a step toward his rise as a public figure in the sixteenth century. A country boy from Sora, who had once been abandoned by his own father and thus had to depend on the charity of Philip Neri and a Roman noble family, became a confidant of popes and powerful monarchs. He was elevated to the cardinalate. And he barely missed being elected pope in two conclaves. The success of the *Annales* as an effective weapon of the Counter-Reformation and the emergence of Baronius as a powerful figure in the Vatican form a single story of a man and his book which will be treated as such in the following pages.

Acknowledgments

Professor Eric W. Cochrane of The University of Chicago has been to me what St. Philip Neri had been to Baronius, a constant inspiration, except that in this case the mentor extended his help in many tangible ways as well. He will have my enduring gratitude.

Professors Hanna Holborn Gray and Donald F. Lach of The University of Chicago, Professor Hans Baron of The Newberry Library and The University of Chicago, Professor George H. Williams of Harvard University, Professor Matthew A. Fitzsimons of the University of Notre Dame and the late Professor John T. McNeill of the Union Theological Seminary have read the manuscript in various stages and offered many helpful suggestions. I extend my gratitude to them.

The generosity of the late Archbishop Bernard J. Sheil of Chicago and his Educational Trust enabled me to travel in 1964 to Rome to collect the data for this book. The hospitality of the late Eugene Cardinal Tisserant enabled me to live in Rome for a year. His kindness also helped me obtain free access to the Vatican Library, of which he was the director at that time, and to the Vatican Archives. To them my undying gratitude.

Doctor Sergio Mottironi of the Vallicelliana Library and his staff were most helpful to me during my tenure in Rome. When the librarians of The University of Chicago kindly accepted my rather preposterous suggestion of microfilming all the Baronius documents at Vallicella, Doctor Mottironi and his staff spent countless hours helping in the tedious process. And it was they also who responded promptly to my many requests for additional microfilm copies of various documents. My profound gratitude to them.

To all the librarians of the various libraries of The University of Chicago, especially those gentlemen and ladies of the Swift

Library, who have been most gracious in permitting me what amounted to a monopolistic use of the microfilms, books, and other documents relating to Baronius studies that were acquired from Europe, my many thanks.

My heartfelt thanks also to Miss Emily Schossberger and Mr. John Ehmann under whose directorship of the University of Notre Dame Press the process of the publication of this book was initiated, and to Mr. James R. Langford under whose directorship it was completed.

My thanks also to Mrs. Emmy Lou Papandria who was very tolerant in preparing the final copy of the manuscript from my unmanageable longhand.

I must express my gratitude also to the American Council of Learned Societies which saw fit to give a grant to the University of Notre Dame Press toward the publication cost of this work.

Finally, my eternal gratitude to my wife, Elizabeth, and our little daughter, Kavita, of whom I made undue demands and whose understanding and affection sustained me during the preparation of this book.

1

Early Years

Caesar Baronius was born on Wednesday, October 31, 1538. His parents, Camillo Barone[1] and Portia Foebonia, were leading citizens of Sora, an ancient city in the kingdom of Naples about seventy miles north of the capital. The family was rich and had been well-known for generations. It was also noted for its piety, or at least for its performance of what then were considered the essential external signs of piety—not the least of which was paying for extensive repairs on the long decayed and delapidated monastery of Casamare. It was this generous deed, as well as its established reputation in the community, that led the king of Sicily, Ferdinand II, to confer the title of nobility upon it on February 8, 1497.[2]

By the time of Caesar Baronius, however, the family fortunes had dwindled, even though the noble traditions were kept.[3] The deep religious devotion fostered in the family was characterized by the piety of Portia Baronio, recorded by Caesar himself and his early biographers. Caesar described his mother as a "very holy woman."[4] Barnabeus, author of the first published biography of Baronius, related that while Portia was pregnant with Caesar she always felt the child in her womb moving with joy every time someone mentioned the name of the Virgin Mary—an obvious reference to the experience of Elizabeth when visited by Mary, bearing Jesus.[5] As soon as Caesar was born, his mother offered him, as the very devout women did in those days, to the Virgin Mary.[6]

Several extraordinary incidents of the early childhood are recorded by Baronius' biographers which also would indicate the deeply religious nature of the environment he was reared in. One was the miraculous cure of Caesar. When only an infant of two, Baronius had been grievously ill. His mother had taken him to the

1

little Church of the Madonna, a mile from home, and had spent three days there praying to the Virgin.[7] Another incident was the prediction by a beggar about the greatness Baronius was to achieve in the Church. Such extraordinary occurrences and premonitions would naturally prompt a devout woman to raise her offspring in an especially religious manner, and thus she did according to Marzia Baronio's testimony. Giving Caesar special religious instruction and introducing him early in life to charitable practices were some of the things she did in order to make him worthy of the high ecclesiastical position she believed he might one day be accorded.[8]

The peculiar nature of the piety practiced by the people of southern Italy at this time is indicative of their aloofness from the mainstream of Renaissance culture which was flourishing in the north. The south, particularly the backwoods areas of the Abruzzi region, was relatively untouched by the humanistic activities of the northern cities. At the very beginning of the Renaissance period, to be sure, the kings of Naples, most notably Robert of Anjou, vied with the other Italian states to play host to Petrarch and other first-generation humanists. But the communal and quasi-republican structure of the northern city states, which seems to have been very conducive to the growth of the humanist movement, had long since vanished from the south.

The kingdom of Naples, as we know, had been tossed around for the previous four centuries in the Angevin-Aragonese and then the Habsburg-Valois dynastic power play. As a result, whatever national consciousness the Neapolitan monarchy had once created completely vanished, and a new one was not to appear again until the second half of the seventeenth century. Thus, the lack of proper political climate and patronage, it seems, was at least partly responsible for the stagnation of the humanist movement in the south.[9]

Conversely, the kingdom of Naples failed to benefit from one of the most important effects of humanism which was very prominently seen in northern Italy; that is, the strengthening of civic consciousness and local patriotism. Whatever humanistic influence the kingdom experienced was forced to remain either a largely court phenomenon, Lorenzo Valla's for example, or a purely literary effort, like the scholarly work of Giovanni Pontano, which was wholly unpolitical in its nature and implications. Thus, Naples escaped completely the fusion between politics and letters that did so much to reinvigorate the Florentine Republic from the time of Leonardo Bruni till the time of Piero Soderini and Niccolo Machiavelli.[10]

As Naples remained isolated from humanism as a whole, so it was untouched by those specific aspects of humanism that regarded religion. One of the things that the humanists in Italy took a great deal of interest in was the critical revision and interpretation of the Bible. As early as 1311, Pope Clement V established the chairs of the Hebrew, Arabic, and Chaldean languages in Rome in order to stimulate biblical researches. But it was only in the second half of the fifteenth century that the results of this linguistic study began to appear prominently in the exegetical works of several scholars, among them Paolo Burgense (d. 1453) and Alfonso Tostato (1399–1455). Lorenzo Valla's critical interpretation of the New Testament was the most famous of them all.[11] Twenty-two editions of the Vulgate Bible came out from Venice alone between 1475 and 1499, several of them with extensive commentaries, which would indicate the extent of the interest shown in Bible reading and learning in fifteenth century Italy.[12] But this interest was largely confined to northern Italy, particularly the more important city states. The kingdom of Naples remained generally unaffected by it.

Another important by-product of humanism in Italy was the widespread interest in religious reformation. This interest found expression in the many new religious congregations founded in the late fifteenth or early sixteenth century, and the reorganization of the old religious orders at this period. The formation of the Oratory of Divine Love in Genoa in 1497 was perhaps the first organized effort in this direction. The amazing success of this movement was largely due to the wholehearted involvement of leading humanist bishops such as Jacopo Sadoleto, Gian Matteo Giberti, Gian Pietro Caraffa, and Gasparo Contarini.

Sadoleto, bishop of Carpentras, not only lent his aid to the reform movement in Italy, but even tried to enter into a personal dialogue with the Protestants, particularly John Calvin.[13] Giberti combined his humanistic and reform interest when he introduced a thorough-going reform in his diocese of Verona and encouraged his people in the study of the Bible. Caraffa, as bishop of Chieti, was not only involved in the Oratory of Divine Love but also was a leading spirit behind the formation of other religious organizations, most notably the Theatines.[14] His reform measures as Pope Paul IV are well known.[15] Contarini, a Venetian patrician and humanist besides being a supporter of the Oratory, had a strong influence on the papacy's relation with the empire during the Reformation, and as bishop of Belluno after 1536 he also championed the ecclesiastical reformation of his diocese.[16]

The spark that was lit by the Oratory of Divine Love suddenly spread all over Italy and gave inspiration to the founders of several new and more formally organized religious congregations. Among them were the Theatines, the Sommaschi, the Barnabites, and the Oratorians, all religious congregations of men, and the Ursulines, a teaching order of women.

Among the older religious orders in Italy which underwent radical reformation were the Franciscans and the Dominicans. It was Matteo da Bascio, an Umbrian, who led the reform movement within the Franciscan order which eventually ended in establishing a separate order, the Capuchins.[17] The reform of the Dominican order had been initiated in the last part of the fifteenth century by Savonarola, but this reform was given a new direction by Pope Paul III who censured the order severely for the alleged Protestant leanings of many of its members.[18]

All Italian cities were affected by this reform movement in varying degrees. Wherever strong leadership existed, the movement strengthened and produced comparable results: Milan with Carlo Borromeo, Venice with Gaetano da Thiene, Rome with Filippo Neri. Conversely, wherever such leadership did not exist, the movement slackened. Such was the case of Naples.

A branch of the Theatine order, however, was established in Naples, the home town of Caraffa. His sister met with some success in reforming the order of Dominican nuns. Yet by and large, the reform movement did not have any lasting impact on Naples, let alone the interior regions of the kingdom, far removed from the mainstream of Italian life. The people of the Abruzzi, therefore, still followed old religious practices and adhered to traditional religious beliefs, many of which verged on superstition. The piety of Portia Baronio is a case in point. Her excessive devotion to the Virgin (a virgin only very loosely connected with the Mary of Saint Luke's Gospel), her intense devotion to a variety of doubtfully historical saints, and her complete credulity about reported miracles were characteristic of her time and place. And it was this religious world of the Abruzzi, not that of Jacopo Saloleto or Ignatius Loyola, that provided the first formative influence on Baronius' life as a Christian.

Caesar Baronius' formal education was begun in the town of Veroli, about nine miles from Sora, and continued in Naples where he was sent to study law. Naples indeed was a natural choice, not only because of its proximity to Sora, but also because as the capital of the kingdom it offered many opportunities to a young man pursuing a career in law. The city also remained a splendid island in the largely uncultured sea of southern Italy. As Croce pointed out, "Naples, with her university and other schools, her monasteries and the house of the Jesuits, the libraries, the museums, the tribunals, and her most splendid churches and lavish palaces, was always a great center of letters and learning."[19] Therefore, it exerted a great attraction for all ambitious provincials. Thus young Baronius was sent to Naples and not to Bologna or one of the more famous law schools of the north.

When Baronius left for Naples on October 29, 1556, he was only eighteen years of age. But, according to his biographers, he had already shown a decided taste for learning. Barnabeus, for example, related that Baronius spent all the money he could save in buying books and in supplementing classroom learning with private instruction.[20] His stay in Naples ended abruptly when he suddenly was overcome by fear of the imminent danger of war.[21] Pope Paul IV and Henry II of France were planning to invade Naples in order to overthrow the Spanish rule there. As it turned out, the armies of the French king and the pope did not invade the city of Naples. Actually, Rome saw more military action than Naples. However, Baronius had decided to leave for the Eternal City, and he was not going to change his mind. Perhaps the attraction of Rome rather than the fear of war was the real reason for his decision.

He left Naples about the twentieth of October, 1557, in a boat bound for Rome. Giovanni Marciano, who wrote the early history of the Oratorian congregation, recounts a supposedly miraculous incident which occurred to Baronius on this trip. As the story goes, Baronius accidently missed the boat he was scheduled to take. But actually the error was the result of divine protection, because the boat was shipwrecked soon after its departure. Marciano claimed that Baronius himself revealed this to Trojano Bozzuto of the Naples Oratory.[22]

Baronius was well received in Rome, probably through the influence of his father. In one of his letters to his father soon after his arrival in Rome, Baronius made mention of a meeting with a cardinal whom he did not name but who offered him help.[23] At any rate, by November 3, 1557, he was comfortably quartered at the house of one Caterina d'Alvo, together with another youth from Sora.[24] Little is known thereafter of his early career in Rome. He may have been overwhelmed by the new environment, for his father apparently rebuked him for negligence and misbehavior. In a letter to his father dated December 8, 1557, he referred to his father's remarks and asked him to be understanding of his youthfulness.[25] The rebuke was probably unjustified, more the result of young Baronius' modesty than of actual indiscretion. But at least it led him to reiterate his better intentions; for he concluded the letter with a promise never to dishonor his father, his country, or himself.

In this letter of December 8, Baronius also told his father that there were some secrets which he had to keep to himself for the time being. It is possible, indeed, that his father's suspicions concerned these secrets. There is a good chance that these secrets were none other than the first contacts with Philip Neri, which Baronius dared not reveal to his father because of his opposition to his son's religious vocation, an opposition that was to become more vociferous as time went on. Though the letters are silent on the matter, there is good reason to suppose that Baronius had already been attracted towards Neri who was currently one of the most respected and highly regarded men in Rome.

Philip Neri was a Florentine by birth, and a member of a middle class family that had been traditionally notaries for nearly a century. His father was a procurator of the Monastery of San Marco and had become a great admirer of Fra Girolamo Savonarola. Indeed, he may even have gone into temporary exile after Savonarola's fall, as did many of his associates. The spirit of Savonarola, or what Ponnelle rightly called the "cult of Savonarola"[26] still persisted in San Marco when young Philip Neri frequented the monastery for his early education in the 1520's.[27] It is highly likely that he derived from the monks much of his intense piety and his critical attitude toward the institutions of the Church, particularly the papal curia.

Neri once confessed to some Dominican monks that "all I have of goodness in me came from your fathers at San Marco of Florence."[28] There is no doubt that the prophetic posture and the mystical stance he assumed in his later religious career made him resemble, if not the real Savonarola, at least the image of Savonarola created by his Dominican followers of the sixteenth century. And Neri's great interest in liturgical matters, particularly devotional hymns, can be traced without any doubt to the instructions he received from the monks of San Marco, especially from Fra Servatio de' Mini.

At eighteen, Neri was sent by his father to San Germano, a little town at the foot of Monte Casino, to take over the business in-

herited from a childless cousin. He was entrusted with a genealogi-
cal table that demonstrated his noble descent. But he cared little
about either, and within a few months he tore up the genealogy,
abandoned the business, and left for Rome. Rome, during the pontificate of Paul III, had apparently recaptured the splendor of the
days of Leo X and had completely forgotten about the recent
tragedy of the Sack of 1527. But at the same time, it was also
becoming the stage for the activities of various Catholic reform
groups whose efforts were soon to be recognized by the pope himself in his first appointments to the College of Cardinals. It was
also the scene of considerable disquiet—for the more responsible
leaders of the Church were at last becoming concerned over the
spread of the Lutheran revolt in Germany, of the depredations of
the Turks in the Mediterranean, and of the appearance of heretical
movements in Italy itself.

Soon after he arrived in Rome, Neri enrolled himself at the recently organized Sapienza, or University of Rome, as a student of
"humane sciences," namely, classical literature and philosophy. He
then studied theology at the theological school of Sant' Agostino,
belonging to the Augustinian monks. At the Sapienza, Neri's instructor in philosophy was Cesare Giacomelli and at Sant' Agostino his teacher of theology was Antonio Altoviti, both of whom
later actively took part, as bishops, in the Council of Trent. The instruction at both schools was scholastic in content and in method,
very similar to the instructional style of the late medieval school
men. Neri had no quarrels with the theology or even the philosophy of Thomas Aquinas, but the dull and drab dialogues of the
scholastic teachers bothered him. His early training in the Savona-
rolan tradition of San Marco militated against such meaningless
eloquence. In fact, he came to dislike scholasticism so much that
he later discouraged his Oratorian disciples from following scholastic methods.[29] He sought to learn philosophy and theology not
as an empty exercise but as a way to reorder society and the
Church, as all the humanists from Petrarch to Savonarola to Contarini did, but that was exactly what the scholastics did not pay
any attention to. The alienation, therefore, was inevitable.

What most impressed Neri about Rome, however, was its irre-
ligiosity which was shared even by men in the highest ecclesiastical offices, which gave Rome, in the words of her critics, the deri-
sive name of the Babylon of the Apocalypse. And this impression
led to his first vocation—that of reforming what he found reproach-
ful, just like Savonarola. The vocation soon turned into a personal

crusade against sin and irreligion by counsel, persuasion, example, and charitable activities. When Neri was thirty-five years old, his confessor, Persiano Rosa, told him that he could best serve the Church by becoming a priest; and after much hesitation, he finally did so in 1551.

The apostle of Rome, as Neri would be called in later years, was a strange combination of many different qualities and interests. His personal asceticism, his austerity, and his mystical experiences made him a mixture of Savonarola and Catherine of Siena—both of whom he was very devoted to. His great interest in the Scriptures and in patristic studies preserved in him the humanist tradition. His enthusiasm for simple piety and popular devotions reflected the recent evangelical reforms, as well as the long pietistic tradition of the Florentine confraternities.

But Neri was also an innovator. In fact, he founded a religious institution that was largely unprecedented in the history of the Church, namely the Oratory. At first the Oratory was basically an informal forum, where intellectuals and common people alike could go to study and discuss Christian religion in relation to changing times, somewhat similar to the humanistic academies which were popular in Italy during the High Renaissance. It started as a casual reunion of Florentine residents in Rome, but later it expanded as a meeting for all those vitally interested in Christian renewal. Many of those who frequented the Oratory were still Florentine businessmen, but increasing numbers of intellectuals, famous literary figures, high ecclesiastical officials, and members of the aristocratic families of Rome began to attend the meetings. Gianbattista Strozzi and Antonio Quarengho, famous humanists; Pier Luigi Palestrina, famous musician and choir director of the Vatican; Camillo and Hieronimo Pamfili, Roman aristocrats; Onofrio Panvinio, famous historian; and Cardinal Alessandro di' Medici (later Leo XI) were some of the frequent guests of the Oratory, indicating the popularity of the meetings among the elite of Rome.

They all met around Philip Neri, whom they nicknamed the Socrates of Rome, an obvious reference to the school of Socrates as described in Plato's *Symposium*.[30] They read and discussed Christian literature of all periods. Among the early Christian writers they read were Denys the Carthusian, Climacus, Cassian, and Richard of Saint Victor. Among the medieval writers they read were Gerson, Catherine of Siena, Innocent III (his *De Contemptu Mundi*), Serafino da Fermo (*Phareta Divini Amoris*), Feo Belcari (*Life of Blessed Colombini*), and Jacopone da Todi (his hymns, especially the *Stabat Mater*).[31] The texts were read and discussed in such a manner that all the participants would understand their meaning and significance to daily Christian life. The hymns, of course, were intended to strengthen pious sentiments.

As time went on, these informal meetings produced a more formal organization, a religious congregation for secular priests who, without the three traditional vows of the religious orders, wanted to live a common life in pursuit of spiritual perfection. Thus, the Oratorians were organized. But Neri's initial informal meetings were never given up. Indeed, they were improved as the Oratorians served as the permanent organizers of such meetings.

Another of Neri's innovations was the pilgrimages to the seven basilicas of Rome. As a young layman, he had often visited the various churches of the city and the tombs of the martyrs alone. He then turned what had been a private devotion into a public observance, without losing its original informality and simplicity. Although the aristocrats and cardinals of Rome joined him in his pilgrimages, as well as the common people, their common hymn singing—one more of Neri's innovations—and their conviviality helped to maintain the simplicity of the affair, without turning it into yet another ponderous religious ceremony. Hymns were also sung during the meetings at the Oratory. Some of the leading musicians of Rome, like Giovanni Animuccia (an early member of the Oratory and successor of Palestrina as the choirmaster at Saint Peter's) led the singing on these occasions.

Visiting the poor in their homes and the patients in hospitals was still another of Neri's personal pious practices, and it also became common practice among his growing number of followers. Such visitations were being encouraged by many Church reformers and indeed they were formally incorporated into the program of many religious confraternities. For instance, the Oratory of Divine Love, founded in Genoa in 1497 and brought to Rome in 1517, considered this one of its important functions. The humanist reformers like Jacopo Sadoleto and Matteo Giberti who joined this Oratory had helped to establish the San Giacomo Hospital for the incurables. What Neri and his followers did was take advantage of an already existing trend and strengthen it in order to help the needy and sick of Rome. In any event, this activity had, as did his other devotional practices, made Neri one of the most lovable and popular figures in Rome by the time young Baronius arrived in the city.

Francesco Zazzara's *Memoirs* is the earliest source that makes reference to Baronius' first encounter with Neri.[32] What brought them together, apparently, was their common interest in the conversion of a certain Marco da Casalvero, who reportedly had been alienated from the Church. Since Baronius frequently visited this man who lived close to the Church of San Girolamo della Carità (then the residence of Neri), it is very probable that Baronius made a visit to the famous Neri on his own initiative. In any event, soon after Baronius' arrival in Rome he started to frequent Neri's residence, according to the Oratorian chronicler, Zazzara. He also chose Neri as his regular confessor and imbibed from him, among other beliefs, a conviction that "divine law is better and richer than laws of men."[33] Thus the desire for a professional career in the tribunals, a desire after all that had been put in him by his father, gradually waned.

Soon the change in Baronius was irrevocable. And that Neri was largely, if not wholly, responsible for it, is suggested by the fact that the text of the anonymous *Vita* of Neri, in which this matter is related, was edited by Baronius himself. The conversion of Baronius was so total that he wanted to leave the world immediately and join a religious order. That he did not do so was also due to Neri's influence; for Zazzara recorded that Neri refused to give his penitent permission, saying that better things were awaiting him. Neri advised him, instead, to continue his legal and humanistic studies, while not neglecting, of course, his spiritual development.[34]

There are no contemporary sources available that would indicate the nature of Baronius' education in Rome. We come across only some brief and casual statements about this matter in the early biographies. Barnabeus, for example, passingly mentions that Baronius went to Rome to study civil and ecclesiastical law and that he studied in Rome under Cesare Costa, who later was made archbishop of Capua.[35] It is to be assumed, however, that Baronius received a strongly humanistic education because the academic circles of Rome, as well as the general atmosphere of the city itself, were permeated with what may be called the humanistic spirit. Even the faculties of philosophy and theology, which Neri had found some fifteen years before adhering to the old scholastic methods, came under strong humanistic influence. The Church's top leadership had been promoting the cause of humanism for more than a quarter of a century since the movement had once been all but destroyed in the aftermaths of the Sack of Rome.[36]

One of Paul III's first acts after his ascension to the papacy in

1534 was to create a number of cardinals, among them some very famous humanists. Jacopo Sadoleto, Reginald Pole, Giovanni Battista Cervini, Gasparo Contarini, Giovanni Morone, and Pietro Bembo were the cardinals of Paul III who were well-known for their humanistic learning as well as their interest in Church reform. The pope gave Bembo the job of publishing the stylish *Briefs* which Paul himself had once composed for Leo X. He entrusted Cervini with the organization of the Vatican Library and the cataloguing of the manuscripts. Paul sent his scriptors to search for Greek manuscripts among the Maronite monasteries of Lebanon and among the Greek settlements in southern Italy. During his pontificate, Greek texts were being printed at the Vatican, often with accompanying commentaries. Vernacular editions of the Bible were encouraged under Paul, and the Vatican even printed an Ethiopic New Testament in 1548–49. Paul was so widely acclaimed as the patron of humanism that numerous works by humanist authors of Europe were dedicated to him, including the revolutionary work of Nicholas Copernicus, *On the Revolution of the Heavens.*

Paul III's fifteen-year reign was followed by the five years of Julius III and the twenty-two days of Marcellus II. Julius languished under the weight of his responsibilities and passively let the years of his pontificate go by without accomplishing anything. Marcellus' reign was too short-lived to leave any impact. Humanistic scholarship, therefore, was left unaffected during the years, 1550–55.

In 1555 Gian Pietro Caraffa became Pope Paul IV, and the luxury-loving curia was transformed into a terror-machine, striking out at anyone the pope suspected of heretical sentiments. But even under Paul humanism survived unscathed, because the pope himself was a lover of letters. He commanded considerable scholarship in Greek and Hebrew in addition to Latin. He had become a friend of Erasmus when they met in England and encouraged the great humanist to publish his edition of Saint Jerome.[37] As papal nuncio to Spain, he had encouraged Cardinal Ximenes in the publication of the polyglot Bible. Paul, therefore, was not opposed to humanism, even though he charged some of the leading humanists, including Cardinals Pole and Morone, with heresy and subjected them to intense persecution. Hence, humanism was still flourishing when Caesar Baronius started his education in Rome. Furthermore, there is no question about the humanistic leanings of Cesare Costa, Baronius' early instructor in Rome, who praised the city as "al-

ways adorned with precious stones, in every way blessed and advanced."[38] Only a humanist-classicist could describe the Rome of
that time in such glowing terms.

The interest in humanism was matched by an overwhelming
desire for religious reform. This was true of most of the humanists
in Rome, as well as the popes themselves. As the Protestant revolt
became a real and serious threat to the unity of the Church, and
as the outcry for reform within Catholicism increased in volume,
many of the humanist reformers intensified their efforts. The tempo of the whole city of Rome was charged with anxiety and excitement and larger numbers of people became willing to respond
to the call for reform. In this atmosphere, Baronius found no difficulty in reconciling his humanistic studies with his new enthusiasm for the kind of religious devotion he discovered in Philip
Neri.

If anything, he was willing to sacrifice his studies for the sake of
his religious devotions. In fact, he did so when he started to spend
most of his time in spiritual exercises and charitable works. One
of the charitable works, mentioned prominently by all his biographers, was his daily visit to the Hospital of the Holy Spirit in
Rome. As Zazzara testifies, Baronius went there every morning
and afternoon to console and counsel the sick, and he did this for
more than nine years without missing a day, even when he himself was ill.[39] In fact, he seems to have recovered every time he
visited the hospital under the weather himself, and he made it a
point to attribute this to the superhuman intervention of Neri.

He thus came to regard Neri as a miracle-working saint. A particular miracle left a lasting impact on him. One evening, as Baronius declared under oath at the canonization proceedings of Neri
many years later, he went to confess to Neri, as was his usual custom. But this time, Neri, without hearing his confession, told him
to go immediately to the Hospital of the Holy Spirit and inquire if
something had to be done. When Baronius said that there was
nothing to be done, since everything had been taken care of shortly
before, Neri demanded obedience. Baronius obeyed, of course, and
upon reaching the hospital found a dying man who, through an
error, had not been administered the sacraments. Immediately, Baronius brought a priest who gave him the last rites; moments later
the man died, as if his death was somehow delayed just for this
purpose. Baronius narrated the whole incident to Philip Neri who
then told him, "Learn to obey without questioning."[40] He had already been a docile disciple of Neri, but this made him even more

so. He not only considered Neri his spiritual mentor but even swore to obey him under all circumstances. He continued to adhere to the rules of the Oratory, where he frequently received the Eucharist, attended all the assemblies, participated in all the liturgical functions, and performed acts of charity.[41]

Baronius' strong attachment to Neri was viewed with alarm by his father, who had been planning a career for his only son in the interest of the family. Various entreaties to abandon his new religious interests met with no response, which infuriated his father, who finally cut off his allowances. Zazzara reports that Neri subsequently arranged accommodations for his disciple in the house of his friend, Giovanni Michele Paravicino.[42] Baronius lived with this family from about the middle of March, 1558 until he was ordained a priest on May 27, 1564.[43] One of his duties in this household was to tutor the six children of the family, one of whom, Ottavio, later became a cardinal.

Alienation from his father only helped to strengthen Baronius' decision to enter the religious life. He intensified the austerity of his daily life by extra penances, frequent fasts and abstinences, and long hours of prayer and study.[44] He also renounced his paternal inheritance and exchanged a series of letters with his father in which he expressed his singleness of purpose.[45] To be a saintly man like Philip Neri seems to have been his foremost desire during this period. He still did not neglect his intellectual training during these trying times, to be sure, as the above testimonies might indicate. But the important fact is that his intellectual preparation, just as his every other endeavor, was directed at that one goal of achieving superior sanctity.

At this time, Philip Neri had already converted his residence at San Girolamo della Carita into the Oratory as a meeting place for the reform-minded Catholics of Rome. The custom of common readings from Christian writers and public discussions had already been established. Occasionally, Neri would call on one of the lay persons in the group to give a short speech on some devotional subject in order to inspire the audience. On one of these occasions, on the vigil of the feast of Epiphany in 1558 to be exact, Neri called upon Baronius to make a few remarks. Though only a young man of about twenty years, he moved his audience deeply by his sincerity, devotion, and mature reasoning. Neri, therefore, invited him frequently to make short speeches. Barnabeus considers that Baronius' speeches were so full of spiritual fervor that they had the extraordinary power of moving even hardened hearts. In fact, he

claims that one speech of Baronius was responsible for the conversion of a prelate of the Roman Curia and three Roman aristocrats.[46]

There must have been some truth in these claims, for we see
that Neri soon made Baronius a regular speaker at the Oratory.
The topics he chose for his talks were inspirational in nature, and
often were intended to instill the fear of God in the hearts of the
listeners. Zazzara reports that in those days Baronius was "always
talking about frightening things like death, hell, and judgment."[47]
His frequent treatises on such subjects might have been a reflection
of his own inner conflicts at that time because, as he himself revealed to a colleague, this was the time a strong temptation against
the virtue of purity started to afflict him. This temptation continued to torment him all through his life. Baronius, however, considered this as a providential arrangement to keep him humble.[48]
In order to overcome this and other temptations, he practiced
many penances, some self-imposed and others suggested by his
spiritual mentor, Philip Neri. That Neri imposed many penances on
Baronius is beyond doubt, whatever the reasons may have been.
Baronius himself wrote to his parents on December 16, 1560,
about the rigorous discipline under which Neri kept him.[49]

Sometime in 1558 Neri asked Baronius to substitute his usual
moralistic sermons at the Oratory with a series of lectures on the
history of the Church, from the beginning to contemporary times.
In retrospect, it seems that Neri made this move because of some
premonitions about a disturbing event that was to occur in the following year. Matthias Flacius Illyricus and his group of scholars
brought out the first volume of the *Magdeburg Centuries* in 1559;
and the work caused great consternation in the Catholic world.
Baronius' biographers, all of whom believed in Neri's prophetic vision, contend that Neri had seen the threat the *Centuries* was going
to pose against the Church, and therefore he commanded Baronius
to prepare his speeches on the history of the Church so that eventually he would be able to refute the Protestant work.[50]

Apart from the prophetic powers of Neri, this contention cannot be validated. For one thing, Neri could not have known the
exact nature of Flacius' work a year before its publication, even
though European scholars were aware of the researches being done
by Flacius and his colleagues. At any rate, it can be definitely
proven that Baronius' original purpose of making speeches about
the history of the Church and of writing the *Annales* was not to refute the *Magdeburg Centuries*. One of his own letters renders clear

evidence in this case. This letter was addressed to Cardinal Guglielmo Sirleto and dated May 16, 1577, nearly eighteen years after the appearance of the *Centuries*. [51]

In his letter, Baronius requested Sirleto to recommend him to the cardinal of Pisa so that he might obtain permission to own and to read the *Magdeburg Centuries*. Of course, as a "heretical" work, it could be read only with ecclesiastical permission. As reason for this request, Baronius mentioned that he was beginning to rewrite his work on the history of the Church, in view of publication. It is, therefore, clear that Baronius definitely did not own a copy of the *Centuries* until 1577. Even if he had previously read the work with temporary permission of his superiors, it would not have sufficed for a refutation. The fact that he did not make an attempt to get permission to own and read the book until this time, until the time he was ready to rewrite the *Annales* for intended publication, shows that he did not originally intend to refute the *Centuries*. However, it should be pointed out that in the intervening years from 1577 till 1588, the year Volume I of the *Annales* was published, Baronius changed his mind; as a finished product, the *Annales* indeed was intended to refute the *Centuries*.

There is a perfectly reasonable explanation for Neri's command to speak about the history of the Church. It concerns the interests of the men who attended the sessions at the Oratory. They were humanists and Church reformers. Humanists had always been historically minded. The history of the early Church and the Church fathers intrigued almost all of them, from Valla and Erasmus on. Neri himself was fascinated by the catacombs, the ancient monuments of Rome, and the tombs of the early martyrs. It was only natural, therefore, to agree on such an interesting topic as the history of the Church for their discussions. Consequently, Baronius was prevailed upon to undertake these lectures. This, of course, turned out to be a providential arrangement, for after the appearance of the *Magdeburg Centuries*, Neri commissioned him to the more important task of writing the *Annales Ecclesiastici*.

It is not clear exactly when Neri commissioned Baronius to write the *Annales*, but indications are that it was soon after the appearance of the *Centuries*. It is certain, however, that Baronius started the actual work on the *Annales* before the end of May, 1564. His letter to Cardinal Ottavio Paravicino, which is inserted in the fourth volume of the *Annales*, refers to the work as a grown tree "once planted as a tiny sprout in your house while I was staying with you as a young man." [52] Since Baronius left the Paravicino

household immediately after his ordination to the priesthood on
May 27, 1564, the work on the *Annales* must have started before
that date.

Baronius was bewildered by Neri's command to commence work
on a history of the Church. He had no taste for it, nor was he willing to do it. But Neri insisted that he should. He thus testified at
the canonization proceedings of Neri,

> He ordered me to talk about the history of the Church. When
> I replied that it was not to my taste but that I would rather
> treat spiritual matters for the sake of compunction, the Father
> insisted that he wanted me to talk about the history of the
> Church. Besides this, he seriously urged several times that at
> any rate I should talk on Church history. These circumstances
> caused me to think that the Father, enlightened by the Holy
> Spirit, wanted such a work, useful to the Church of God, to be
> done. As I have recognized from certain experiences, this work
> of the publication of the *Annales* has come to be more the result
> of his prayers than my work. He made me speak on this topic
> in the Oratory continually for thirty years and he made me re-
> peat it entirely over and over again. Needless to say, I have
> found myself doing this work. As proof of this, I would like to
> add that many times I have wanted to become a religious—a
> Capuchin, Theatine or a member of any other reformed order—
> and I insisted persistently. But he would never give me permis-
> sion. Many religious persons were thus scandalized when the
> Father said that, in his opinion, people would not need to enter
> religious orders; but this scandal happened because they did not
> see what God had shown to the said Father.[53]

The same story is repeated in Baronius' essay dedicating the
eighth volume of the *Annales* to Philip Neri.[54] Even after repeated
commands from Neri, however, Baronius seems to have been hesitant about undertaking the task of writing the *Annales*. What made
him finally change his mind was a vision he had, as Zazzara reported in his *Memoirs*.[55] In this vision, said to have been recounted
by Baronius himself, a celestial voice resembling that of Philip Neri
sternly told him that he was the one to write the history of the
Church, and that he should not hesitate or try to escape from the
responsibility. At the time of this vision, Baronius was trying to
persuade Neri to entrust this work to Onofrio Panvinio, who was
already working on a history of the Church.

Compared to Panvinio, Baronius saw himself utterly inadequate
for the task. He said that his Latin was poor, his knowledge of history and literature was weak, and his experience in writing all but

non-existent. These objections were recorded by a contemporary disciple of Neri in a work about Neri's life which was edited and corrected, although not published, by several Oratorians, among them Baronius.[56] Therefore, it is beyond doubt that he raised these objections. But the will of Neri prevailed, and Baronius, a young man in his early twenties, set himself to the arduous task of composing a monumental work. Nearly thirty years elapsed, however, before the first volume appeared. And it was during these thirty years that Baronius matured, through many labors, as the author of the first comprehensive history of the Church in modern times.

2

The Philipine Circle

By the middle of 1558, the young man from Sora was thoroughly engrossed in the new way of life that Philip Neri had shown him. The spiritual and intellectual stimulation he received in the Philipine circle from the most enlightened and learned men of Rome was a new experience the eager youth relished completely. The congenial character of Neri attracted all sorts of men with widely varied talents, interests, and backgrounds. Two of his early disciples, Giovanni Severiano and Paolo Aringhi, were interested in the catacombs. Indeed, they were the pioneers with Neri himself in discovering some of them; previously only the catacomb of Saint Sebastian was known. Antonio Bosio, most fortunate of the pioneers, profited a great deal from the discoveries of Neri and his two disciples. What attracted them most was the hope of finding relics of the early martyrs and saints of the Church and of using new inscriptions for enriching their biographies.[1] Neri's interest in Church history may thus have originated in the catacombs.

The Philipine circle was frequented by members of the most well-known noble families of Rome: Altoviti, Colonna, Massimo, Savelli, Salviati, Farnese, Altieri and the like who gave it an aura of respectability. Among those who attended the functions at the Oratory were also well-known scholars: Gian Battista Modio, physician and prominent man of letters; Francesco Maria Tarugi, courtier, writer and the most noted orator of the time; and Giacomo Marmita and Gabriele Tana, both poets. Neri's close friends in the Dominican monastery of Santa Maria sopra Minerva should also be considered as members of his circle, even though they did not frequent the Oratory. Among them were Vincenzo Ercolani and

Paolo Bernardini, both eminent theologians and scholars. The two famous Borromeos, Carlo, later archbishop of Milan, and Federico, nobleman, intellectual, and eventually Carlo's successor, were also part of the circle. Brilliant composers and musicians like Giovanni Animuccia performed in the Oratory, adding color to the religious functions. Francesco Bozzio, Tommaso Bozzio, Giovanale Ancina, Silvio Antoniano Valier, Gabriele Paleotti, Agostino Cusano and the Abate Maffa—all well-known humanists—were members of Neri's group. Andrea del Monte, converted rabbi and famous speaker; Michele Mercati, botanist; Antonio Talpa; and numerous other men of varied talents and interests were also associates.

There is no doubt that the young student from the south was dazzled by such an august company and stimulated by its vibrant intellectual and spiritual activities. He may have revealed to his family his decision to follow the path of Neri by the year 1558, for his father, alarmed about the prospect of losing his only son, demanded his immediate return to Sora. We have a letter from Baronius, dated June 5, 1558, in which he requested his uncle Marco Barone, a canon of Sora, to persuade his father not to recall him because he did not want to lose the excellent opportunities in Rome.[2] On June 24 of the same year he wrote his parents that he wanted to stay in Rome because that was "better for the well-being of my soul as well as body."[3] However, in a letter to his parents of December 16, 1560, he made mention of a visit to Sora in 1559.[4] The visit must have been very brief for it was abruptly ended when his father insisted that he get married.

By the end of 1559 Baronius' desire to follow the path of Neri found concrete expression in his attempt to join a religious order, although he does not seem to have any specific one in mind. However, Neri continually dissuaded him from becoming a religious. [5] Zazzara reports that Baronius, anxious to make a decision about this matter, frequently went to his confessor, Constanzo Tassone, for guidance.[6]

Meanwhile, a series of unusual incidents occurred which seemed to have convinced Baronius that divine guidance was coming to him through Neri. Zazzara again reports that one morning in mid-year 1559 Neri asked Baronius to go immediately to Constanzo Tassone, who at that moment was celebrating Mass at the main altar of the church of Girolamo della Carità. He said that Tassone would have a message about the will of God regarding Baronius' future. Upon meeting Baronius, Tassone told him that the will of

God would be known to him in five months, and that during this time he should meditate and pray constantly about the impending revelation. On the vigil of the feast of the conversion of Saint Paul, in January 1560, Neri and a large number of his followers, including Baronius and his confessor, were en route to visit the Basilica of Saint Paul. Among the group was Tassone who dramatically revealed the divine will: Baronius should become a secular priest.[7]

Having received such a seemingly authentic revelation about his vocation, Baronius proceeded on the road to priesthood. In 1560, he was initiated into all the minor orders. Before taking the important and irrevocable step of the major orders, he tried once again to placate his irate father through a carefully composed letter, written on December 16, 1560.[8] This letter, in which he expressed his unshakable decision to his parents, is full of allusions to the express will of God, revealed to him through his spiritual mentors, and exhortations to his parents about the necessity of their resigning whole-heartedly to the divine will. For him it was a clear and definite call by Christ, similar to the call of the apostles. From now on his soul and body would be completely at God's service, he said. This complete sense of dedication would become characteristic of his future life, his personal devotions, and his intellectual labors. Any work he would undertake from this point on would have one unmistakable goal—the glory of God through the service of his Church.

Several letters which Baronius wrote to his parents during the years 1560 and 1561 again indicate his total dedication to religion and his almost fanatical determination to serve the cause of the Church.[9] The extraordinary nature of his religious zeal is evident from his many unusual and, ordinarily-speaking, unnecessary acts of devotion. For example, as a cleric destined for the secular priesthood, he was not expected to take any special vow of obedience or poverty. However, he insisted on taking a vow of obedience to Neri, even before he took any of the major orders. This vow, by which Baronius voluntarily took it upon himself to obey Neri all through his future life and in every conceivable matter, was formally administered to him by Neri. Similarly, he took a vow of poverty, which also was not a practice incumbent upon secular priests.[10] He displayed excessive humility in his great reluctance to receive the major orders, perhaps in imitation of the saints of the Middle Ages, particularly Saint Francis of Assisi. As Zazzara reports, he showed extreme reluctance to proceed any further after having received the order of subdiaconate on December 12, 1560.[11] Neri had to order him, under pain of sin, to receive the next major order, the diaconate. Baronius did so on April 5, 1561.

The same year Baronius also attained the initial goal of his visit to Rome: a doctorate degree in law. But by this time his mentality had changed so much that he did not find any meaning in an academic degree. He had continued his legal studies only very reluctantly, and upon Neri's insistence. He also had thought, perhaps, that the degree might appease his irate father, who had sent him to Rome for that purpose. Thus, he completed the studies for the doctorate despite his own unwillingness, expressed in several of his letters to his parents.[12]

At that time the degree of doctor of laws was normally conferred on candidates by the College of the Consistorial Advocates at a formal ceremony that was solemn and quite expensive. But distinguished professors sometimes took the privilege of granting degrees to their disciples in private ceremonies. However, when Pope Paul IV ascended the throne, he, in his characteristically strict manner, forbade all private granting of degrees outside of the Consistorial College. Baronius had planned to receive the degree privately at the house of Cardinal Santa Fiore or some other prelate.[13] But because of Paul IV's order, he had to receive the degree in the colorful public ceremony of May 20, 1561. The expenses for the degree were met by an uncle, Paul, who was a military captain.[14]

"I have fulfilled a debt I owed you," Baronius wrote to his father after receiving the degree of doctor of laws.[15] In these words he made an allusion to his true sentiment, an aversion for worldly honors and distinctions, which was also to characterize his subsequent actions. He then destroyed the diploma and refused to use the title of doctor after his name.[16] In order to emphasize his total aversion to what he called "worldly wisdom," he destroyed with the diploma a collection of poems he had written some years before.

Baronius' attitude towards learning and letters was made more clear in a letter to his father dated January 7, 1562. He said: "Who adds learning adds sorrow."[17] In this instance, he was writing about the suggestion of the newly appointed bishop of Sora, Tommaso Gigli, that he should study theology and philosophy further. This would have meant the postponement of his ordination to the priesthood. Baronius, of course, did not see any value in this suggestion. "It is enough for me to look at the Scriptures and the writings of the holy Doctors (of the Church) in a positive manner, without laboring over speculative theology and philosophy," he remarked in the same letter to his father. This might indicate that Baronius was averse only to the scholastic approach to dogmatic theology, and not to the study of the Scriptures and Church fathers, which, of course, was made popular by the humanist reformers of his time.

Neri advised Baronius against prolonging his studies. Obviously, Neri wanted him to continue the research he had started on the history of the Church rather than spend his time in more formal education for the priesthood, which consisted mainly of studies in speculative theology, philosophy, and canon law, rather than history. Bishop Gigli, of course, was representing the feelings of the fathers of the Council of Trent, who at that time were concluding their deliberations. One of the most important reforms they called for was a strong theological education for the clergy. Perhaps the bishop thought that such a promising priestly candidate as Baronius should especially have the benefit of such an education so that he could be called upon to teach future seminarians. As it turned out, however, Baronius received only a minimal training in theology. Very little mention is made in his correspondence or in the memoirs of his contemporaries about his theological education, except for the spiritual guidance he received from Neri and his active participation in the discussions at the Oratory. But these could not substitute for a formal theological training—at least so thought Bishop Gigli. However, the final decision in this case was made by the more practical-minded Neri, and Baronius continued his preparations for ordination to the priesthood.

Around this time, Caesar's father seemed to have become reconciled to his only son's avowed vocation. Several of Baronius' letters at this time indicate that relations with his father had become cordial again.[18] In his correspondence he expressed great pleasure over the father's change of mind and his newly-found interest in spiritual life. This was in remarkable contrast with the severe criticisms he made against the father's callousness toward spiritual matters, expressed in many previous letters. This improved relationship with his father must have been what prompted Baronius to visit his parents in the summer of 1561.

Also in the same summer, soon after Baronius returned to Rome from Sora, word came to him that he had been given the administration of a large benefice connected with the Hospital of the Holy Spirit in Sora. Contrary to the current common practice of clerics to treat the benefices connected with their offices as personal income, Baronius took special measures to insure that all the revenue from his benefice would go for the renovation of the hospital. He exhorted his father and mother to serve the hospital in every way they could. At his request, the lay confraternity of the Congregation of Charity, which supported the Hospital of the Holy Spirit in Rome, held a meeting in Sora and established a branch of their organization there to support the local hospital. They made Caesar's father the promoter of the organization. Thus, he not only made sure that the income from his benefice would be used for the hospital but also took the necessary steps for the improvement and good administration of the institution.

About this time, Baronius was also offered some wealthy benefices in Parma by one Monsignor Santa Fiore.[19] But he was unwilling to leave Rome, and he refused to hold a benefice *in absentia*. Furthermore, he considered the offers of benefices and opportunities to earn wealth as devilish temptations.

Baronius' involvement in the restoration of the Hospital of the Holy Spirit in Sora occasioned renewed pressures from his parents and countrymen to return home. But he considered his vocation to be the special task, entrusted him by Neri, of writing the history of the Church. Therefore, he decided to remain in Rome, and he wrote to his father that, "I am not going to leave Jerusalem to go to Babylon."[20] He compared this chosen vocation to the martyrdom of the ancient Christians and exhorted his mother to encourage him in it. The early Christians, after all, "considered themselves blessed to be worthy of having a martyr son."[21] The analogy of martyrdom may have been another indication of his resignation to an undesired task, one imposed on him by Neri.

During the early months of 1563, Baronius wrote several letters to his parents which contain valuable insights into his deep personal commitment to the work Neri had entrusted him, and into his growing interest in serving his Church in its war against Protestantism.[22] Imbued with the zeal of a Counter-Reformation religious leader, he relegated to second place all his other interests, including his love and loyalty to his parents and native city. He continuously turned down the requests of his lonely parents who still tried persistently to bring him back to Sora. And he expressed his determination to continue in the way of life he had chosen, and explained the various methods he was trying in order to acquire spiritual perfection, including the then common Oratorian practice of visiting the Basilicas and holy places of Rome.

Baronius' religious zeal at this time seems to have been so intense that apparently he even lost normal human sensibilities. For example, when he heard that his father was ill and bedridden, he wrote that he "should think about death everyday and be prepared for it."[23] He argued that, for a good Christian, death was not a fearful incident, but the end of all evil things and the beginning of all good things. For over a month after this letter, Baronius did not hear about his father's condition, and all during that time he prayed for his soul—not for his health. Finally, when he learned that his father had recovered his health, he exhorted him to be extremely careful about his spiritual exercises.[24]

Almost every letter Caesar wrote to his parents during this period contained long exhortations about spiritual life. He seems to have had a total contempt for even the very basic human feelings such as a mother's love for her son. In many of his letters, he chided his mother for her human affection towards him. What he wanted was a "spiritual love." Finally, when he received a letter from her in late 1563, in which the so-called detached spiritual love was evident, he answered with "great jubilation" because she wrote "not like a mother but like a perfect religious."[25]

The year 1563 saw the conclusion of the Council of Trent. Among the decrees of the Council was an important exhortation to bishops to take all the necessary steps to teach the people authentic Catholic doctrine. This exhortation was especially significant in view of the new definitions made by the Council. In order to make them understandable, the Council had ordered a catechism of Catholic doctrine to be issued as a handbook for laymen. Years before the decrees of the Council were promulgated, the religious education of the laity had been undertaken by many newly founded religious orders, like the Company of Jesus, and by several newly reformed ancient orders. But a new fervor was apparent after the decrees of the Council were sent to all bishops and religious orders. Religious leaders began to take special interest in this matter, and many educated laymen also banded together, volunteering to instruct children and willing adults in Catholic doctrine.

A religious zealot like Baronius was not one to pass up such an opportunity. He volunteered to help a confraternity of men banded together for the purpose of teaching religion to the people of central Italy, and he persuaded one of their members, a man named Mark, to go to the diocese of Sora to organize a similar program there. In a letter dated November 1, 1563, Baronius wrote to his

father about the good news of securing the services of the said
Mark and requested him to make all provisions for setting up an
ambitious program of religious education.[26] He also sent the necessary books and materials for catechism classes, as indicated from
his letter, to the teacher Mark.[27] In subsequent years, he sent other
teachers to Sora for the same purpose, and continued to show a
very keen interest in the religious education of the people there.

There was yet another reform decree of the Council of Trent
that affected the life of Baronius, that is, the decree that required
the bishops to take extraordinary care for the academic and moral
training of the new clergy and the reformation of the old. Accordingly, bishops all around the world, especially in areas where Protestantism posed a threat, began to establish seminaries and training centers for priests. The bishop of Sora was anxious to establish
such a program, and the first man he approached for help was
Caesar Baronius. In a letter Caesar wrote to his parents on April 9,
1564, he says that "the Bishop wanted to do me a great favor by
granting a canonicate at Saint Mary's so that I may reform and instruct the clergy according to the decree of the Council."[28] Considering that Baronius was only a deacon at the time, this offer
seems to be an important testimony to his reputation for learning
and good character. Predictably, this offer was turned down because his prior commitment to write the *Annales* was more important to him.

After Baronius' ordination, the bishop was to renew his request
again, and in fact he conferred the canonicate on him, even without his consent. Baronius' answer again was in the negative. The
insistence of the bishop was partly the result of the maneuvering
of Caesar's father in order to induce him to come home. He, therefore, wrote to his father on June 4, 1564, expressing his determination not to accept this offer. "I will never give my consent to
that," he wrote.[29] Later on the bishop came to Rome and tried
personally to persuade Caesar to accept the offer, but to no avail.[30]

Baronius was ordained a priest on May 27, 1564, at the age of
twenty-six. Neri had been, for nearly three years, anxious to have
him ordained, so much so that he even had obtained a special permission from the Roman Curia in 1561 for Baronius' ordination
before the legal age of twenty-four.[31] It was only the reluctance of
Baronius that delayed the step until this time. And even then, except for Neri's stern demand, he would not have taken the step, as
Zazzara reports in his *Memoirs*.[32] A deep feeling of humility and a
sense of unworthiness overwhelmed him so much that he thought

the minor orders were as far as he should go. But the obedience he
pledged to Neri proved to be an even greater influence on him.

Baronius' ordination coincided with an important step in his
career as an historian. In 1564, just a few weeks before the ordination, he completed the first cycle of his oral narration of the whole
history of the Church at the Oratory. Before publishing the first
volume of the *Annales*, he was to repeat it six times, each time
adding the insights gained from his continuing research. Needless
to say, this repeated oral rendition and the concurrent dialogues
with the intellectual elite of Rome who attended his lectures were
an excellent training for his future as the author of the *Annales*.

Soon after his ordination, Baronius was sent to the church of
San Giovanni, the parish church of the Florentine residents of
Rome. This church had recently been entrusted to the care of
Philip Neri. The Florentines in Rome, naturally, wanted their famous fellow countryman to be their pastor. Accordingly, they had
sent a petition to the pope, and obtained their wish. Baronius
served in the parish as an assistant to Neri. He was the first among
the disciples of Neri to become a priest, but soon after his ordination several others were also elevated to the priesthood. Neri arranged for all of them to live together at San Giovanni dei Fiorentini, thus forming the first nucleus of men who made up the future
religious congregation of the Oratorians.

Baronius entered the life of the congregation enthusiastically.
At San Giovanni dei Fiorentini he cooked and washed more than
his share, to the point, indeed, that it became a joke among his
colleagues, and Baronius perpetuated the joke by writing with a
piece of charcoal on the wall of the kitchen, "Caesar Baronius,
perpetual cook." His colleagues affectionately remembered this,
and after his demise erected a slab with this inscription on it. This
slab is still preserved in San Giovanni.

All the contemporary co-religionists of Baronius who left any
kind of written statement about him, invariably mentioned his
great piety and religious zeal. Thus, Matteo Ancina, Paolo Aringhi,
and Pompeo Pateri describe in their memoirs the extraordinary
piety of their fellow Oratorian.[33] They praise lavishly his unusual
religious fervor, hard work, constant prayers, and charitable disposition. For example, Aringhi reports that Baronius' fear of sin
was so great that he seemingly felt severe pain while hearing about
the least sins of his penitents in confession. Once the Abbot Marc'
Antonio Maffa, an apostolic visitor to the religious, remarked after
confessing to Baronius that "Father Caesar sighs so much while

hearing my confession, as if I have killed ten men or committed some such terrible sin."[34] Even though the remark was intended to be humorous, it touched a note of realism in the religious attitude of Baronius.

Baronius' ascetic attitude at this time was so severe that he did not have any hesitation in demanding monastic austerity even from ordinary lay people. The demands he made on his parents, especially on his mother that she should forget her maternal affection for him, is a case in point. Still another instance would bring to sharper focus the extreme nature of his ascetic attitude. It concerned his paternal aunt, Marzia, who was widowed shortly after her only son was born. She returned home to live with her brother, Camillo Barone, Caesar's father. After some years of widowhood, she was seriously considering a second marriage, which was quite natural since she was only about forty years of age and in perfect health at that time. She, therefore, wrote a letter to her nephew, the new young priest, seeking his advice in this matter.

In one of the longest letters he ever wrote, Caesar gave a very one-sided answer to the lonely woman.[35] He completely discounted the possibility of a lonely middle-aged woman desiring to enter into a legitimate marital relationship with a man for her personal fulfillment. The devil will say, he wrote, " 'marriage is a holy thing; it is a sacrament; it is a state of life established by God himself. Besides there will be more resources for almsgiving.' Oh! What a diabolical deceit! Oh! What an infernal cunning!"[36] In order to prove his point, he brought in examples of "holy widows" like the prophetess, Anna, from the Old Testament, but he ignored the remarried widows, like Ruth, who were similarly holy. This one-sided outlook seems to have remained with him all during his life, as future events would testify.

Meanwhile Baronius was kept busy by the many works imposed on him by Neri. After his ordination, he was required to perform the normal functions of a parish priest at San Giovanni dei Fiorentini. Daily mass, confessions, counseling, and various other routine tasks were to be attended to. Besides these, he had to continue the regular narration of the history of the Church in the Oratory at San Girolamo della Carità. In 1565 Neri ordered him also to preach at San Giovanni on feast days. Thus Baronius had an oppressive schedule to follow, but he seemed to have relished this new function of preaching because many people who heard his sermons became his "spiritual children."[37]

Caesar's sermons were full of inspirational stories about the lives and miracles of saints, particularly of the Blessed Virgin, which were meant to elicit religious devotion in people. One miracle supposedly worked by the Virgin Mary in connection with the Turkish siege of Malta in 1565 was a favorite of Baronius at this time. The Turks besieged Malta, the headquarters of the Spanish corsairs, but after taking one of the three main forts they were obliged to withdraw. Rumor had it that the Blessed Virgin appeared in battle array before the Turks, completely stupefying the Turkish soldiers; some of them fell on the ground while others fled. Whatever may have been the validity of this story, Baronius used it to demonstrate to his "spiritual children" the value of devotion to the Blessed Virgin. He wrote to his parents about this miracle in very glowing terms, and exhorted them to show more devotion to her in thanksgiving for such a great favor done for the Christians of Malta.[38]

One of the things that constantly tormented the young priest Baronius was the division in the Church created by the rise of Prottestantism. Like most pious Catholics of that time, he believed it to be the work of the devil. His feelings against heresy became intensely personal not only because his personal involvement in the reconstruction of the history of the Church placed him squarely against the most talked about Protestant scholars of the time, the authors of the *Magdeburg Centuries*.

Perhaps it was to bolster his own inner strength at this time that Baronius began to cultivate a special devotion to Saint Peter, the symbol of unity and authority for Catholics. In fact, it became a daily practice for him to visit Saint Peter's Basilica and perform several devotional rituals. Some of his contemporary co-religionists described his daily visits to Saint Peter's as follows:[39] First of all, he would walk into the Basilica and, kneeling before the bronze statue of Saint Peter on the throne, he would place his hat at the foot of the statue and kiss the feet saying, "Peace and obedience. I believe in the one, holy, catholic, and apostolic Church."[40] Then he would go down to the basement of the church, to the site of the apostle's tomb and prostrate himself on the floor, praying to the saint that he should deliver the Church from infidels and heretics. Such intense devotion to the Apostle Peter, upon which rock the Church was founded according to traditional Catholic belief, demonstrated Baronius' dedication to the authority of the papacy and indicated a sense of mission about the history of the Church he was going to spend his life on.

Sense of mission notwithstanding, Baronius found his task very difficult to pursue. First of all, his priestly functions constantly interrupted his researches. Then, he was confronted with the staggering problem of collecting data for the *Annales*. He was, of course, in a unique setting in Rome, with the Vatican archives and the many manuscript collections and libraries. But the libraries were not yet properly organized, and he had no catalogue to consult, no authority with whom he could discuss. Indeed, he was engaged in a pioneer project. Besides the burden of collecting data for the work, he was also required to organize the material for immediate delivery to a distinguished audience. Ceaseless research and hard work, therefore, became necessary.

His fellow Oratorians who lived in the same house with Baronius testified that he spent most of the day and night in his room pouring over books and manuscripts without sufficient rest or relaxation, which adversely affected his health.[41] He found himself ill several times during the second half of the 1560's. But miracles were a plenty in Philip Neri's pocket, and he helped to cure his favorite disciple every time he was afflicted with an ailment.

Baronius, himself, gave a description of one of these miracular cures in his testimony during the canonization proceedings of Neri.[42] He said that he had been feeling severe pain in his stomach for some time during 1566. He could not eat for any kind of food would increase his pain and make him utterly incapable of doing any work. Then, one day Neri called him to his room and pointing to a large loaf of bread and a piece of lemon demanded that he eat all of it. Naturally, Caesar dreaded the consequences, but being a man of heroic obedience, he did what was demanded of him, and behold! he was instantly cured of the stomach ailment.

Baronius fell ill also on many other occasions, and every time he got well he quickly attributed his recovery to Neri's intercession. So strong was his belief, indeed, that he claimed even to have visions on the subject. One such vision occurred in 1572, and Baronius and his biographers—all of them devotees of Neri like himself—describe it in the following manner.[43] Baronius fell seriously ill with a fever and was apparently at the point of death. Neri, therefore, administered the last sacraments to him. Immediately after Neri anointed him with the holy oils, the "dying" Baronius had a vision. He saw Christ in heaven, sitting on his throne, with the Mother of God on his right side. Neri was standing at the feet of Christ, and he begged him innumerable times to save the life of Baronius. But Christ adamantly refused to grant his request. Then, Neri turned to the Blessed Virgin and begged her to intercede with her son. Needless to say, Christ granted the wish, and Baronius instantly recovered! Pious biographies of saints and churchmen written by their devotees always included legends of miraculous events. Only that in this case the Oratorian biographers of Baronius and Neri were recounting the miraculous cures one of their venerable members experienced through the intercession of their founder.

However, the exaggerations and blind faith in visions and dreams display the lack of a proper theological perspective among the early members of the Oratory. Most of them had no theological training, other than the spiritual and ascetical principles they learned from Neri. This may have been the reason the vicariate of Rome asked the Oratorian priests to take an oral examination in theology, probably some time in 1567. The Oratorian chronicler who reports about this examination says that it was prompted by some malicious complaints about the supposedly poor theological training of Neri's priests.[44]

Complaints aside, such examinations were usually given to young priests by all bishops, according to the directives of the Council of Trent. At any rate, this examination helped to throw some light on the subject of Baronius' familiarity with theologians and Church fathers. As the chronicler reports, he not only exhibited a thorough knowledge of the teachings of Augustine, Ambrose, Thomas, and other Church fathers, but he was also able to quote verbatim from their works. His colleagues performed well, too. In fact, they did so well that Cardinal Savello, who was the papal vicar administering the Roman diocese at that time, requested Neri to send them to hear the confessions of suspected heretics incarcerated by the Holy Office. Leaving even a wide margin for the exaggerations of this prejudiced chronicler, it is safe to conclude that Baronius did have a familiarity with the works of the Church fathers.

Several letters which Baronius wrote to his parents in 1567 also contain information about the nature and extent of his scholarly endeavors. In one of them, written on May 29, 1567, he requested financial aid from his father for securing books needed for his work.[45] He mentioned particularly the works of Venerable Bede (673-735), the author of the *Ecclesiastical History of the English People* and numerous other works; those of Saint Prosper (d. 463), the fifth century defender of Augustine and the author of the *Chronicle*; and the *Summa Theologica* of Saint Thomas Aquinas.

These selections clearly indicate his predominant interest in ecclesiastical history; indeed, he had already launched into the field of historical research which was to bear fruit several decades later.

In the same letter to his father, he also mentioned that he had been selected to preach on four consecutive days to the general chapter of the Capuchins, assembled in Rome at that time. Such a rare distinction again was an indication that his scholarship had been well established. Still another recognition was accorded him when Neri entrusted him with the responsibility of the Lenten sermons of 1568 in San Giovanni dei Fiorentini, at the request of the congregation of that church.[46] Calenzio suggests that Baronius' familiarity with the Scripture and the Church fathers and the sincerity of his sermons must have endeared him to that congregation.[47] Considering that the parishioners of the church were mainly wealthy Florentine merchants and sophisticated professionals, it is safe to assume that Baronius had exhibited more than ordinary learning and religiosity to elicit such an enthusiastic response from them. Baronius' fame as a distinguished scholar and preacher must have spread far beyond the city of Rome by 1568, for in that year he received an invitation from the famous reformer-bishop of Milan, Carlo Borromeo.[48] The invitation was not accepted because neither Neri nor Baronius wanted the work on the history of the Church to be interrupted.

Neri's reputation of extraordinary sanctity and his many seemingly miraculous deeds had already attracted several young men, including Baronius, to his company. The increased devotional and intellectual activity in his Oratory aroused the interest of more seriously minded young men who joined Neri's company and eventually were ordained priests. In order to house these priests and some of his dedicated lay followers, Neri had his fellow Florentines build an Oratory connected to their Church of San Giovanni. This house, built only in 1574, soon became too small for the growing numbers of his followers. By 1577, Neri had thirteen disciples in holy orders and several other lay followers who resided in the Oratory.

Meanwhile, in 1575, he obtained from Pope Gregory XIII a long awaited document, officially recognizing Neri and his group of priests as a congregation of secular priests. Thus, the Oratorian congregation was officially established. Together with this recognition, the pope also gave them the Church of Santa Maria in Vallicella as their own. Neri immediately went to work. He demolished the old church, and built a new one, together with a large

residence adjoining it in order to house all his disciples. By April
of 1577, the Oratorians were in their new headquarters. However,
the change in residence did not alter Baronius' rigorous schedule.
In spite of the increasing pressures of his priestly duties, he continued the narration of the history of the Church, and by 1578 he
had retold it from beginning to end for the fourth time.

3

Formation of a Historian

Suddenly, in 1578, Baronius was faced with a choice of careers. That year, Tommaso Gigli, bishop of Sora, was transferred to the see of Piacenza at his own request. The reigning pontiff, Gregory XIII, was, therefore, looking for a worthy candidate for the vacant bishopric. Gigli may well have recommended Baronius as his successor because of the special interest Baronius had shown during the preceding years in the religious education of the people of Sora. But most probably Pope Gregory had already made up his mind. After all, he knew Sora to be Baronius' native city; and he was also well aware of his reputation as a scholar and a priest.[1] The prospect was certainly a very attractive one. But Baronius finally turned it down. For by now he was completely committed to the project to which he was to dedicate most of the rest of his life: the history of the Church.

There are indications that his research was progressing well at this time and that it was being remarked upon by persons in high places in the Church. In one of his letters to his father in 1578, Baronius mentions the help he was receiving from Cardinal Guglielmo Sirleto.[2] As a leading humanist and Church reformer, Sirleto must have been extremely interested in Baronius' work. Because he was librarian of the Church, Sirleto was also in a position to help Baronius in his research. Indeed, the cardinal lent him many ancient books and documents from the Apostolic Library and from his own personal collections. He also read parts of Baronius' writings, and he was extremely pleased. Sirleto, therefore, praised Baronius exceedingly and urged him to continue his work.

Baronius' relationship with Cardinal Sirleto indicates the widening range of his scholarly associations. In the succeeding years he would consult personally with many more contemporary scholars and carry on extensive correspondence with many others. There is no way of determining, however, how much progress he had made in his writing by 1578, but his apparent eagerness to consult with well-known scholars would indicate a certain amount of maturity and self-confidence which he had lacked previously. Also a marked change in his attitude toward his work is evident from his letters at this time: the original reluctance and fear had given way to eagerness and enthusiasm.[3]

Around this time Baronius also finished the fifth cycle of his expositions of the history of the Church at the Oratory. Whether he had already started compiling the *Annales* by this time cannot be ascertained. However, a general plan of the work which he organized sometime during this period gives us an understanding of the nature of his projected work as well as the depth and extent of his research. This general plan, which must have been one of the final outlines Baronius used for the *Annales*, is contained in a Vallicelliana codex.[4] In this outline he divided the history of Christianity up to the time of Charlemagne into five parts: (1) From the birth of Christ to the death of Constantine (A.D. 1-337), (2) From the time of Constans to the death of Theodosius II (A.D. 337-450), (3) From the time of Marcian to the death of Maurice (A.D. 450-603), (4) From the death of Maurice to Charlemagne (A.D. 603-768), and (5) Charlemagne and successive emperors (A.D. 768-). For each part he listed a number of sources which he had consulted or intended to consult. For example, he listed Eusebius, Josephus, and Philo as sources for the earliest history of the Church. For the development of dogma and church discipline in the first period (A.D. 1-337), he listed Epiphanius, Philastrius, Augustine, Tertullian, and several other Church fathers. For the second period (A.D. 337-450), his sources included Rufinus of Aquileia, the continuator of Eusebius, Severus Sulpicius, Sozomen, Theodoretus, Athanasius, and Gregory Nazianzen. For the third period (A.D. 450-603), Procopius, Evagrius Scholasticus, Aimonius, Paul the Deacon, Nicephorus Calistus, and Cassiodorus. For the fourth period (A.D. 603-768), Adonis of Vienna, Saint Bede, Saint Eulogius, Marianus Scotus, and several papal documents. For the era of Charlemagne and successive generations, Nicephorus Gregora, Georgius Pachimerus, Gulielmus Tyrus, Polidorus Virgilius, Sabillicus, Papirius Massonius, and popes John VIII and Gregory VII. His selections were mostly original sources contemporary to the particular period, but he also made reference to numerous sources of subsequent periods including works of his own contemporaries like Papire Masson (Papirius Massonius). At the conclusion of the outline, he added the following note to himself, which can be considered as a statement on the guidelines which he would use in selecting and evaluating historical sources:

> First of all, one rule should be observed in all these (historical research and writing). That is the chronological sequence. If this is violated, insurmountable difficulties will arise and errors will occur. Let the chronicles written by diverse authors for diverse times guide you in this. Such chronicles could be the annals compiled year by year during the reign of an emperor or jotted down for some other reason.
>
> You should, first of all, read in chronological order the authors who wrote about the events of their own times. If such authors are not available, at least the authors closest to the times should be selected. But the later ones should be trusted only in as much as they rest on the authority of earlier writers.
>
> Among the histories written by contemporary authors, some are more preferable and more trustworthy. Such are histories made known through correspondences and histories interwoven with other kinds of writings written for other purposes.[5]

Baronius remained faithful to these rules. He compiled the *Annales* in chronological order, presenting the historical events under three concurrent dates representing the year of Christ, the year of the ruling emperor, and the year of the reigning pontiff. In fact, the chronological placement of the events was so important to him that where dates of events were not ascertainable, he included doubtful dates in his narrations, thus incurring the criticism of subsequent historians. Although he occasionally misread his sources, particularly those in Greek, which he understood poorly, he was always very scrupulous about adhering to the principle of temporal priority in selecting the sources of his narrative.

Baronius, then, was totally committed to the huge project of the *Annales* in 1578. But the beginning was slow because even as he had finally made up his mind to dedicate himself wholly to history, he was sidetracked with a special commission—one requested of him by a churchman so eminent that refusal would have been impossible.

Carlo Borromeo, cardinal archbishop of Milan, wanted some historical illumination on a subject that aroused some controversy in his archdiocese. The argument was about the propriety of clerics growing beards, a subject that would seem trivial to us today but

was of some significance for a man so encumbered with detail as
Carlo. Baronius, accordingly, prepared a learned essay on this subject, proving from reason, authority, and historical practice that
growing whiskers indeed was proper for clerics.[6] He completed the
essay by May 24, 1578, when he sent it to Borromeo through a
certain Monsignor Cessare Speziano. This and similar distractions
delayed his work on the *Annales*, no doubt, but they also sent him
back to the historical sources he had already picked out and made
him learn them more thoroughly.

Distractions notwithstanding, Baronius completed work on the
first volume of the *Annales* by the early part of 1579. In a letter
dated April 25, 1579, he conveyed the good news to his father.[7]
He told Camillo Baronio that his book had been examined by ju-
dicious men who had only praise for it. He wanted the credit and
the honor for it to go to the entire Oratorian community at Vallicella, but his colleagues, after having deliberated on the matter,
decided that the work should be published under Baronius' own
name. Thus, the title was to read *Historia Ecclesiastica Controversa
R. P. Caesaris Baronii Sorani Presbyteri Collegii S. Oratorii etc.*
Therefore, he told his father, "be happy and praise the God 'who
elected the feeble to confound the mighty.' "

The volume was ready; but it was not actually to be published
for another eight years. Several things intervened which made it
impossible for him to concentrate on the publication of the *Annales*. First of all, a personal tragedy; Portia Baronio, his mother,
died on July 25, 1580, leaving behind a bereaved husband and a
son whom she had been longing to see at least once more before
she died. Several communications between the son and his parents
during late 1579 and early 1580 reveal the deteriorating health of
the mother and the concern of the son.[8]

It may have been this concern that caused a telepathic vision
which Baronius experienced at the moment of Portia's death.
While he was hearing the confessions in the church at Vallicella on
the morning of July 25, 1580, he reportedly saw her soul rising to
heaven. Wondering about this vision, he immediately sent a mes-
senger to Sora who met at some mid-point his counterpart from
Sora coming to announce the sad news to Baronius. It was later
verified that Baronius had the vision exactly at the moment of his
mother's death.[9] When she died, it became the responsibility of the
only son, Caesar, to console his father and to assist him in adjust-
ing to a new life. Characteristically, young Baronius exhorted his
father to lead a better spiritual life in imitation of his departed

mother.[10] Through letters he also aided his father to make decisions about property arrangements, and sent from Rome an inscribed marble monument to be placed at the grave of Portia. Her death disturbed him a great deal. But, as a faithful religious, he did not let this purely personal affair affect his work on the history of the Church or other duties. What really interfered with the publication of the *Annales* were the tasks imposed upon him by Pope Gregory XIII in connection with the revision of the *Roman Martyrology*.

In 1580, after having set in motion the elaborate process of establishing the new calendar which is known by his name,[11] Gregory decided to revise the *Martyrology*. Several *Martyrologies* existed at that time, all of them prepared at different times for the use of regional churches, and therefore very different in the number and identity of the saints commemorated. Such diversity had once bothered no one; but in the context of the centralizing and uniformizing tendencies of the post-Tridentine Church, they were no longer admissible. The pope felt it highly desirable, therefore, to prepare a new *Martyrology*, which he wanted to establish as the official version to be used universally in the Church. For this purpose, he appointed a commission of learned men, one of whom was Caesar Baronius. In one letter to his father, Baronius related with enthusiasm how Cardinal Sirleto, who had become his friend and patron, had recommended him to the pope, and what an honor he considered it to be a member of such a commission.[12] While appointing Baronius to this commission, the pope offered to grant him a sumptuous pension in order to employ a copyist. Baronius refused this offer because of his vow of poverty. But the pope insisted that he should at least accept a monthly allowance of ten Roman *scudi*. Pompeo Pateri in his memoirs and Barnabeus in his biography of Baronius make mention of this fact.[13] Baronius also made reference to this allowance in a letter to his father in which he offered to send him four of the ten *scudi* every month.[14]

The commission established for the revision of the *Martyrology* was composed of at least the following men: Cesare Baronio, Antonio Geronio, Curzio Franchi—historians; Silvio Antoniano, Pietro Ciacconio de Toledo, Gerardo Vossic, Antonio Angellip—theologians; Latino Latini—literary critic; and Luigi Lilio—astronomer. Several other famous names, such as Robert Bellarmine, are often mentioned in connection with the project, but their participation has not yet been proven.[15] Cardinal Sirleto appears to have been the coordinator and overseer of the project.[16] As the work progressed, however, Baronius emerged as the most prominent member of the commission; his unique experience of more than twenty years of historical research could not be matched.

The commission was urged to complete the work before the inauguration of the new calendar on October 5, 1582. This deadline was met, but at the cost of issuing only a partial version in April, 1582, just enough to cover the remaining months of the first year. Two complete editions were made in 1583. Haste still took precedence over accuracy, since the publishers put pressure on the commission in order to meet public demand. As a result these editions contained many errors. Consequently, none of them was thought worthy of the official approval of the Church. It took the commission still another year to remove most of the errors contained in the first three editions, and bring out a fourth with the official approval of the Church. With the brief *Emendato Jam*, Gregory XIII finally approved the fourth edition on January 14, 1584.

Revision of the *Martyrology* was largely a historical task. What the commission had to do was weed out the mythological and unhistorical saints from the existing *Martyrology* and provide more complete information about the lives and works of those accepted, as well as to include the lives of the later saints. Since in the early Church saints were named and venerated by popular acclaim rather than by official canonization, a universally accepted list did not exist. Each local church had its own cluster of saints, and its own *Martyrology* which contained their stories and commemorative prayers. Often mythical saints were venerated based on alleged miracles accepted by local traditions. Only towards the close of the eleventh century did the popes, recognizing these abuses, begin to impose restrictions on the practice of popular recognition of sainthood. Thus, Urban II, Calixtus II, and Eugene III recommended that this role be relegated to the general councils. Alexander III wanted it to be controlled by the papacy. But the final and decisive step to reserve the right of declaring saints to the papacy was taken only in 1634 by Urban VIII. Even then, a correct procedure to beatify and canonize saints was lacking. Such a procedure was introduced only in 1748 by Benedict XIV, with the publication of his famous work *De Servorum Dei Beatificatione*. In the meantime, saints whose historicity and sanctity were questionable continued to be venerated in many local churches.

To exclude popularly venerated saints from a *Martyrology* that would bear the official approval of the universal Church was a delicate matter, one which could have resulted in serious division unless such decisions were based on undisputable historical evidence. Therefore, as basic historical sources, the revisers used several texts, the authenticity of which were generally accepted at that time. Among them were the medieval *Martyrologium* of Usuard, a Benedictine monk who prepared the work in the ninth century at the request of Charlemagne; the *Martyrologium* of Saint Bede; an ancient *Martyrologium* of the Church of Santo Ciriaco in Via Lata; and a Greek menology recently translated into Latin by Cardinal Sirleto.[17] Besides these, the commission collected from all parts of the Christian world manuscripts and printed works dealing with locally venerated saints. Interested bishops and churchmen could send to the commission any document that existed about their saints, and in cases where they had no documents, written description of the local tradition about them. It seems that every saint who had the backing of any kind of a written document, inscription, or local tradition was accepted by the commission, unless there was strong historical evidence to the contrary, or if the sanctity or theological orthodoxy of the recommended saint was seriously in question. Several cases in which decisions were made on Baronius' initiative would support the above observation.

In the correspondence of Baronius, we find a letter written by his father and addressed to a certain priest, Francesco di Messer Pietro, in the little south Italian town of Trasacco. In this letter Camillo Baronio asks the priest to send the names and relevant information about the patron saints of that town to his son, Caesar, so that he may include them in the new *Martyrology*.[18] The priest must have sent the petition, because we see the feast of Santo Cesidio and companions, holy martyrs, was set for August 31 in the same revised *Martyrology*.[19] But judging from this correspondence, very little was known about these martyrs; only the local legend or tradition and the patriotic loyalty of the townspeople were their support. However, to Baronius the historian, legend alone could not lend any weight to the historicity of these saints. Hence, he added the following note about Santo Cesidio of Trasacco in his *Notationes* to the *Martyrology*: "He is celebrated for the many daily miracles; since it is my mother's birthplace, I am talking about the things witnessed and experienced."[20] Baronius, in other words, looked for some sort of justification for including this saint in the *Martyrology*. He could not fully accept the saint without the support of some sort of written record. But he could not exclude Santo Cesidio either, for Baronius accepted fervent piety as at least a good indication of the veracity of the object of piety—a critical principle that apparently had the support of his colleagues, however inadequate it may have been for forming a valid historical judgement.

The case of Cesidio was difficult enough. But the one that really troubled Baronius was that of Pope Felix II, who most probably was an Arian anti-pope appointed by Emperor Constantius in place of Pope Liberius whom he had exiled.[21] The Arianism of Felix and his usurpation of the papal throne was recognized by many scholars at that time, even though his name had been found in many ancient *Martyrologies* as a confessor and martyr. The commission, therefore, was not willing to give an honorable mention to him in the *Martyrology*. Baronius particularly was against Felix, and in order to prove and justify his position, he even prepared a treatise on the life and work of the anti-pope. But there were strong allies on the side of Felix who were convinced of his sanctity and martyrdom, the most important of whom was the influential Cardinal Santori di San Severina.

The argument was raging between the two sides, when behold! a miraculous discovery occurred. Some thieves, who were digging for hidden treasures near the tombs of Saints Cosmus and Damianus in the Roman Forum accidentally came across several new tombstones and sarcophaguses. One of the marble sarcophaguses had the following inscription on it: "The body of Felix, Pope and Martyr, who condemned Constantius."[22] This occurred on July 29, 1582, the eve of the feast day of Felix in the old *Martyrologies*. The miraculous discovery had an immediate effect on those who were skeptical about the sanctity of Felix, including Baronius, who unanimously agreed to place him on the roster of saints. A modern historian would be puzzled by the easy credulity of the commission, particularly of Baronius the historian, as there is no indication that the commission made any attempt to examine the inscription carefully in order to determine its authenticity. Baronius did not give the matter close attention. But, in a day when multiplication of miracles was encouraged as an argument against the Protestants, and long before the more spectacular unmasking of fake archaeological remains in the eighteenth century, he too, like all his colleagues, bowed before what they were certain was a direct intervention of God. Here again we have to understand the peculiar nature of the subject under investigation; that is, the recognition of the sanctity of a person which was more in the realm of faith than scientific history. Therefore, this is not an instance where Baronius' critical approach to historical sources may be validly judged. That has to be done when we discuss his major historical work, the *Annales*. The work on the *Martyrology*, however, constituted an important part of his preparation to become a historian, and as such is significant.

In a work of this nature, the commission seems to have determined, that positive historical proof of the saint's historicity and sanctity could be overlooked in deference to the strong tradition among the faithful and supporting divine signs like miracles. But statements or beliefs about saints that could be proved wrong by authentic sources were rigorously excluded. In fact, the main purpose of the Gregorian revision of the *Martyrology* was the removal of such errors; that is, those errors which became obvious for historical reasons but not those which did not have the support of historical sources one way or the other. The revisers were fairly successful in achieving this limited goal.

Cardinal Sirleto wanted to be doubly certain about the historicity of the recognized saints, and he also wanted to provide more historical information about them than was possible in the *Martyrology* which was mainly intended for daily devotional reading. Therefore he appointed Baronius, the most competent historian among the members of the commission, to prepare critical commentaries on the texts in the *Martyrology* pertaining to the lives of all martyrs. Baronius started this work even while the final draft of the *Martyrology* was being prepared for the press.[23] He completed the commentaries in 1584.[24] But he must not have been ready to send them to the press yet, for the Gregorian edition of the *Martyrology* came out in the same year without them. However, they were published together with his own revised edition of the *Martyrology* in 1586, from the press of the same Domenico Basa who had published the previous edition.

Baronius patterned his commentaries after a similar work prepared by Pietro Galesino and published at Milan in 1578. Galesino's commentaries were placed in the appendix of the Milan edition of the *Martyrology* in order to throw more light onto the history of the saints. But his approach was purely hagiographical and only secondarily historical; he sought not to establish the truth about the past, but to inspire piety. Baronius' commentaries, on the other hand, were placed underneath the text dealing with the saints of the day, and were characterized by exactness of information, richness of references to ancient sources, and the critical selection of such sources.[25] The Baronian edition of the *Martyrology* was prefaced by a treatise in which he dealt with the history of *Martyrologies* from the beginning to his own times. This scholarly treatise remains even today as the preface to most approved editions of the *Roman Martyrology*.

This was the first work Baronius had ever published, but the learned world received it with great enthusiasm. The famous critic

Latino Latini considered it very erudite.[26] Guglielmo Lindano, bishop of Ruremonda and famous theologian, praised it as a "golden" work.[27] Great scholar and critic Cristoforo Plantino, called it "most scholarly."[28] Theologian, Giorgio Colvenerio commented, "most erudite and most useful."[29] Abbot Jacobus de Marquais of Tours considered it "useful and necessary to the Church."[30] Noted scholar, Niccola Seraio, and French philosopher and theologian, Papire Masson, called it "most erudite."[31] Dominican theologian, Vincenzo Giustiniani, termed Baronius' commentaries "angelical annotations";[32] and famous Parisian scholar, R. Viseur, "divine and in every respect golden."[33]

Any version of the *Martyrology* would normally have been a best seller at the time because every priest, religious, and pious layman used it for daily devotional readings. The scholarly annotations of Baronius were an added attraction, particularly to the educated Christian who could appreciate historical knowledge. Thus, the demand for this edition of the *Martyrology* became so great that at least seven printings were made during the lifetime of Baronius: in Rome, Venice, and Antwerp. Two of these printings were actually new editions, emendated and elaborated by Baronius. Several more editions of the Baronian *Martyrology* were published until Benedict XIV made another revision of the work in the 1740's. Even after that, however, most editions carried Baronius' *Notationes* and *Tractatus* on the *Roman Martyrology*. The great diffusion of this work made Baronius well-known not only among the learned circles of Europe but also throughout the Catholic world. And because references were made about his forthcoming *Annales Ecclesiastici* in all editions of the Baronian *Martyrology*, the new work was well advertised long before it was sent to press.

Even while Baronius was busy with the *Martyrology*, still other functions competed for his time and attention. One activity which interfered with the progress of the *Annales* was a commentary on the *Acts of the Apostles* which he delivered weekly at the Oratory from May 12, 1580. It cannot be ascertained whether or not Philip Neri asked him to do this, but it is safe to assume so in view of the already mentioned relationship between the two men. In any other case, Baronius might not have been willing to further divert his attention from the all important task of preparing the *Annales*. The series of commentaries were continued through the rest of the year 1580. Manuscript copies of these lectures are preserved in the Vallicelliana Library.[34] Biblical commentaries eventually became a tradition in the Oratory, and its institutor was Baronius. Whoever conceived the idea, Neri or Baronius, it certainly was a reflection of the interest in biblical learning prevalent in Rome at this period.

Still another work interfered with the preparation of the *Annales*. Pope Gregory XIII was extremely devoted to his namesake, Saint Gregory Nazianzen. In 1580 he built a new altar in Saint Peter's Basilica in honor of the saint and transferred his remains with great pomp and ceremony from the Church of Santa Maria in Campo Marzo to the new location. Pope Gregory was a great benefactor of the Oratorians, and they thought it proper to join him in celebrating the occasion in an active manner. Baronius, therefore, prepared a biography of Saint Gregory (probably at the suggestion of Neri) and presented it to the pontiff. This work remained in manuscript form until the Bollandists published it, without any change, in their *Acta Sanctorum* in 1680.[35] A revised and enlarged edition was published by an Oratorian successor of Baronius, Albericius, in 1760.[36]

In 1582, still another task was imposed on him by Cardinal Felice Peretti (Montalto), who was to become Pope Sixtus V. The cardinal was preparing an edition of the collected works of Saint Ambrose, and he wanted to preface it with a carefully written biography of the saint. Being a friend of Baronius and being aware of the research he had been doing in the early history of the Church, it was only natural for the cardinal to request him to prepare the biography he needed. Baronius, however, was extremely reluctant to undertake this task, fearing that this would further delay the publication of his *Annales*.[37] But the cardinal was finally able to prevail upon him, and Baronius immediately started to work on this project along with his other research.

The biography of Saint Ambrose was completed in 1584 and was published in 1587 in the sixth volume of Peretti's edition. This, again, contributed to Baronius' renown as a scholar. Later, he inserted much of this biography of Saint Ambrose in the fourth volume of the *Annales*, published in 1593. The biographies of Saint Ambrose and Saint Gregory Nazianzen distracted Baronius from his major work on the history of the Church. But his critical and objective approach to the lives and works of these saints was a pioneer experiment and a departure from the hagiographical writings of previous Catholic biographers. His method was imitated by later patristic scholars, among them the Bollandists and the Benedictines of Saint Maur.

In 1583, Baronius was called upon by Pope Gregory XIII to undertake an important mission. As Calenzio reports, a new heresy appeared in Naples regarding the Eucharist.[38] The heretic in question reportedly denied the presence of the blood of Christ in the consecrated host. Once, after receiving communion, the above mentioned heretic furtively removed the host and hid it in a handkerchief. As the story goes, this host miraculously took the shape of a blood-stained crucifix, thus lending divine authority to the presence of Christ's blood in the consecrated host. But the report of such a heresy, in the wake of the Reformation, was a terrible shock to the pope, and he immediately sent Baronius to Naples with instructions to meet with the religious authorities there and to take the necessary steps to suppress the heresy before it spread. Details of this mission are not known; secrecy was imposed in order to prevent news of the heresy from reaching the public. However, on the way to Naples Baronius paid a visit to his father in Sora, and on his return to Rome wrote a letter to him describing how well he was received by the archbishop, the papal nuncio, and other dignitaries.[39] His being sent on such an important mission, again, was a recognition of his learning and orthodoxy. It was also an indication of his growing influence in high places.

Camillo Baronio died in 1583. Several letters Baronius wrote to his father in the latter part of that year reveal his affection and deep concern for him.[40] The father had become quite fond and proud of his son after the long period of cold relations. There is no indication that Baronius went to Sora at this time, but the emotional strain over his father's death and the consequent family settlements must have had at least some adverse effect on his work.

All these activities, concerns, and other routine religious functions consumed practically every moment of his time in the early 1580's. Being one of the founding members of his religious congregation, he also was constantly called upon to undertake more than his share of responsibilities. In 1583, for example, he was asked to lead the reorganization of the Oratory, and to preach the Lenten sermons.[41] In 1584, he was elected prefect of the Oratory.[42] In the same year he was also appointed librarian of the Oratory, a most appropriate choice considering his own scholarly interests.[43] His characteristic religious zeal often got him involved in the counseling and conversion of sinners and criminals. A famous case in this connection was the conversion of the notorious criminal, Bartolomeo Catena, who had been committing many atrocities in Campagna. Hearing about this, Baronius prayed and did penances for him, and sent a letter to him through some Capuchin priests. When finally the criminal was apprehended while passing through Rome and was condemned to death. Baronius was there to hear his confession and prepare him for death.[44]

Another prominent case in which Baronius played the role of the spiritual father was the trial of the famous heretic, Giacomo Massilara, better known as Paleologus. An ex-Dominican priest, he married in defiance of the law of the Church, and he had preached anti-Trinitarian doctrines in Poland and Germany. Apprehended by the Inquisition in 1584, and ordered to recant the heretical beliefs, he remained obstinate. Arguments by theologians like Robert Bellarmine were of no avail. He was, therefore, condemned to die at the stake as an obstinate heretic. When he was being led to the scaffold erected in Rome's Campo dei Fiori, Philip Neri intervened, and by his characteristic simplicity and compassion saved the man from immediate execution. He also succeeded in persuading Paleologus to renounce his beliefs publicly. In order to converse with him further and help him to regain his faith, Neri sent two of his disciples, Baronius and Giovan Francesco Bordini, to Tor di Nona, the prison where the condemned man was kept. It is recorded that Baronius' counsel was particularly helpful due to the erudite manner in which he handled the theological and historical questions of Paleologus.[45]

Many of these works were undertaken by Baronius on his own accord while others, such as the work on the *Martyrology*, the biographies of Saint Ambrose and Saint Gregory Nazianzen, and, of course, the trip to Naples, were imposed on him by his superiors. In any case, he was unable to bring out even the first volume of his most important work on the history of the Church which, in his own words, had been ready to go to the press since 1579. Some of his letters during this period reveal his regrets and impatience about this matter.[46] Perhaps Philip Neri, who was even more interested in this project, felt the same way for we have a record showing that he appointed Tommaso Bozzio, a member of the Oratory, to assist Baronius in the publication of the first volume of the *Annales*.[47] But this did not work out because Bozzio was not willing to help Baronius; he wanted to work on his own project of preparing a similar history from Adam to Christ.[48] In fact, he prepared such a work in twelve volumes of which only the first was published. The other volumes still remain in manuscript form in the Vallicelliana Library.[49]

Even though Baronius did not receive any assistance from Bozzio, he was able to make some progress with the *Annales* in 1587. The most time consuming task of the *Martyrology* was out of the way, and his oral renditions of Church history at the Oratory, of which he was on the seventh cycle, was only an occasion to crystalize his ideas and organize his material. He was now recognized as an accomplished scholar. And recognition acted as a stimulus on him as well as on Pope Sixtus V, who granted him an annual pension of four hundred *scudi* to be used for the preparation of the *Annales*. In 1580, when Gregory XIII offered him a large pension, he had refused it. But this time he seems to have been anxious to receive it.

An incident illustrates Caesar's new attitude toward financial help and even more importantly towards the cause for which it was intended, namely the *Annales*. As his contemporary biographer Paolo Aringhi relates, Baronius was not only happy to receive this grant, but he was also unwilling to let the money leave his hand and be used for anything except the *Annales*.[50] For the first time, we see him attempting to go against the will of his spiritual mentor, Philip Neri, who wanted this money to be placed for the common use of the Oratory. Neri even had to threaten him with expulsion from the congregation before Baronius complied with his wish. Aringhi's relation of the story leaves the impression that Neri was only testing the obedience of his favorite disciple, and that he did not really intend to interfere with the publication of the *Annales*. If so, Baronius passed the test. His initial reaction, however, is a certain indication of his revitalized personal interest and commitment to this work.

This renewed personal interest, coupled with the insistence from interested Catholic leaders and scholars, proved to be the strong incentive that kept him working at full speed on the final preparation for publication of the first volume of the *Annales*.[51] The stage was all set when in 1587 Sixtus V, his long-time friend and patron, offered him the facilities of the Vatican Press, newly established that year. The pope also offered to employ a proof reader to assist him. Baronius preferred to enlist his own co-religionists instead, probably because he thought they might be better at it and be able to prepare the index at the same time. The proofs were sent to the Oratory at Naples, which had been established in 1586; and there two young Oratorian priests, Tommaso Galletti and Francesco Bozzio, were entrusted with the task. Baronius' longtime friend and co-religionist, Antonio Talpa, was to oversee their work and suggest any further corrections and additions. Himself an erudite person, Talpa accordingly made many suggestions, particularly regarding the format of the book, and these were all incorporated.[52]

Several of Baronius' letters to Talpa, written between November of 1587, and April of 1588, contain detailed descriptions of the work in its different stages.[53] On January, 1588, for example, he wrote that the work was going at a feverish pace because he wanted to publish the first volume at least in March. In the same letter he mentioned that he intended to carry the first volume up to Trajan because that would cover nearly the first hundred years from the birth of Christ, the second up to Constantine to cover approximately the next two hundred years, and the third up to Theodosius covering only about seventy years because of the amplitude of material. This plan was changed later, but at least it shows that Baronius had already started preparing the materials for the next two volumes.

In these letters to Talpa, he also reveals numerous difficulties he encountered in the process of printing the *Annales*. First of all, it was extremely difficult and time consuming to send the proofs all the way to Naples and back again. Then the corrections his readers made were not often satisfactory to Baronius. The indexes they prepared were disorderly. The Naples Oratory did not have all the books and codices Baronius used, and the readers were, therefore, unable to double-check references. The members of the Roman Oratory for one reason or another did not provide the help Baronius needed. Thus, much of the mechanical work also fell on the shoulders of the author. Moreover, the incompetence of the Vatican Press, which was not yet well organized, also created problems for him. Many errors crept into the first edition, even after some of the material had been done over several times. Some errors were so displeasing to Baronius that he inserted an announcement in the first volume that a second edition with corrections and additions would soon be forthcoming.

Even while the printing was in progress, many cardinals of the curia and learned men of Rome, anxious to read the long awaited work, sought for press proofs.[54] This shows the great interest with which the Catholic world awaited the book. Finally, some time in June or July of 1588, the printing of the first volume was completed. This volume was dedicated to Sixtus V who was greatly interested in the work, and Baronius personally took a copy of it to the pontiff. The pope, reports Baronius, was extremely gratified with the work, and exhorted the author to continue and complete it.[55]

The *Annales* was received by Catholics everywhere with great enthusiasm. For many of them this was the God-sent work to refute authoritatively the Magdeburg Centuriators. The receptive at-

titude of the Catholic world guaranteed success to the work. But
the world of erudition was also to recognize it, not without merit,
as one of the richest treasuries of historical learning ever produced.
Not only would the *Annales* make publishing history, but it was
also to touch off a literary polemic unprecedented in history. The
amazing story of the *Annales* had just begun.

4

The Success of a Book and a Man

When the first volume of the *Annales* was published in 1588, Baronius was a few months short of fifty years old. For the previous thirty years he had incessantly labored over the preparation of the *Annales*. Those were the years of relative obscurity and toil. In contrast with the past, the remaining nineteen years of his life would be characterized by fame, glory, success, and influence in the highest echelons of ecclesiastical and civil society. He would become a cardinal of the Church, would be nominated for the papacy—though unsuccessfully—in two conclaves, and he would enjoy the confidence of popes and monarchs. It was not noble birth or familial connections that made him so eminent. His scholarship and the prodigious success of his *Annales* were his only credentials. His Church, long beleaguered by Protestant onslaughts and deprived of her once unchallenged intellectual leadership, was successful in regaining much of her lost prestige and leadership partly due to his work, and she was grateful. This was the background of his ascendancy in the ecclesiastical hierarchy. His personal success and the success of his major work, the *Annales*, were so interrelated that one cannot be treated without the other.

The ready reception and the overwhelming applause given to the *Annales* by the Catholic world—clergy and laity alike—have to be explained in context with the setback the Church had suffered at the appearance of the *Magdeburg Centuries* some three decades before. The *Centuries* was mainly the work of Matthias Flacius Illyricus. Born in 1520 in Istria and introduced at an early age to Lutheran ideas and writings by a cousin, an ex-Franciscan provincial, he was sent to Venice and Basel for a humanistic education in 1539. From there Flacius went to Tubingen and finally to Witten-

49

berg in 1541 where he received his theological training under Melanchthon. He spent most of the 1540's in Wittenberg. It should
be remembered that this was the period during which Luther lev-
eled his most virulent attacks against the papacy, and the proximity of the Reformer must have had a hardening effect on the already cultivated anti-Catholic attitude of Flacius. In 1544 he was
made professor of Hebrew at the University of Wittenberg, and in
1546 he received his doctorate in theology under Melanchthon.
Soon Flacius was found to be openly critical of his mentor, Melanchthon, particularly with the latter's mild and conciliatory attitude towards the Catholic side. This eventually resulted in Flacius'
departure from Wittenberg in 1549. He then went to Magdeburg
where he spent the major part of his life, and accomplished the
monumental task of editing the *Magdeburg Centuries*. He died in
1575 at Frankfurt.

The *Magdeburg Centuries* was the culmination of a series of attempts by Lutheran writers to explain the history of the Christian
religion in such a way as to lend authority and justification to the
Protestant positions in dogma and religious practice. Such a historical explanation was absolutely necessary because Luther had
rested his case for separation from Rome mainly on a historical
argument, namely the gradual evolution of the hierarchical system
of the Church contrary to the design of Christ. This argument was
a central theme of all his sermons and writings.[1] To bring this argument to clearer focus, Luther also had outlined the general
course of a new historical approach to Church history in 1536
in his preface to the *Vitae Romanorum Pontificum* by the ex-
Augustinian, Robert Barnes. In it, all the evils that had come
about in Christendom during the previous centuries were attributed to the popes. Another work, published twelve years later by
John Bale, an ex-English Carmelite, also followed the same trend.
This work, *Acta Romanorum Pontificum,* which was published in
1584 at Ipswich as part of a larger work on English literature, contained virulent criticisms of the papacy. These were the pioneer
works in confessional historiography from the Lutheran side.

The strong anti-papal tone of these works was not only imitated
but even intensified in the works of Flacius, for he himself was
firmly convinced that the pope was the anti-Christ.[2] Brilliant scholar that he was, his natural inclination was to establish this position by marshaling authentic historical sources. Flacius' first attempt in this regard resulted in his work, *Catalogus Testium Veritatis*, which appeared in 1556 from Basel. The main purpose of

this work was to prove from history that under papal leadership the evolution of the Church from early middle ages actually constituted a departure from practices of the early Christians; that Lutheranism was not an innovation but only a restoration of Christianity in its pure form. For substantiation he rallied the authority of four hundred witnesses, selected from different ages starting with apostolic times. Among these witnesses were Augustine, Bernard, and Tauler, all of whom could be interpreted to have favored some aspect of Lutheran doctrine.

While working on this book, Flacius conceived an idea of preparing a comprehensive history of the Christian religion. The ultimate purpose of this history again was to justify the Lutheran position by demonstrating the historical development of the hierarchical Church as the result of a deliberate plot by the Roman pontiffs. Realizing the importance and the extent of the work, he organized a group of men to help him with the collection and the processing of data. He sent many agents to the various libraries and archives of Europe to collect manuscripts and rare books dealing with the history and development of Christian religion from its earliest times. After having spent several years collecting the necessary data, around 1557 a committee of five men under the leadership of Flacius began to compose the work. At least nine others were enlisted to aid this committee in the capacity of coordinators or research assistants.[3] The multi-volume work was published by Johannes Operinus at Basel from 1559 to 1574.

The work appeared with an imposing title: *Ecclesiastica historia integram Ecclesiae Christi ideam quantum ad locum, propagationem, persecutionem, tranquillitatem, doctrinam, haereses, caeremonias, gubernationem, schismata, synodos, personas, miracula, martyria, religiones extra Ecclesiam et status Imperii politicum attinet, secumdum singulas centurias, perspicuo ordine complectens: singulari diligentia et fide ex vetustissimis et optimis historicis, patribus et aliis scriptoribus congesta per aliquot studiosos et pios viros in urbe Magdeburgica.*

Altogether thirteen volumes were published, each covering a century. Each volume is generally divided into sixteen chapters, dealing with various aspects of the Christian religion such as doctrine, ceremony, ecclesiastical government, synods, etc. Every chapter in turn is divided under appropriate subtitles. For example, chapter four of volume one which deals with doctrinal matters contains separate treatises on God, creation, Scriptures, sin, divine law and justification, faith, sacraments, the Church, etc. Nearly a

third of the work is devoted to the nature and development of
doctrine. The growth of the Church and the historical development of her organization are outlined in the framework of an eternal conflict between good and evil, God and devil.

The papacy is portrayed as the instrument of the devil which
from century to century increasingly obscured the real teachings
of Christ and obstructed the freedom of the faithful. The primacy
of the pope, naturally, is denied, and papism is compared to the
beasts of the Apocalypse. The pontiffs who played a greater role
in establishing the papal authority are called monsters, among
them Gregory VII who "was most monstrous."[4] The validity of
tradition is denied. The old Catholic saying attributed to Pope
Stephen I in support of the validity of tradition, "nihil innovetur
nisi quod traditum est," is replaced by the principle "falsum quod
posterius immissum."[5]

With the elimination of tradition as a basis of argument, the
Centuriators reserved the whole realm of theological interpretation
to biblical exegesis and patristic writings. With a great number of
such sources at hand, they were able to develop in their volumes a
convincing argument in favor of the Lutheran position. The immense array of documents they presented in support of their arguments and the professedly scrupulous selection of such documents as to their authenticity lent more credence to their position. What the Centuriators did in essence was to use historical
arguments to prove their theological positions.[6] This new approach indeed was very timely and effective in view of the questioning attitude which became prevalent among the Christians of
Europe in the wake of the Reformation.

The appearance of the *Magdeburg Centuries* with all the trap-
pings of critical history, claiming to be the authentic interpretation of the history of the Church, created great consternation
among Catholics. Naturally, they wanted to refute the Centuriators, but there was no one man or one group equipped with the
necessary talent and erudition. However, several attempts were
made by Catholic scholars, but none to be compared with the
magnitude or documentary wealth of the *Centuries*. Onofrio Panvinio, an Augustinian priest and the best Catholic historian of the
time, attempted a systematic refutation of the Lutheran work.
With the aid and encouragement of Philip II of Spain, he prepared
the *Chronicon ecclesaie usque ad Maximilianum II* which was published from Cologne in 1568. He was also preparing another three
volumes entitled *De primatu Petri et Apostolicae sedis potestate*

to refute the anti-papal position of the Centuriators, but sudden death in 1568 put an end to his effort. His work, however, was posthumously published in 1589, and it earned him the title of "father of all history."[7] Other Catholic scholars also attempted to refute the *Centuries*. Dr. Conrad Braun of Augsburg, a friend of Peter Canisius, was one of them. William Eisengrein was another who published a book pointing out the flaws in the first volume of the *Centuries*. Later, two Englishmen, Alan Cope (a canon of Saint Peter's) and Nicholas Harpsfield, wrote against the Centuriators.

All these works, however, were fragmentary, and therefore did not constitute a systematic refutation. Realizing this, Pope Pius V requested the Jesuits of Germany, particularly Canisius, to refute the Protestant work.[8] Accordingly, Canisius published his *De Corruptelis Verbi Dei* in 1571. He followed this with two more works. The first one was devoted to John the Baptist and it sought to refute the Protestant position on justification by faith alone. The other dealt with Mariology, and it sought to reaffirm the Catholic practice of the veneration of the Virgin. But like the previous Catholic publications, these works of Canisius were not complete and therefore ineffective in refuting the *Centuries*. Besides, the Jesuits of Germany were faced with the immediate problem of the reconversion of Protestants and thus were not able to spend the time and effort needed for such a systematic theologico-historical work.

In 1571 Pius V established a commission of cardinals to study ways and means of adequately refuting the *Centuries* and checking the adverse influence of the work on the Catholic church. Cardinals Sirleto, Hosio, Maffei, Montalto, Colonna, and Guistiniani, all prominent in the Roman Curia, were members of this commission. But nothing of real importance was accomplished by the commission because of the death of Pius V in 1572.[9] Isolated authors like the Englishman Thomas Stapleton,[10] Robert Bellarmine, and the editor Marguerin de la Bigne still continued to produce apologetical works defending the Catholic church. But a comprehensive work, comparable to the scope and documentary wealth of the *Centuries* had yet to be produced from the Catholic side, and this need was widely recognized by Catholics all over Europe. This is the background in which the *Annales* made its appearance. The elation with which the Catholics received the work, therefore, is understandable.

The wide demand for the work, naturally, was anticipated by everyone concerned, not excepting the author. At a time when

copyrights were not generally recognized, the possibility of un-
authorized publication was very real, and it is for that reason
Baronius requested and obtained an order from Sixtus V prohib-
iting anyone from publishing the *Annales* for the next ten years
without the permission of the author.[11] This step was justified by
the popular demands for the book that were to follow. Even while
the first volume was being printed at the Vatican, Christophorus
Plantinus, the famous Antwerp publisher who had previously reprinted Baronius' *Notationes* to the *Martyrology*, requested permission to reproduce the *Annales* from his press. But the author
was unwilling to have the work reprinted until after the necessary
corrections were made. He subsequently made these corrections
with the help of fellow Oratorians, Giovenale Ancina and Silvio
Antoniani. Plantinus was later authorized to publish the second
edition of the work.[12] This second edition of the first volume,
which came out in 1589, met with such great demand in all parts
of Europe that the publisher, Plantinus, raised the price by one-
third.[13] Still they were so widely purchased that shortly afterwards "no more copies were left," as Jacobus de Marquais wrote
to Baronius soon after this edition was published in Antwerp.[14]

The learned world of Europe, particularly Catholic intellectual
circles, reacted with great enthusiasm as soon as the first volume
of the *Annales* hit the market. Streams of laudatory letters poured
onto Baronius' desk from all parts of Europe. The president of the
University of Louvain, Henricius Gravius, wrote with lavish praise
of his erudition and congratulations for the significant success of
his work.[15] Laevinus Torrentius, bishop of Antwerp and a noted
scholar, sent a letter congratulating Baronius. He later wrote an
encomium on the *Annales* which he requested to be inserted in the
next edition;[16] and Baronius obliged. Francesco Panigarola, bishop
of Asti and one of the most popular preachers of the time, who
later prepared an Italian compendium of the first volume., wrote
in his preface:

> I have never seen such a rich work; it is to me like seeing an
> ocean of beautiful things; it is like reading not just one book
> but four complete books, all of them classics; a competent
> history of the Church, a most learned commentary on the New
> Testament, a brave disputation against the modern heretics, and
> a most minute collection of all the ancient customs.[17]

Panigarola concluded his preface with an exhortation to the reader
to pray so that "the Lord may keep our most beloved Father

Caesar long enough to complete this work, which work, in my judgment, is the most useful to God's Church, of all the works produced in many centuries, printed or in manuscript." Numerous other noted scholars and Church leaders also expressed their admiration for the work, so that Baronius was making only a modest statement when he wrote to Talpa on October 22, 1588, that the *Annales* "was accepted by the men of letters beyond all my expectations."[18] Reviewing the impact of the *Annales*, a modern historian (Pope John XXIII) wrote the following:

> The enthusiasm with which the *Annales* were received and which surrounded the person of Baronius in all of Europe is almost incredible. The appearance of the first volume gave such a relief to everyone, as if an enormous danger threatening the fatherland had been magically removed.
> The pope, the kings, the princes, the scholars, Catholics from every country turned their eyes and thoughts to Baronius. They waited the successive volumes with anxiety. And from all over the world came into the poor cell of the Oratorio letters of applause and encouragement, and often documents so that the work which had begun so well might be completed successfully.[19]

While the appearance of the *Annales* was creating such a wave of enthusiasm in learned circles, many persons suggested to Baronius that an abridged version of the book be prepared for the use of the common people.[20] Since the author himself was engaged in the compilation of the successive volumes, he entrusted this work to his Oratorian confreres of Naples, who at that time were helping him to make the necessary emendations in the work.[21] But in the meantime, the aforementioned Francesco Panigarola offered to do an Italian compendium of the *Annales*.[22] Realizing that a vernacular version of the work would be much more useful for the common people, Baronius accepted this offer and subsequently asked his Neapolitan colleagues to discontinue the work on their Latin compendium.[23]

While authorizing the Panigarola version, Baronius also was hoping that it would open the door for still other abridgements in other languages so that his work would become accessible to the peoples of different countries.[24] This hope was partially realized when Marcus Fugger, baron of Kirchberg and Weissenhorn, and counselor to the Holy Roman Emperor, requested permission to prepare a German translation of the *Annales*.[25] Of these two versions of the work authorized by Baronius, Panigarola's Italian compendium was the first to be published in 1590 from the press of Giovanni Gigliotto at Rome. Marcus Fugger's German translation appeared in 1594 at Ingolstadt. Neither of these versions went beyond the first volume of the *Annales*, partly because the translators were unable to cope with the immense volumes Baronius was bringing forth at very short intervals. However, these set the example; and others were to follow in due course.

In the meantime, spurred on by the universal acclaim for his work, Baronius was eagerly working on the successive volumes. But an oppressive number of sacerdotal functions continuously obstructed his progress. Neri did not show any inclination to relieve him from any of these functions. Desperately, therefore, he requested his more sympathetic co-religionists of the Naples Oratory to intercede with Neri on his behalf.[26] However, there is no indication that his efforts were rewarded. Instead, Neri imposed more burdens and humiliating penances on his famous disciple. Every time Baronius presented a new volume of the *Annales* to Neri he would order him to do some penance like serving as an altar boy at several masses.[27] Neri also subjected Baronius to various kinds of humiliations, such as publicly ridiculing him, dubbing him with laughable names like "barbarian" and degrading his achievements in the presence of other scholars.[28]

In view of Philip Neri's continued enthusiasm about Baronius' work on the history of the Church, the seeming obstructions he placed on the historian's path become difficult to understand. The only valid explanation is that Neri, as a true ascetic, placed humility and personal sanctity above scholarly accomplishments, and that he wanted to protect his favorite disciple from the temptations of pride which could have resulted from his success in the world of learning. Baronius would later affectionately call these his spiritual father's "tyrannical" impositions in the essay of thanksgiving to Neri which he inserted in the eighth volume of the *Annales* soon after his death. In the same essay the author of the *Annales* gives all the credit for his accomplishments to the stern discipline of Neri, which removes any doubts about the purpose of such humiliating impositions.[29]

Neri's precautions against the possibility of Baronius becoming too proud may have been justified in view of the amazing rise in the latter's popularity and renown. Within the two years that elapsed between the publication of the first and second volumes of the *Annales*, 1588-90, Baronius received universal recognition and so many honors that Neri could have feared that his disciple's personal sanctity might be adversely affected. For example, soon after the publication of the first volume, Baronius was offered the bishopric of Teano by Sixtus V. Vincenzo Brancaleoni, the bishop of that diocese, had died in 1588, and Cardinal Giulio Antonio Santoro (Cardinale di Santa-severina), himself a scholar and a patron of scholars, had recommended the author of the *Annales* for the vacant bishopric.[30] Two years later, late in 1590 or early in 1591 (around the time the second volume was published) another bishopric was offered to Baronius. Francesco Maria Enrici, the bishop of Sinigaglia, had died, and the duke of Urbino in whose territory the diocese was located requested the reigning pontiff, Gregory XIV, to appoint Baronius to that see.[31] Baronius rejected both these offers because he was unwilling to discontinue his scholarly work. But rumors still persisted in Rome that he was soon going to be elevated to high ecclesiastical office, possibly to the College of Cardinals.[32] All these offers and rumors seem to indicate the prominence he had achieved after the publication of the *Annales*.

In late 1590, the Vatican Press published the second volume of the *Annales*. As soon as it came off the press Plantinus at Antwerp started to reprint it, as he had the first volume, for the larger market of central and northern Europe. Baronius' original plan had been to bring out a volume every year, but he was slightly behind schedule because of the immense quantity of material he had to work with and because of the lack of any substantial assistance. In the prefatory essay dedicating Volume II to Sixtus V, Baronius explained that "ponderous things can hardly move at the pace of a race."[33] This explanation may have been given in view of the pontiff's special interest in the speedy completion of the *Annales,* which he also considered as a refutation of the *Magdeburg Centuries.*

The pope's interest had been manifested previously by the pecuniary donations and the encouragement he gave to Baronius. These were again repeated at the completion of the second volume. Sixtus V sent a hundred *scudi* and made some promises to Baronius of which he mentioned in a letter to his close friend, Talpa.[34] In this letter, Baronius requested Talpa to pray that these promises not be fulfilled, which cast some mystery over the nature of the promises. Calenzio considers that the promise was to elevate Baronius to the cardinalate, which seems to be quite probable under the circumstances.[35]

After the death of Sixtus, the succeeding popes also encouraged
Baronius in his work. During the brief reigns of Urban VII, Gregory XIV, and Innocent IX, he continued to receive special favors
helpful to his work. Gregory XIV, for example, granted him the
privilege of taking home some manuscripts from the Vatican Library, which indeed was a very unusual favor.[36] Clement VIII,
soon after his elevation to the papacy in 1592, began to consider
Baronius as a member of the papal household and allowed a pension of two hundred *scudi* in support of his work.[37] Also, around
this time, Baronius was offered by a Portugese prelate a donation
of three hundred *scudi*, which he did not accept.[38]

Indeed, such was the attention Baronius was receiving that it
eventually aroused jealousies even among his fellow Oratorians.
One man was particularly envious: Antonio Gallonio, a fellow
member of the Roman Oratory, who at that time was engaged in
a scholarly project similar to that of Baronius.[39] His main interest
was to collect and edit the lives of all the saints of the Church,
something like what the Bollandists were to do at a later period.
Gallonio collected from all over the Christian world existing manuscripts of printed works on the lives of the saints. After having collected all the available materials, he began to compile the lives of
the saints in chronological order and transpose them into contemporary Latin. He actually completed two volumes, covering the
saints from Saint Stephen the protomartyr to those who died in
the year 271. But these volumes were never published, probably
because no substantial support or encouragement was given to
them.[40] It seems that popes, prelates, and people alike were already too interested in Baronius' *Annales*, which they considered
to be most beneficial to the Church in the aftermath of the *Magdeburg Centuries*, that they could not find any value in a work such
as Gallonio's which did not have any special significance in the
contemporary context. Gallonio's jealousy, therefore, was understandable.

There may have been other sources too, besides those mentioned above, from which Baronius received material support, because his personal financial position seems to have been substan-
tially improved at this time. In 1591, he was able to bring his widowed paternal aunt, Marzia, to Rome and provide her with a house
adjacent to the Oratory and two maids to take care of her.[41] He
was also able to assist many poor people during the severe famine
of 1591, which affected Rome and all of Italy. Baronius reportedly was very active in bringing relief to the famine-stricken peo-

ple and thus exhausted all his personal resources. He even sold a gold reliquary, which he prized very much, in order to buy food and clothing for the poor.[42]

These charitable activities undoubtedly diverted his attention to some extent. But what proved to be a more serious impediment to the progress of the *Annales* was the disorganized condition of the Vatican Press during the years 1590–92, which saw the elevation of four popes. However, Baronius made arrangements with the Typographia Torneriana in Rome to publish the third volume and it came out in 1592. This volume was dedicated to Philip II of Spain.

Each volume of the *Annales* was dedicated either to the ruling pontiff or to an outstanding Catholic prince. Due to the tremendous popularity of the work, every pope and prince was eager to receive such an honor. When the third volume was dedicated to Philip II, therefore, Baronius understandably suspected that the then reigning pope, Gregory, might be disappointed. In order to neutralize this disappointment, Baronius wrote an essay dedicating the forthcoming Volume IV to Gregory and presented it together with a copy of the third volume.[43] But by the time Volume IV was ready for publication in 1593, Gregory XIV had died. Baronius, wisely reticent to waste his efforts on the dead, changed the dedication for the benefit of Gregory's successor, Clement VIII.

Just as the popes and the most important secular princes of Europe were anxious to have the volumes of the *Annales* dedicated to them, the lesser prelates and princes who had no hopes of receiving such honor sought to get their names in the work somehow or other. One of the ways of accomplishing this was to send essays or poems praising the *Annales* and the author with the request to publish them with the text. Thus, the famous poet from Seville, Consalvus Ponce de Leon, wrote a poem in praise of Baronius, comparing him to Julius Caesar, which was published in the third volume.[44] The poem eulogizing the *Annales* sent by Laevinus Torrentius, bishop of Antwerp, has already been mentioned.[45] Theophilus de Braganza, archbishop of Evora, Portugal, wrote to Baronius describing how "the fame of your name and your piety spread most gloriously in all parts of the world."[46] In a subsequent letter the bishop requested Baronius to include the history of his church and his own life in the *Annales*.[47] He authorized his representative in Rome, Doctor Antonio Gomez, to negotiate this matter with Baronius.

With the publication of every volume, Baronius' renown spread

wider. Even more scholars and churchmen from every part of
Europe recognized his erudition and sought his friendship. For
instance, the famous Louvain theologian, Henricus Gravius, who
recognized Baronius' scholarship soon after the first volume was
published, became one of his close friends. Their friendship was
further strengthened when Gravius came to Rome in early 1591
at the invitation of Sixtus V to become the prefect of the Vatican
Library and the Vatican Press. His unexpected death in June of
that year unfortunately ended that relationship. But in memory of
the friendship of these two men and in recognition of the scholarship of Baronius, the University of Louvain officially enrolled
Baronius in the first order of their theologians.[48]

Others who wrote in praise of Baronius' work and sought his
friendship included Nicolaus Faber, noted theologian and orator
of Paris and counselor of the French king;[49] the president of the
Portugese university of Coimbra;[50] and the archbishop of Coimbra,
who also wrote several letters to Baronius in appreciation of his
work, and sent five hundred gold coins through the archdeacon of
Evora.[51] When Baronius gratefully rejected the gift, the archbishop
sent it again through the famous Dominican scholar and theologian of the Council of Trent, Father Ludovicus Sottomajor, insisting that he should accept it.[52] Baronius, however, again rejected
the gift. The main reason he steadfastly rejected this and other
offers was that, as he himself explained to Sottomajor, the popes
were eager to finance the work themselves, and receiving outside
help would have offended them.[53] Clement VIII especially was
anxious that Baronius should have enough resources for his work,
and soon after the gift of the archbishop was rejected, the pope
granted him an allowance of another two hundred *scudi*; this even
after Baronius intimated that there was no need for it.[54] The pope
wanted Baronius to have "abundantly, and more than just what is
needed.[55]

Among the numerous letters Baronius received around this time
from dignitaries all over Europe was that of Archbishop Stanislaus
Karnakowski, primate of Poland, dated August 5, 1592.[56] After
describing the great impact the *Annales* had on erudite men, the
archbishop requested Baronius' permission to have the work translated into the Polish language for the use of the common people.
Baronius gladly granted this permission in a letter dated September 30, 1592.[57] The archbishop's effort to translate the *Annales*
into his native language was particularly significant in view of his
Counter-Reformation activities. He had recently established a Je-

suit college at Kalisz in order to expedite the reconversion of Protestants. And it was to this Jesuit college he entrusted the job of translating the *Annales*. Obviously, the primate wanted to place the work in the hands of Catholic apologists who were already active in the re-Catholicization campaign in Poland. This purpose was not far from Baronius' mind, either, when he granted the request. He wrote to the archbishop:

> As to your request for permission to translate our *Annales* into the Polish language . . . as you consider that it would be very useful to battle the heretics, it seems to me clearly that you are imitating Patriarch Abraham who considered it was enough to arm the slaves to fight five kings; and you seem to follow David who, rejecting the royal armaments, went to the battle with rustic weapons. You indeed will rightly know that in the new battles the Lord has chosen the weaker one to be more powerful.[58]

Here Baronius seems to view modestly the effectiveness of the *Annales* as a weapon against the heretics, but at the same time he does not fail to point out, through the analogies of Abraham and David, how powerful this weak weapon would become with the aid of divine power.

The battle against heretics in the temporal as well as the spiritual realm was again foremost in the mind of Baronius, when a few years later he dedicated Volume XI of the *Annales* to Sigismund III Vasa, the king of Poland. Keeping in mind two of Sigismund's current enterprises that portended success to the Catholic church—one, by diplomatic and military efforts to regain the Swedish throne from his uncle, Charles IX, who had replaced him after his own deposition because of his attempts to restore Catholicism in Sweden, and, two, his maneuvers against Boris Godunov for his control of the Russian throne through the pretender, Dmitri—Baronius exhorted him:

> Continue . . . and complete the glorious work you have undertaken. Fight the wars of the Lord. . . . You will have angels for your co-fighters. . . . The Catholic Church has already given her contributions of prayers, and the Supreme Pontiff who presides over her imparts the apostolic benediction over this. May Christ in whose name it is done assist you so that not only the tyrannical heretic but even the chief infidel, the unjust possessor of the Oriental Empire, be brought under just arms.[59]

Of course, Baronius was referring to the Lutheran king of Sweden

and the Orthodox monarch of Russia, respectively, by the terms
"tyrannical heretic" and "chief infidel." He obviously was expressing his own wholehearted support and that of the Roman
Curia when he wished Sigismund military and political success
over the "heretics." These dreams of uniting the thrones of Poland, Russia, and Sweden under the banner of Catholicism were
shattered when the Poles were routed in Russia. But the battle of
the book, the intellectual onslaught of the *Annales*, eventually
accomplished better success.

At the commission of the primate of Poland, the Jesuit scholar,
P. Skarge, prepared an abridged translation of the *Annales*, which
was published from Cracow in 1603. The first edition contained
only the first ten volumes of the *Annales*, but a second edition including all the twelve volumes of Baronius' work was released subsequently in 1607. The Polish Catholics, like their counterparts
everywhere else in Europe, received the *Annales* with great enthusiasm and acclaim. The Jesuits and other Catholic leaders found it
an inexhaustible arsenal in their intellectual warfare against Protestants. Thus, the *Annales* played an important role in their successful campaign for the reconversion of Poland.[60]

Aside from the immediate impact of the *Annales* as a Counter-
Reformation weapon, it was to serve in subsequent centuries as an
important vehicle for cultural interaction between the west European Latin Christian world and the Eastern Orthodox world. In
succeeding centuries it also would become an extremely valuable
source in the development of Slavich historiography.[61] The two
main sources from which Slavic historiography received inspiration
in seventeenth and eighteenth centuries, according to Picchio, were
the *Annales* of Baronius and the work of Mauro Orbini on the
Kingdom of the Slavs.

The *Annales* started its travel through the Slavic nations when
Skarge introduced it in the Polish language in 1603. But the wider
diffusion of the work in the Eastern Orthodox world came after it
was translated into Russian in 1678 from Skarge's Polish version
by a monk, Ignatius Muron, at the commission of Archbishop
Josif Rjazan. But by then the original Latin *Annales* had already
become a well-known work of reference in all the Slavic countries,
Russia included. Similarly, Orbini's work was translated into Russian by the order of Peter the Great and published in Saint Peters-
burg in 1722. Subsequently, this became something like a companion volume to the *Annales*, and together they were used by
Slavic historians as sources for reconstructing the history of their
civilization.

The *Annales* became particularly popular because of the patronage of the Orthodox church. During the late seventeenth and early eighteenth centuries there was such a great demand for the book among the Orthodox Christians that their printing presses were unable to meet it. This may have been the reason that many manuscript copies began to circulate in the Slavic world. The work was so well-known that the manuscript copies often carried only the name of the author, "Baronij," as a title.

Due to the extraordinary popularity of the *Annales* among their followers, the Orthodox hierarchy of Russia felt constrained to revise the work, removing whatever was incompatible with views of the Orthodox. The official version allowed so many variations from the original text, that a large number of enlightened readers openly criticized it. Such critics were mainly from the ranks of the "raskol'niki," literally dissenters, or schismatics, who were generally protestors against liturgical forms and gestures. At any rate, a controversy was started within the Russian Orthodox church about the *Annales* of Baronius. The protests of the dissenters, however, were slowly quieted, and the Orthodox church published the official version in 1719 from the press of the Synod of Moscow. This version of the *Annales* was widely diffused and generally accepted throughout the Slavic Orthodox world.

Another abridged Russian version of the *Annales* was published by Andrej Marveev (1666-1728). This edition was based on the original Latin text, and was probably more authentic. But it never attained the popularity of the official Church version, possibly because it was considered a "raskol'niki" version and, therefore, unacceptable to the Orthodox church.

The influence of the *Annales* was considerable also on the secular historiography of the Slavic world. One of the earliest national histories of Bulgaria, for example, was mostly based on the Russian Orthodox version of the *Annales*. This was the work of the Bulgarian monk, Paisij Hilendar, on the *History of Slavobulgaria*. Paisij Hilendar used many east European sources also for the compilation of his work, but his major sources were the *Annales* and the aforementioned work of Orbini. In fact, his dependence on the *Annales* was so great, as Picchio observes, that the last portion of his work, covering the history of Bulgaria from the thirteenth to the fifteenth century for which Baronius could not be his guide, was very sketchy and inadequate in comparison with the earlier parts.[62] These and the previously stated facts clearly indicate that the *Annales* of Baronius, which was originally introduced in Eastern Christendom through Skarge's abridged Polish translation, had a significant role in the development of the ecclesiastical and secular historiography of the Slavic world.

Encouraged by the universal acclaim for his book, Baronius worked with increasing speed. He was able to bring out the fourth volume early in 1593, scarcely a year after the third. By this time there was so much demand for the *Annales*, and Baronius and the Oratorians were financially so much better off, that they were able to establish their own printing press at Vallicella.

The fourth volume, dedicated to Clement VIII, was published from the Vallicelliana Press. Clement was already very favorably disposed towards Baronius and had granted him sizeable pensions. He now felt it appropriate, as some of his predecessors had, to elevate the famous scholar to a higher dignity in the Church. Just what position he had in mind is not clear; but from what can be surmised from Baronius' frantic efforts to get out of it, the pope seems to have been quite determined to give him something significant. Baronius wrote to Talpa that he was having many persons assiduously pray so that there should be a change of heart on the part of the pontiff.[63] He thought of fleeing Rome, he said, but that was of no avail because the work on the *Annales* would bring him back again. The letter reveals an extreme mental anguish over what he considered to be an impending disaster. In a real sense, any important ecclesiastical dignity or office would have been a disaster to his scholarly work, which was by now very dear to him.

In the meantime, Philip Neri, who himself had shunned ecclesiastical dignities, offered help, but in his own peculiar manner. As Paolo Aringhi relates in his unpublished biography of Baronius, Neri played one of his characteristic antics. He had a young member of the Oratory, Agostino Buoncampagni, place a cardinal's hat on the head of Baronius one day when he was asleep in his room.[64] Perhaps this was intended to help Baronius to laugh the matter off and not to take it too seriously, or to remind him of the inevitable and the need for resignation. The prayers of Baronius, however, seem to have been heard, at least for this time, for the dreaded dignity did not descend on him. But he had to suffer other kinds of interruptions, mainly from admiring followers from all over Europe who came to Rome in large numbers to visit him. They wanted to hear his sermons, visit his room, confess to him, and obtain his pictures and autographs.[65] This popularity of Baronius indicates that not only the learned but also the common people of Europe at this time were aware of his work. He was, indeed, looked upon as a hero of the Counter-Reformation.

The international fame Baronius enjoyed seems to have further bolstered his reputation at home among his own fellow Oratorians at this time. The earlier jealousies and lack of cooperation now vanished. Philip Neri, the founder and first superior general, had been ailing for some time and he desired to entrust the administration of the congregation to another man. There seems to have been no doubt in anyone's mind who the next superior general should be. Only a short time before, Neri had chosen Baronius to be his confessor when his previous spiritual father, Giovanni Battista Peruschi, a Jesuit, died.[66] Then in 1593 the Oratorians recorded their unanimous esteem for him when they elected him the rector of the Roman Oratory and the superior general of the whole congregation.

This election was an open testimony not only to Baronius' scholarly achievements, of course, but also to his religious piety, a most important consideration in the election of a religious superior. Undoubtedly he excelled all his co-religionists in scholarship, and his relationships with the churchmen and the people of Rome indicated that he was equally qualified in other respects as well. No wonder, then, that the election of July 23, 1593, was unanimous. Baronius, however, was quite unwilling to accept the office, but his vow of obedience and his respect for duty left him no choice. There are two contemporary accounts of the election, both indicating that not only Neri but also the ruling pontiff, Clement VIII, wanted Baronius to be elected superior general. [67] Two of the most important Italian cardinals, Agostino Cusano and Federico Borromeo, who were present at the election, also expressed their strong approval.

Baronius certainly was a most appropriate choice to succeed Neri, but the new responsibilities brought additional burdens on him which were undesirable at this stage of his work on the *Annales*. In fact, he wrote to his close friend, Talpa, shortly after the election requesting him to pray so that he "may not succumb under the burden."[68] It must indeed have been a very difficult job to succeed Philip Neri, whom not only the Oratorians but the whole Roman populace, from pope to beggar, held in highest esteem. Neri's extraordinary simplicity and good humor endeared him to everybody, and he was the founding father of the Oratorian congregation. Baronius, on the other hand, was of a very serious nature with a scholarly bent, qualities which were not in themselves likeable to the rank and file of the congregation. But the reports of contemporaries show that he lived on cordial terms with them all during the three years he held the office of superior general.[69] In fact, he elicited high praise from his subordinates. The only criticism that can be found among the reports of contemporaries is that he was too "credulous and little practical"[70] in administrative affairs, which is understandable in the background of his characteristic simplicity and the life-long occupation with speculative matters.

In the meantime, the *Annales* continued to gain greater and greater following. New editions of the first two volumes were prepared by Baronius in 1593-94 and published from two presses in Rome, the press of the De Angelis and that of the Oratorians at Vallicella. The first edition of the fifth volume of the *Annales* also came out in 1594 from the Vallicelliana Press. This volume was also dedicated to Clement VIII. But it included a second dedicatory note, addressed to William, duke of Bavaria, which won the author a generous donation from the flattered recipient.[71]

While the whole Catholic world enthusiastically welcomed the *Annales*, a note of disapproval came from Spain. Baronius distressingly described in a letter to Talpa dated June 29, 1594, a rumor that was spreading in Rome that the *Annales* was going to be put in the Index of forbidden books by the Spanish Inquisition.[72] The Inquisition was not in the habit of giving any reason for its actions, but it is probable that the prohibition of the *Annales* was contemplated as a reprisal against Rome for having included in the Roman Index a book against the freedom of the Church written by one Giovanni de Roas. This particular book had been published with the approval of the Council of State of Spain and with the blessing of one of the inquisitors; hence, the ire of the Spanish Inquisition.[73] Baronius certainly had nothing to fear because Cardinal Federico Borromeo, the prefect of the Congregation of the Index at Rome, was his personal friend and Pope Clement himself was a great supporter of the *Annales*. In fact, only a few months later Baronius was to be selected as Clement's confessor.[74] Whether any action was taken by these men is not clear, but for the time being the *Annales* was spared from the hands of the Spanish Inquisition. Baronius would, however, come to clash directly with the Spanish monarchy at a later time and suffer severe consequences. This rumor was an omen of events to come.

5

Splendid Years

The most important theological problem facing Clement VIII in 1594 was the question of the acceptance of Henry of Navarre back into the Church. A simple theological question in this case was immeasurably complicated by the political machinations of the Spanish court. In making this difficult decision, Clement sought the advice of his confessor and trusted friend, Baronius. The role of Baronius in the reconciliation of Henry IV made him *persona non grata* in the Spanish court. There is no doubt that the Inquisition had this in mind when it considered action against the *Annales*. The significance of Baronius' role can be realized from a survey of the events that led to the absolution of Henry of Navarre from heresy.

All the details related to this event are well documented in three codices of the Vallicelliana Library.[1] Indeed, these records are quite thorough and they enable us to reconstruct the circumstances of this historic drama vividly and accurately. The papers include a full account of the solemn ceremony of absolution by a personage of no less importance than a master of ceremonies to the pope, Paolo Mucante.[2] The climax occurred on September 17, 1595, at the Portico di San Pietro when Clement ceremoniously absolved the French king, represented by his ambassadors who knelt before the pope and did public penance in the name of Henry. It was a solemn occasion; and the repetition of the age-old formula led to rejoicing in Rome and Paris.

But the rejoicing contrasted sharply with the air of turbulent controversy that had reigned until that moment. It all started when Henry, after having secured the throne of France and established a program of reconciliation between the warring religious factions, set out to settle an issue of his own conscience.

On July 25, 1593, on the feast day of Saint James the Elder,
Henry had knelt at the main altar of the Church of Saint Dionisius
in Paris, abjured his Calvinistic beliefs, and requested to be received into the Catholic church. At the same time he had also sent
a request to Rome for a formal absolution. There was nothing extraordinary about this procedure, which had become rather common at the height of the Counter-Reformation as many lapsed
Catholics returned to the fold, especially in France. But Henry's
case was somewhat different. After all, he had lapsed not once,
but twice; and on the second occasion Sixtus V had issued a special bull of excommunication. Gregory XIV also had formally
condemned him for the same reason. Such public condemnations
against Henry, no doubt, were induced by political reasons, in the
context of the religious wars in France. However, when a new attempt at reconciliation was made, his previous record was naturally cited against him. The political circumstances in which he
sought to be reconciled also cast doubts upon his motivation.

But what made the reconciliation even more difficult was the
opposition of Spain. Henry's acceptance into the Church would
have strengthened immeasurably his position on the French throne
which Philip II of Spain was claiming on behalf of his daughter by
his third marriage with Elizabeth of Valois, sister of Henry III.
As soon as word was out about Henry's attempt to reenter the
Church, Spain mobilized her diplomatic forces around Europe and
particularly in the Vatican. A very strong contingent of Spanish
cardinals in Rome, headed by the influential Franciscus Penia,
auditor of the Rota Romana, stood ready to checkmate every attempt by the French to effect the reconciliation. In fact, the Spanish party launched its attack with a booklet prepared by a number
of Spanish theologians under the leadership of Penia, entitled *De
veris et falsis remediis Christianae Religionis instaurandae, et Catholicos conservandi.*[3] This booklet was given personally to Clement
VIII, who unfortunately was thus caught in the middle of a political controversy in theological guise. Penia had thus succeeded
turning a political question into a theological one—the question,
that is, of whether a public figure who had relapsed into heresy
might be absolved. And a resolution could no longer be made according to purely political criteria.

Clement had only one way out: an appeal to his personal conscience. Instead, then, of consulting an authoritative college of
theologians, he turned to his confessor, Baronius. Accordingly,
Baronius wrote a small treatise, refuting point by point the argu-

ments of the Spanish theologians, and submitted it to the private use of the pope. He wrote his remarks directly on the very copy of the booklet the Spanish party had presented to the pope. Clement wrote on the book in his own hand: "Hunc librum Nobis Clementi Octavo dedit Franciscus Peyna Rotae Auditor: adnotationes autem vel censurae sunt Caesaris Baronii."[4] Thus, Baronius helped the pope make a private decision.

At the same time, Clement VIII permitted the question to be discussed publicly. The way he did so was again through Baronius, who elaborated his earlier private arguments in a letter dedicating the fifth volume of the *Annales* to Clement, which came out in 1594.[5] A discussion on the subject of receiving back into the Church relapsed heretics was not totally inappropriate in this particular volume because this covered a span of time (395–440 A.D.) which saw the rise and fall of many heresies. But no one was so naive as to fail to notice the contemporary significance of such a discussion. Baronius' central argument was that the Roman pontiff, as the vicar of Christ and dispenser of graces, had the right and duty to absolve all penitent heretics, even lapsed ones. The conduct of the Church through the centuries bears ample testimony to this, he said, and any prejudicial treatment of lapsed sinners ran counter to the specific examples of prophets and saints, like David and Peter, who themselves were lapsed sinners.

Such an open stance in favor of Henry of Navarre was not at all palatable to the Spanish party in Rome, especially because the author of the article was not just anybody, but the confessor of the pope. The Spanish diplomatic machine started grinding again: Baronius and the pope himself came under public and private pressure. In 1595, therefore, Baronius felt impelled to write an apologetical work in support of his own public statements and the implied stance of the pope.[6] In this work, Baronius again put his historical erudition to good use. He argued from the tradition of the Church, that dealing mercifully with lapsed heretics, especially princes, was necessary—not only for the spiritual welfare of the immediate beneficiaries, but also for the good of countless numbers of their subjects.

To be sure, this pamphlet did not put an end to the controversy. The Spanish soon came out with a counter-pamphlet which claimed to be a definitive refutation of Baronius' historical arguments. It was prepared by an anonymous bishop, obviously an expert in history as well as in civil and canon law; and it struck directly at Baronius' strongest argument, that of precedent. All the cases Baronius cited as precedents were inapplicable, the pamphlet declared. How could the case of King George of Bohemia be cited here, the pamphlet asked, for he never abjured publicly the Catholic faith and was never publicly condemned by the Church. In the case of the absolution of Emperor Henry IV at Canossa by Gregory VII, was it not proven by later historical events that this was a mistake as the apparent penitence of Henry was nothing but a political strategy in order to appease the rebelling Saxons? Did they not see in their own times the same kind of Machiavellian political guile exhibited by Henry VIII and Queen Elizabeth? How could Henry, born and brought up in heresy and after having fought so valiantly for so many years against the Catholics, suddenly become a loyal son of the Church? Should not a public absolution, if one should be given at all, wait for public acts of penitence and humility which would insure the sincerity of the king's motive? The Spanish pamphleteer was, however, very careful not to offend the pope: he did not deny the pope's authority to absolve even relapsed heretics. Rather, he cleverly directed his arguments in order to cast doubt on Henry's sincerity.

This pamphlet also reached the hands of Clement who may have been perturbed by the tenacious position of the Spanish party. In order, therefore, to reassure the pope and to refute the new arguments, Baronius was impelled to write still another treatise, *Ad apologeticum apologia*, during the summer of 1595.[7] Even this pamphlet did not succeed in appeasing the Spanish faction in the Roman Curia whose mood was still rebellious—so much so, indeed, that even a strong-minded pontiff like Clement did not dare to take a definitive step about the absolution of Henry IV against their wishes. It was at this juncture that Baronius took two unusual steps which seem to have had a tremendous impact on the pontiff's ultimate decision. First, using his authority as the confessor of Clement, he declared that he would deny him absolution unless he granted the legitimate request of the French king—a declaration that required no little courage, given the respective positions of the confessor and the penitent.[8] Secondly, he consulted privately with each of the curial cardinals in the hope of persuading even some of the Spaniards to favor the cause. His efforts were successful and when Clement introduced the case in a subsequent consistory, he was assured of approval of the absolution.[9]

For the part he played in this drama, Baronius received the eternal gratitude of Henry IV. The king considered him a trusted ally in the Vatican and on many occasions corresponded with him. For example, he wrote to Baronius on June 7, 1599, expressing his desire to preserve the traditional title of the French kings as the "Firstborn Son of the Church and Most Christian King."[10] In another letter, dated August 30, 1599, he profusely thanked Baronius for all the favors he had done for him.[11] Baronius in turn, dedicated to him the ninth volume of the *Annales*.[12] The grateful monarch saluted the author with warmth and admiration in several letters and sent him an extremely valuable miniature silver chapel through the French ambassador to Rome, while requesting the continuance of his good offices at the papal court.[13] Henry also gave Baronius a pension of 1,200 lire per annum.[14]

On the other hand, Baronius incurred the eternal hostility of the Spanish court for his role in Henry's absolution. Indeed, the ire was soon transformed into threats on his life.[15] And it was to continue for the rest of his life as Baronius was yet to involve himself in still another controversy against the Spanish—the controversy over the governance of Sicily. Eventually it would cost Baronius, if not his life, at least the papal tiara.

Even while he was thrust into the middle of the international rivalries of Europe, Baronius could not neglect his modest duties as the religious superior of the Oratorians. Under his fervent leadership the congregation was steadily growing. Two more houses were opened—one in Fermo and another in Palermo—and new houses meant additional load of administrative details. But he soon had to bear a still greater burden when Philip Neri died in 1595. True, he had long since taken over the responsibility of governing the congregation during Neri's protracted illness. But the lingering life of the founder was still the focus of inspiration to the Oratorians; and when that was extinguished, Baronius had to fill the vacuum.

Neri was a colorful personality, one who evoked deep feelings of loyalty in all the people he came across, be it the Roman populace or the Roman pontiff. His personal charisma and the miracles he was said to have performed earned him a great following. His exit from life was no less dramatic. He fell seriously ill early in May, 1595, and after having received the last sacraments from Baronius, he lay prostrate for nearly a month, expecting death. Suddenly on May 26, his illness left him—miraculously, of course. He got up and celebrated Mass with great fervor. A few hours later, his illness returned, and within a matter of moments he was dead.[16] Only a short while before, he had worked a similar miracle on no less a person than Pope Clement VIII himself, curing him instantly from a serious attack of gout. The pope himself gratefully told the members of his court and visiting churchmen about this miracle.[17]

Such dramatic incidents skyrocketed the saintly reputation of Neri among the clergy and common people of Rome, not to mention the members of the Oratorian congregation. The shoes of such a man had to be filled by the scholarly and bookish Baronius who had none of the charismatic qualities of his predecessor. To add to his troubles, the controversies about the nature and structure of the congregation, which had laid dormant during the founder's lifetime, seem to have erupted with sudden fury after his death, and Baronius was left alone to deal with them.

The chief disagreement seems to have been about the question of religious vows—whether the Oratorians should remain a congregation of secular priests or accept the religious status with the three traditional vows. Some members apparently believed that a religious status was somehow more conducive to spiritual perfection. Neri wanted to keep the congregation a society of secular priests, but when he left the scene, those members of a different persuasion raised the issue with vehemence. Two letters Baronius wrote to the Naples Oratory immediately after Neri's death testify to the seriousness of the matter. The first, written the very next day after the death of Neri, declares that the will and testament of the founder called for keeping the congregation a secular institute.[18] On June 10, 1595, he wrote again to Naples, this time declaring the approval and the ardent wish of the pope himself that the Oratorians should not change their constitution.[19] These letters and other admonitions were written with such urgency that they suggest the continued pressure and very sharp differences among the members of the congregation.

The death of Neri marked the end of a phase in the development of the Oratorian congregation. As the founder, Neri could administer the congregation in a personal manner. But this was not possible for the next superior, Baronius, who felt the need for codifying the aims and procedures of the congregation clearly and precisely. Accordingly, Baronius called a general meeting of the Oratorian membership in Rome on May 26, 1595, even while the body of the founder lay in state. The chief document they adopted at this meeting was very fundamental to the structure of the congregation. This decree bound every member to the secular status of the congregation and prescribed that any member who wished otherwise should be excluded.[20]

Within a fortnight, other legislation also was adopted in order to give lasting stability to the congregation, thus far only loosely organized. One such law set the term of the superior general at three years, with provisions for a re-election for only another term.[21] Another law prohibited the residence of prelates in the Oratory and the acceptance of responsibility for the care of monasteries, seminaries, and colleges.[22] This law was intended to insure the freedom of the congregation and its members so that they could concentrate on the spiritual needs of the general public, as Neri always wanted. Still other legislation limited the membership of the congregation to the houses of Rome, Naples, and Sanseverino.[23] This was to insure the utmost efficacy of the free and secular institute and to guard against the dangers of over-expansion that had afflicted so many of the Counter-Reformation religious organizations. The efforts of secular priests in other parts of Europe to organize in the fashion of the Oratorians could be encouraged, and even supported by the Filippini, but no formal connection could be established. Hence, by an act of legislation at the very beginning of his tenure, Baronius strengthened the organizational aspect of the congregation. He thus facilitated its transformation from a group of followers around one dynamic leader into a permanent institution.

Still other matters called for his attention: the decoration of Chiesa Nuova, for instance, and the reconstruction of the sacristy and the library at Vallicella. Perhaps the most important accomplishment of Baronius' generalship, indeed, was the tremendous enthusiasm for intellectual activity which he generated among members of the Oratory. With his encouragement and guidance a great many books were published by the Filippini in various branches of learning. Most of them were pious and apologetical in nature, like so much of the literature of Counter-Reformation Rome. Antonio Gallonio, for example, translated into Latin his earlier Italian work on the sufferings of the martyrs and enlarged it to include the recent persecutions of the English martyrs.[24] Tommaso Bozzio published his widely circulated work against the heresies, *De Signis Ecclesiae contra omnes haereses libri XXIV*.[25] He also brought out five different treatises against various aspects of Machiavelli's philosophy, which were considered to be at variance with Catholic doctrines.[26] The Oratorians also published several musical compositions, originally produced for singing at the Oratory by such great masters as Pier Luigi da Palestrina, Giovanni Animuccia, and Francesco Soto.[27]

Another important activity that consumed the time and energy of Baronius at this period was the canonization proceedings of Philip Neri. Within two months after Neri's death, the Vatican established a commission to investigate his life and virtues. Considering that normally it would take scores of years before the Vatican would approve such a procedure, it is ample testimony to the high esteem in which Neri was held in Rome. Perhaps this also is a testimony to the influence of Baronius in the Vatican.

In the meantime, Baronius was becoming a dignitary of the Church, in spite of all his efforts to avoid high ecclesiastical positions. His function as the confessor of the pope, his renown as the author of the *Annales*, his office as the superior general of the Oratorians, all made him eligible for high honors in the Church. He had successfully resisted previous attempts to make him a prelate, but at last time ran out. On November 21, 1595, Clement VIII, after having gone to confession to Baronius, suddenly declared that he had decided to raise his confessor to the dignity of protonotary apostolic.[28] Then followed the tragi-comical scene in which two palace prelates tried to subdue physically a protesting Baronius and forcibly to dress him in the appropriate habit. He was, however, able to plead with them and the pope to get an extension of one day before accepting the dignity. This delaying tactic and his many supplications to Clement did not help him, however. Finally, the purple vestments of a protonotary apostolic were sent to the Oratory from the papal palace and he was thus forced to don this insignia of his new dignity.

Where other men might have rejoiced in these honors, Baronius lamented. Yet he had to resign to the will of the pope; the most he could do to neutralize the effects of the new status was to avoid wearing the colorful vestments except when absolutely necessary, and to instruct friends and subordinates not to show him any deference.[29] Amidst all this confusion, he somehow managed to publish the sixth volume of the *Annales*, comprising the history of the Church between 440 and 522 A.D. This volume also was dedicated to Clement VIII.

Baronius at this time may have been entertaining the hope that he would be relieved of the burden of the superior generalship at the close of his first three-year term, which was soon to end. If he did, he was sorely disappointed. When the Oratorians met in general council in May of 1596, they did not deliberate too much on the subject. Baronius was re-elected for another term. However, very shortly Baronius was to be relieved of this duty because a still higher dignity would be accorded him; and this new condition would be infinitely more unbearable to him.

It was in May of 1596 that Baronius was forcibly vested with the insignia of a protonotary apostolic. There seems to have been no doubt in the minds of Vatican watchers that this was only the first step towards higher dignities. Rumor mills began to grind, this time with much more accuracy. A consistory was going to be held in June of that year to create new cardinals, and it was inconceivable that such an eminent figure as Baronius could escape nomination. Soon the topic was on the lips of all Romans; and inevitably it reached the ear of Baronius.

As could be expected from previous experiences, he tried to avoid being promoted, resorting to every means and invoking earthly and heavenly forces to his assistance. He sent his friend, Talpa, to the pope to implore him in the name of the Oratorian congregation not to take their superior general away from them.[30] To rally the heavenly forces on his side, Baronius made a vow that he would visit the seven Basilicas of Rome, barefooted and sackclothed, if only he would be spared the cardinalate.[31] Still seeing no sign of change, he contemplated fleeing from Rome.[32] But this was not a feasible thing for a renowned figure; besides it would have been childish and scandalous, he thought. Then as an evasive measure, he made a suggestion to the pope. Would not Francesco Maria Tarugi, archbishop of Avignon, be a good choice for cardinal? His hope was that if Tarugi, an Oratorian, were selected, perhaps he himself would be spared. Two cardinals from the same small congregation, created at the same consistory, would not look very proper. The pope did accept his suggestion: Tarugi was to be a cardinal too. But Baronius was not allowed to escape.

Then he put forward another, seemingly very convincing, argument to the pope. What would the Protestants say, who were looking for any opportunity to criticize and discredit the *Annales*, if its author were made a cardinal? Would not they trumpet that Baronius was defending the Church and the papacy only because he had an eye on the cardinal's hat? Would not that ruin the value of the very work for which he was going to be honored? Besides, would not that be scandalous? But these arguments were of no avail. Finally, as a last resort, Baronius begged the pope, with tears in his eyes, that he please be spared from the honor. The pope, also as a final resort, ordered Baronius to accept it or be excommunicated. He was named a cardinal of the Roman Catholic church in the consistory of June 4, 1596. And *ipso facto* he was relieved of the superior generalship of the Oratorians.

"As soon as one is made a cardinal, his friends, servants, and relatives would think, and wish, that he would become pope; the

worst of all is that often he himself would suddenly begin to aspire
to become pope."[33] These were words Baronius reportedly told
his Oratorian co-religionists as soon as he returned home from the
consistory. For the rest of his life he would be concerned about
how not to become pope. As his story unfolds further, we will see
how, through the antagonism of the Spanish party in the curia, he
barely escaped becoming pope.

Zazzara has a theory that Baronius actually took a vow that he
would never do anything that might make him a favorite for that
position. Furthermore, Zazzara says, he "knowingly, voluntarily,
and freely wrote against the Monarchy of Sicily" in order to guarantee the opposition of the Spanish party to his election to the papacy.[34] Granting that the Oratorian chronicler was prone to pious
exaggeration, we still can be certain that Baronius would undoubtedly have foreseen the consequences of such a treatise against the
political rights of the Spanish crown.

On the other hand, Baronius did not desist to cultivate good relations with powerful members of the College of Cardinals. Copies
of several letters he wrote soon after his elevation to the red hat,
saluting Cardinals Federico Borromeo, Alessandro Medici (later
Leo XI), and others are preserved in the Vallicelliana archives.[35]
But these were only letters of courtesy, often to long-standing
friends (like Borromeo) who normally expected such greetings.

It is quite probable that as soon as word got back to Sora about
the elevation of Baronius, his relatives sent requests for positions
in Rome, considering the still prevalent custom of nepotism among
higher clergy. At least one letter which he sent back to a relative
refers to the matter with stern indignation.[36] He did not want anyone to come to Rome, he warned, seeking positions in the papal
courts. His characteristic strictness was also exhibited in the style
of life which he chose after his elevation to the cardinalate, which
was not much different from the one he had maintained in the
Oratory. He moved into an apartment assigned to him in the papal
palace, with servants and attendants appropriate to a cardinal, but
the luxuries of heavily cushioned furnitures, silken upholsteries,
valuable vases, and rich foods were not part of his appointments.
After all, was not he still a spiritual son of Philip Neri?[37]

After the initial panic and resistance to the dignity, Baronius
seems to have resigned himself to make the best of it in a spiritual
manner. His choice of a titular church in Rome amply testifies to
this saintly determination. When, according to the ancient custom,
Clement VIII convened the new cardinals in order to assign to

them titular churches in the Eternal City, there was no one willing to take the old and dilapidated church of Saints Nereus and Achilleus. This was a fourth-century church, long neglected and badly in need of repairs, and devoid of rich benefices. But historical-minded Baronius saw the importance of the church and volunteered to take it, regardless of the financial liability.[38] Understandably, the pope was very pleased about this, as Baronius noted.[39] For the next year Baronius directed much of his energy towards the renovation and appropriate decoration of this ancient church, with the material assistance he received spontaneously from many sources.[40]

The crowning point for Baronius' endeavours came on May 11, 1597, when relics of Saints Nereus and Achilleus, together with that of Saint Flavia Domitilla, were transferred to the renovated church in a colorful procession. The relics were removed from the church of Saint Adrian, their resting place for the previous three and one-half centuries, and brought to the Campidoglio where the great procession started and wound its way through the Foro Romano, then beneath the triumphal arches of Septimus Severus, Titus, and Constantine, and finally reached the titular church of Baronius. There crowds of people waited, with their candles flickering in the Roman dusk to receive the relics of the saints and, no doubt, their bearer who was then the proudest Roman.[41]

It was Baronius' finest hour. The intellectual elite of Rome joined Baronius in celebrating the occasion by presenting numerous poems in honor of the saints, and of Baronius.[42] Clement VIII expressed his appreciation by granting a plenary indulgence to everyone attending the ceremony, and to those who would visit the church during the annual feast of the saints.[43] The pope also entrusted the church to the perpetual care of the Oratorians, through a papal bull, issued probably at the request of Baronius.[44]

Baronius' scholarly friends around Europe were delighted about his elevation to high dignity, and they sent him congratulations; Peter de Villars, archbishop of Vienna,[45] and Abbot Jacobus de Marquais,[46] for example. But at the same time, they were also concerned about the future of the *Annales*, now that Baronius was burdened with the duties of a cardinal. However, their concern was unfounded: Baronius had no intention of abandoning the *Annales*. In fact, he published Volume VII within a few months. This volume, covering the history of the Church between 518–590 A.D., was also dedicated to the reigning pontiff, Clement VIII. In the letter of dedication Baronius humorously blamed the pontiff for causing the delay in the publication of this volume by forcibly conferring on him several dignities with their varying costumes to get accustomed to.[47]

However, this friendly criticism did not dissuade Clement VIII from giving Baronius still another laborious honor. In April of 1597, the aged Antonio Cardinal Colonna died, thus vacating the prestigious position of the librarian of the Holy Roman church. There were many cardinals who wished to obtain this position, but the pope's choice was Baronius. However, he was to serve without any salary. There is no indication why the pope made such an arrangement; it is more surprising because only a few years before Sixtus V had raised the salary of the librarian to the tidy sum of two hundred *scudi* a month.[48] But Baronius was happy to serve at this post, perhaps the only promotion he was heartily delighted about.

Over and above all these duties, Baronius also served as the papal theologian after the death of the venerable Cardinal Toledo nearly a year before. Holding, thus, so many important positions, so close to the seat of supreme power in the Church, Baronius emerged as the single most important figure in the Vatican besides the pope himself. Suddenly he was thrown into the middle of ecclesiastical and secular politics for which he had no taste or any preparation. Therefore, what onlookers saw as a splendid career was to him a torture and an agony. He secretly yearned to return to the simple religious life of the Oratory and to devote all his time to the *Annales*. But how could he abandon the purple? Would not that be considered a betrayal of religious duty imposed on him by the vicar of Christ? Such questions constantly disturbed his peace of mind.

In moments of personal agony, the only man Baronius could turn to for counsel was his friend and confidant, Talpa, to whom he wrote several confidential letters.[49] These letters reveal a bookish scholar and a simple religious caught inescapably in the quagmire of practical politics. Baronius seems to have suffered indescribable agony every time he was called upon to offer practical advice to the pope concerning public matters. He had scruples about his own personal salvation in dealing with such matters. The childlike innocence of the man was to the point of being simplistic—it sounds insincere. Yet, he certainly was sincere. As a close associate recorded, Baronius tried to renounce the cardinalate at least three times during the pontificate of Clement VIII.[50] Only the pope's strong opposition prevented him from doing so.

Even while Baronius was seriously considering leaving the Vatican, he was pushed deeper into the thicket of papal politics. Alfonso d'Este II, duke of Ferrara, died in 1597 without a legal heir. As a feudal dependency of the papacy, his duchy had to be handed over to the papacy at the death of Alfonso.[51] But immediately after his death, Alfonso's cousin, Cesare d'Este, had the bishop of Ferrara crown him duke at the cathedral. Clement VIII considered this act an outrage. He convened the cardinals to discuss the steps to be taken. "Decretum est bellum" was the cry from the Quirinale.[52] All the cardinals favored war except Baronius, who agonized about the impending disaster to the Church if she were to become involved in a war. As a first step, Clement VIII imposed a censure on Ferrara. He then let it be known to Cesare d'Este that the legions of the papacy were standing ready to march on Ferrara.[53] Cesare d'Este yielded and retired to his other capital at Modena.

In order to celebrate the victory and personally to establish his authority, Clement undertook a visit to Ferrara, bringing the whole papal court along with him. The triumphal expedition passed through various Italian towns, making stops at Terni, Ancona, and other places. Finally, the papal party solemnly entered Ferrara "with great religion and glory," Baronius wrote.[54] The whole episode must have been a painful experience to him, particularly the political procession led by the pope, reminiscent of the times of Julius II. The few things that he may have really enjoyed during this journey were his meeting with a famous lay apostle of Brescia, Alessandro Luzzago, his side-trip to the Camaldolese monastery near Padova, and above all the companionship of Robert Bellarmine.

Bellarmine, though only a priest at that time, was already a famous theologian and, therefore, was a congenial companion to Baronius. Together, they made a side-trip to Venice, more in the mood of an excursion, with Baronius dressed as a simple priest— all of which made them closer personal friends. In fact, their friendship became so celebrated that a biographer of Baronius likened them to Peter and Paul, "the twin lights of the eyes" of the Church.[55] Baronius soon had an opportunity to prove his friendship.

Early in 1599, Baronius recommended that Bellarmine be promoted to the cardinalate. The recommendation was well received because Clement, after having had to encounter political resistance from Ferrara and having already experienced the political machinations of the Spanish court through their cardinals in the Vatican, had decided to create a number of new cardinals "who would not be dependent on princes."[56] Evidently, the pope wanted to shift the balance heavily towards his side, because he had already seen signs of an impending conflict with the Spanish crown. Bellarmine, of course, was eminently qualified for the dignity. He was already celebrated for his role as a Catholic apologist and for his famous theory of the "indirect power" of the spiritual over the temporal, which strengthened some of the temporal claims of the papacy. The pope was also inclined to take heed of Baronius' recommendations; indeed, in the same consistory he also promoted two other candidates Baronius had suggested, namely Silvio Antoniano, respected humanist, and Monsignor Visconti, at that time papal ambassador to the court of the emperor.

The crowning event of Clement VIII's visit to Ferrara was the double royal wedding between Philip III of Spain and Margaret of Austria, and between Archduke Albert of Austria and the Spanish Infanta Eugenia on November 17, 1598. The august gathering in Ferrara, assembled in renaissance splendor, offered one of the rarest spectacles of pomp and pageantry. It gave Baronius, among other things, the opportunity to rub elbows with the high and mighty of Europe. With obvious delight he wrote to Talpa about his visits with the members of the two royal families, particularly the new queen of Spain and the queen mother.[57] They all had heard about the famous scholar. The royal ladies were interested especially in discussing spiritual matters with the confessor of the pope—these spiritual discussions, of course, were the reason for Baronius' delight.

The festive mood of Ferrara must have been marred by Clement's insistence that Philip III should put an end to the interference of the Spanish court in the ecclesiastical administration of Sicily. Indications are that Philip's answer was very negative. Why else should it be that one of the first things Clement did after he returned from Ferrara was to convene a public consistory in which strong declarations were made about ecclesiastical jurisdiction? In this consistory, held early in February, 1599, Baronius made very strong public statements about the rights of the Church, obviously aimed at the Spanish.[58] Of course, his statements pleased the pope immensely, but on the other hand, they also infuriated the Spanish court and the Spanish cardinals in Rome.

Baronius' involvement in papal politics was distracting and disturbing enough, but he had to suffer even more interruptions because of his position as a cardinal. As his years in the Sacred Col-

lege proceeded, he was forced (his earlier protestations notwithstanding) to accept several ecclesiastical benefices. After all, he
had to maintain the dignity of his status and support his servants
and subordinates. Also against his own decision, he had to break
down and give support to some of his poor relatives in southern
Italy, whose case was convincingly represented by his own Oratorian friends.[59]

In a revealing letter to his friend, Talpa, Baronius exposed his
financial status in 1598.[60] He had an income of four thousand
scudi a year, besides a one hundred *scudi* a month allowance which
Clement VIII provided for poor cardinals. But this allowance was
to last only for the duration of Clement's life. Therefore, when
Clement offered him the priory of San Fortunato d'Arpaia, with
an annual income of five hundred *scudi*, he accepted it. He thought
this priory which was only twenty miles from Naples, would offer
him an excuse to visit his friends in the Oratory of that city.[61]

Another benefice he received at this time was the abbacy of Canosa in Bari, with an income of about six hundred *scudi* a year.
Since the episcopal jurisdiction of the area was part of the obligation of the benefice, Baronius hesitated to accept it, for he had no
desire to hold it in absentia.[62] But the pope seems to have forgotten the decrees of the Council of Trent, and Baronius was given
the benefice anyway. The best he could do, then, was to use the income for the welfare of that forgotten part of the Church. He sent
a representative to Bari who brought back word about the people
and priests there in "the depth of ignorance and sin." Consequently, he found a conscientious priest to reside with the congregation
and take care of their spiritual needs. He also made arrangements
to make needed repairs on the old church. Thus, he returned to
Canosa all the money he collected, without keeping a penny for
himself.[63]

Although Baronius tried very hard to provide for the spiritual
welfare of the people of Canosa, he met with failure, partly because the priest he put in charge there was more interested in himself. Baronius, therefore, suggested to the pope that the territory
of Canosa be joined to the diocese of Minervino. However, the
pope did not heed his suggestion. Instead, he tried to ease Baronius' conscience by pointing out that it was perfectly in accordance with the decrees of Trent to be absent from a benefice as
long as arrangements were made for the spiritual welfare of the
people. The pope also gave an additional allowance of one hundred
scudi for that purpose. Finally, however, Baronius was able to pre-

vail upon the pope, and he renounced the benefice in the year
1600. But he received a compensation in the form of another benefice, this time an abbacy in the diocese of Benevento which had
been assigned by Sixtus V for the Vatican librarian. It provided the
same income of five hundred *scudi.*[64] Still another benefice, in the
archdiocese of Benevento, was given to him but Baronius relinquished this in favor of the other Oratorian cardinal, Tarugi. In
lieu of this benefice, he was given a pension of one thousand
scudi.[65]

One of the benefices Baronius received during his career as a
Vatican prelate was the abbacy of Monte Celio. On April 27, 1602,
he wrote thus to his friend, Germanico Fedeli:

> You may know that His Beatitude has made me the Abbot
> of San Gregorio, with very little income, but with much expense
> and grave complications. The income at the most (as they say)
> is some 1200 *scudi*, but there are many expenses, many litiga-
> tions. His Beatitude wants me also to take care of the monks
> with regard to their regular observance. I believe, therefore,
> these are going to give me some trouble.[66]

Indeed, he was right in describing the nature of the benefice in this
manner. The monastery, which had been established by Pope Saint
Gregory, stood at this time in a dilapidated condition, a poor
house for the precious relics of early Christianity. Historically-
oriented Baronius, therefore, started to restore it immediately. He
employed one of the talented artists of the time, Guido Reni, to
do the painting in the chapel.[67] He restored the Gregorian spirit
of the monastery by reinstating one of the ancient customs Saint
Gregory himself had introduced. Gregory, as tradition holds, had
kept a table in the monastery for feeding the poor. Once Christ
himself had appeared in the guise of a beggar, and ate at that table.
Accordingly, Baronius had the monks keep a table in the monastery on which they were to entertain as many poor persons as it
would hold, every year on the feast day of Gregory. All the poor
who could not be seated were also to be entertained.[68] Thus, Baronius succeeded in restoring to the monastery of Saint Gregory, not
only its physical structure, but also at least some of its traditions.

Baronius, indeed, accepted benefices because sixteenth century mores dictated that a Roman cardinal should be maintained
through them. But he could hardly be numbered among those
greedy prelates who bled the people and deprived their churches
of spiritual leadership. On the contrary, Baronius made best use of

all income he received from his various benefices for what he thought was the good of the Church. An informal account of his financial dealings which he revealed to his Oratorian colleague, Francesco Zazzara, on May 18, 1607, a few weeks before his death amply testifies to this fact.[69] He helped fourteen young relatives to enter different monasteries, giving a gift of one thousand *scudi* each as patrimony to the religious houses they entered. He gave five thousand *scudi* for the Capuchins of Sora, spent five thousand for the restoration of the church of San Gregorio at Monte Celio, and used up seven thousand for the renovation of his titular church of Saints Nereus and Achilleus. He spent a great deal of money for other charities too, he told Zazzara, so much so that he was left practically penniless and even in debt. He wanted his debts to be paid by selling his library and personal belongings after his death.

Baronius was not sorry for all the charitable works he had been able to do, but his disappointment about being saddled with what he considered was a futile dignity continued. When Zazzara reminded him that without the cardinalate he would not have been able to do so much charity, he wryly remarked: "What charity! I have given nothing of my own." This may well be taken as a statement of principle about benefices: indeed, a refreshing view in an age when most higher clergy still handled the wealth of the Church as their own.

The result of all the distractions that the dignity of the cardinalate brought to Baronius was that the *Annales* became not his principal occupation but an occasional escape and Volume VIII was delayed for nearly three years. Finally when it appeared in the middle of 1599, it contained a letter of dedication to Clement VIII and an essay of tribute to Philip Neri, both reflecting on his extrahistorical preoccupations. In the dedicatory letter, Baronius attempted to justify Clement's action in annexing Ferrara to the papal states, basing his argument on the Donation of Constantine, the essential authenticity of which he still maintained.[70] In the tributary essay he once again expressed, with touching tenderness, not only his devotion but also his indebtedness to Neri for guiding him to religious vocation as well as for "tyrannically" imposing on him the oppressive task of the *Annales*.[71]

While Baronius was slow in bringing out the eighth volume of the *Annales*, other scholars and publishers around Europe were busy preparing translations and abridgments of the work in order to make it accessible to the largest number of people. Two Parisian publishers, Sebastianus Nivellius and Gullielmus Chaudiere, for example, contemplated publishing a new edition of the *Annales* in small print in order to place it in many more hands and to decrease the high price of larger editions. Their plan was not carried out, even though they obtained the author's permission.[72]

However, several compendia of the *Annales* were published at the same time. One was prepared by the Jesuit, Giovanni Gabriele Bisciola, under the supervision of Bellarmine.[73] Baronius was so pleased with it that he preferred it to one by his Oratorian colleague, Camillo Severino.[74] Another compendium was published in Germany by Kornelius Schulting, as a direct blast at the contemporary Lutherans and Calvinists.[75] A history of the lives and works of the popes was then compiled from the *Annales* by the Oratorian, Francesco Bordino, who succeeded Cardinal Tarugi as archbishop of Avignon.[76] A similar *Lives of the Popes* based on the *Annales* had been prepared by a Simone Maiolo, bishop of Vulturara, although the unexpected demise of the author interrupted its publication.[77] Baronius also had given permission to some unknown Spaniards to prepare a work on the lives of the saints based on the *Annales*, but this did not seem to have materialized.[78] At the same time, two new complete editions of the *Annales* were begun in 1601. One of them came from Mainz[79] and the other from Venice.[80] Few works of this period enjoyed such widespread interest and publicity.

Urged on by the Catholics of Europe and provoked by Protestant critics, Baronius started to work on the *Annales* in a faster pace. He was thus able to publish the ninth volume within ten months of the eighth. In this, as in previous volumes, the content was made actual in the dedication. The period covered (714–842 A.D.) included the reigns of Pepin the Short, Charlemagne, and Louis the Pious. Baronius, therefore, fittingly reminded Henry IV of France, to whom the volume was dedicated, of the many favors his predecessors had done to the Catholic church and exhorted him to show the same loyalty to her. He closed the dedicatory essay, offering felicitations over the recently celebrated marriage between Henry and Marie de Medici, and wishing that there may arise from this union other Pepins, Charlemagnes, and Louis the Pious's.[81]

The appearance of the ninth volume of the *Annales* in the year 1600 coincided not only with the traditional Jubilee, but also with the culmination of many successes the Catholic church experienced since the time of the Reformation. The Jesuits were by now strongly entrenched in central Europe. They systematically reconverted much of Germany under the leadership of such outstanding men as Peter Canisius.[82] In France, the conversion of Henry IV could be considered as a victory for the Church. In England, an underground church was enjoying at least some sort of an uneasy peace under Elizabeth. On the literary front, Baronius' *Annales* had already eclipsed the *Magdeburg Centuries*. Throughout Europe the numerous religious orders and congregations which sprang up in the wake of the Reformation were making considerable progress. All things considered, the Church was experiencing a surprising reinvigoration as a result of the Counter-Reformation. It was in a spirit of triumph, therefore, that Clement VIII opened the great door of Saint Peter's in the symbolic ceremony, inaugurating the Jubilee celebrations of the year 1600.

Throngs of pilgrims poured into Rome from all parts of the world. It was like the old days again, as if the Reformation had never taken place. Even some Protestants who felt a kind of nostalgia for the old days visited Rome. The city was well prepared to receive them. The religious houses in the city shared the responsibility of catering to their spiritual and bodily needs. The Oratory was especially equipped for this because of the Ospedale della Trinita dei Pellegrini, founded by Neri and served now by all the Oratorians, even by the two Oratorian cardinals, Tarugi and Baronius.

Baronius walked to the four main basilicas of Rome at least some thirty times during that year in order to gain the Jubilee indulgence, as one of his biographers reports.[83] Besides the indulgences he also had some very special reasons for rejoicing. The *Annales* were becoming famous, and better yet, they were proving effective as a means of conversion. Reports came in from different parts of Europe that Baronius' work was instrumental in stemming the tide of heresies and opening the eyes of even hardened heretics. Two of these converts contacted him directly and confessed their debt to the *Annales* in changing their faith. One was Casper Schopp. He was a well-known Lutheran scholar, engaged in Protestant apologetics. But having encountered doubts about his faith, he began to search beyond it. As he himself recalled, many "great and important persons" had tried to convert him, but they failed.[84] Finally, a friend, one G. M. Wacker, suggested that he read the *Annales*. Suddenly, as he said, the way opened to him. Thus he became a Catholic; and in 1599 he came to Rome to visit Baronius and to present him with a letter eulogizing the salutary effect of the *Annales* on him. He published this letter with an apologetical pamphlet he wrote about Catholic scriptural interpretation.[85] It is possible that he was also the author[86] of the extremely caustic pamphlet against Nicola Crasso (pseudonym of Giovanni Marsili) who had attacked Baronius' *Paraenesis ad Rempublicam Venetam*.[87] The most important thing about his conversion was that Rome considered it a great propaganda victory over Protestants.

The other prominent convert of Baronius was a man who bore the family name of Calvin and possibly was a relative of the Reformer. Giustus Calvin was on the Protestant theological faculty of Heidelberg, and he experienced a change of heart in the Jubilee year of 1600. He wanted to come to Rome, visit the basilicas, and become a Catholic. He wrote to Baronius, "the prince among the prelates of the Roman church and among the proclaimers of true and stable justice, who unnerved all the forces of the anti-Christ and restored to the Church all that had been removed from her!"[88] A series of letters followed between Calvin and Baronius which lasted for more than four years.[89] Calvin described to the cardinal his earnest desire to embrace the Catholic faith. He also mentioned the terrible persecutions he and his family had to suffer from the Protestants on account of his Catholic leanings. His attempt to go to Rome in the Jubilee year was not realized; an unexpected illness delayed his trip. Finally, Calvin arrived in Rome in 1602; and Baronius received him with outstretched arms. Clement VIII himself administered the sacrament of confirmation in a full color ceremony at the Lateran Basilica.

As a gesture of esteem and gratitude to his friend and guide to the faith, Calvin relinquished his family name and adopted that of Baronius. After a long stay in Rome, he went back to his native Germany, visiting en route the shrines at Loreto and Siena. He carried in his pocket a letter from Baronius, thanking the archbishop elector of Mainz for all the assistance he had extended to the family of Giustus, residing in Mainz at that time, and asking that he continue his protection.[90] The new convert, accordingly, settled with his family in Mainz, and continued his apologetical works for the Catholic church.[91] Thus, at the close of the sixteenth century, Baronius' *Annales* was not only a most popular work but also an effective tool of the Counter-Reformation; and the author was a most important prelate in Rome, perhaps the most influential churchman after the pope.

6

The Tribulations
of a Curia Cardinal

In 1602, a Roman artist, Francesco Villamena, engraved a portrait of Baronius with the following caption:

> Caesar Baronius, Cardinal of the Title of
> Saints Nereus and Achilleus, Librarian of
> the Sacrosanct Apostolic See, Eminent
> Author of the *Annales* in His Sixty-Fourth
> Year.

> Baronius Lives by History and Piety:
> One Light Complements the Other.[1]

This caption epitomized Baronius' life very well, perhaps with one exception: it missed the priority of piety to history. And piety meant to him essentially the service of the established order of the Church. However, he preferred to serve the Church as a simple Oratorian priest and a historian rather than a high dignitary. This was the reason Baronius had declined offers of bishoprics and other high offices on several occasions. But eventually he had been forced to accept one of the highest dignities in the Church, the cardinalate. As a cardinal of the Vatican curia, he received some excellent opportunities to serve his Church, but his position also required that he embroil himself in ecclesiastical politics—which, indeed, was a tribulation to a scholar dedicated to the monumental task of the *Annales*.

As Baronius' years in the Vatican went on, Clement VIII increasingly called on him for settlement of complex public issues as well as for personal counsel. New problems sprang up year after year, but what attracted Clement's attention in the first year of the seventeenth century was some of the unfinished business of

Trent, not the least of which was the revision of the *Breviarium Romanum*, the daily prayer book of the clergy. The Council had recommended such a revision,[2] and one had actually been begun at the time of Pius V. It soon became apparent that the new edition still contained many errors. Clement VIII, therefore, appointed a commission for a second revision; and Baronius, being the leading historian in the curia, was made a member, as was Bellarmine, by then a leading theologian.[3]

The commission's task was to check on the accuracy of biblical verses in the *Breviarium,* correct theological errors and ambiguities, and insure the historical validity of martyrs and saints commemorated. This work was completed within a year, and Clement inaugurated the new breviary with the bull, *Cum in Ecclesia*, on May 10, 1602. What could best be said about this new edition was that it was an improvement over the previous one though it still contained many errors. It was surprising that Baronius and Bellarmine would allow this to stand. A better edition was to be produced only in mid-eighteenth century, under Benedict XIV.

Clement also made the necessary emendations in the *Roman Pontifical* and the *Ceremonial of the Bishops*, with the aid of other commissions of which Baronius also was a member.[4] But the most important book of Catholic worship still remained to be updated, nearly forty years after the conclusion of the Council of Trent which had strongly urged its revision. That was the *Missale Romanum* which contained the prayers and rubrics of the Mass. The *Missale*, in fact, needed very thorough revision, because many of the prayers used in the Mass were taken from the old Vulgate version of the Bible which had since been revised by Pope Sixtus V. The updated version of the biblical passages had to be entered in the new *Missale*, and more importantly, many additions and changes had to be made in the ceremonies of the Mass. Clement VIII, therefore, appointed another commission for this purpose, and he made Baronius a member of this one, too. This work was finished by the middle of 1604, and Clement promulgated it with the bull, *Cum Sanctificemur*, on July 7 of that year.

At the same time, Baronius was a member of still another commission, the Congregation of the Index, which the Vatican had established for the review and proper classification of books. Of course, the extensive use of the Index of Forbidden Books was one of the measures the post-Tridentine Church undertook for the suppression of heresy. Along with Cardinal Antoniano, Baronius had the special task of reviewing books in the fields of humanities, history, and medicine.[5] This was a very time consuming obligation, given the broadness of these fields. Therefore, the two cardinals were assisted by several subordinates who shared the bulk of the responsibility of reviewing books.

Baronius served in yet another Vatican congregation, the Congregation of the Rites. This was a branch of the Curia Romana which examined devotional books for the use of the faithful, and oversaw the canonization procedures of saints. All devotional books were to be approved by this congregation for their theological content and ceremonial propriety prior to publication. Canonization procedures had to follow the guidelines established and strictly enforced by this congregation. Besides these procedural matters, the congregation was also charged with reviewing testimony of witnesses and of making judgments based on the arguments presented by the postulator and the "devil's advocate." Many devotional books published at this time carried the approval of Baronius. For example, a booklet containing pious readings intended for the octave of Saint Spiridion carried the following approbation: *Ego Caes. Card. Baronius vidi supradictas lectiones, et signavi ex eis aliquas mutandas, reliquas recipiendas, et populo in ecclesia recitandas esse censeo.*[6] Similarly, Baronius read and approved the pious readings on the lives of the patron saints of Poland,[7] several "divine offices" of the Church of Lyons,[8] and numerous other devotional books of that time.[9] All these would indicate not only Baronius' deep involvement in the work of the Congregation of the Rites, but more importantly his profound influence on the liturgical and devotional practices of the time. Indeed, he had a great share in shaping the religious character of the post-Tridentine era.[10]

Still more crucial, perhaps, was Baronius' generally unrecognized role in keeping the theological controversy over the nature of divine grace from boiling over. While the Church saw the return of civil peace in France and the Netherlands and the gradual waning of wars among the great Atlantic powers in early seventeenth century, it had the misfortune of witnessing a war on the theological front. The argument on free will and grace, on which Martin Luther and Desiderius Erasmus took opposing sides, was once again the issue that divided Catholic intellectuals. Like Luther and Calvin before, the seventeenth century theologians searched in the writings of Augustine, the "Doctor of Grace" and "Father of the Church," for answers related to the nature of grace and the extent of man's freedom in attaining salvation.

Two theologians especially dedicated to the study of Augustine early in the century were Cornelius Jansen and Louis de Molina. Jansen's researches, however, did not come to fruition until his famous work was ready for publication in 1638, just a short time before his death. It was actually published posthumously only in 1640.[11] The Jansenist controversy, therefore, did not gather full steam until some years after the death of Baronius. But Molina's work, the treatise on *Free Will and Gifts of Grace*,[12] came out with a blast in 1588. Thus, it was Molinism that Baronius had to confront as papal theologian in the early seventeenth century.

As a true son of Saint Ignatius, who had emphasized the independence of the individual in shaping his own salvation,[13] Louis de Molina upheld that man is almost completely free in doing good works, in other words, unimpaired free will. God has only a "mean knowledge" in these matters, he said, even though he did not quite deny the existence and the need of divine grace as an assistance to man in doing good works. Molina's position was slightly different from that of the traditional Thomists who upheld the existence of two different kinds of grace. The first, which they called "sufficient grace," is the very basic assistance that God gives to every man to enable him to attain salvation. The second, "efficacious grace," they said is the divine assistance that should precede before the conception and execution of each and every good work; without it men are unable to act at all, they considered.

Aside from these theological differences, the matter of the prestige of two rival religious orders also became a hidden, but very important issue in this controversy. It was not surprising, therefore, that two armies of theologians soon joined in battle. The leader of the Jesuits, of course, was their outstanding theologian from Spain, Molina. The Dominicans provided a battery of them: Deomenico Banez, Thomas de Lemos, and Didace Alvarez.

The open theological battle between the two most important religious orders of the Church, which was continuously worsening after the appearance of Molina's book, disturbed Clement VIII a great deal. Only a few years before, his predecessor, Pius V, had to take stern measures against a similar controversy about the nature of grace, including public condemnation of no less a figure than Michel de Bay (Baius), chancellor of Louvain University. Fortunately, Baius had submitted humbly to the decision of the pope and retracted his statements. Baius' teachings had been dangerously close to the Lutheran position of the complete denial of free will, and therefore, it was easy for Pius V to make a decision against them. But Molina's position was not so clearly opposed to the accepted doctrine of the Church. Besides, it was generally supported by the pope's own most loyal soldiers, the Jesuits. However, the controversy it provoked was scandalously dividing the Church and disturbing its peace everywhere. In 1597, therefore, Clement established a special "Congregatio de Auxiliis" comprised of eminent theologians and charged it with the duty of investigating and settling once and for all the whole issue of divine grace. As papal theologian, Baronius served as a member of this congregation, too.

The congregation's task was very difficult because it had to be tactful in dealing with an issue involving the prestige of two prominent religious orders. Moreover, the line separating the two sides was often thin and ambiguous—so much so that the Congregatio de Auxiliis soon declared itself unable to settle the controversy. Clement, therefore, instructed the warring parties to tone down discreetly their volatile argument. In 1605 Clement's successor, Paul V, explicitly forbade that either side should refer to the matter publicly. Finally, a somewhat inconclusive solution was found in 1607: both sides were allowed to hold their own views, but they were admonished not to criticize each other publicly.

Even though the papacy allowed the Jesuits to hold their views on divine grace as a temporary solution to the controversy, Clement VIII took certain measures which would eventually assure the triumph of Thomistic teachings. It was at the height of the controversy *de auxiliis* that Clement formally requested the General of the Society of Jesus to establish a *Ratio Studiorum* for the order in accordance with the teachings of Thomas Aquinas. Even though the idea was highly disagreeable to the Jesuits at that time, they could not resist it in the long run; after all, had not Ignatius Loyola himself required them to follow Thomism in all questions of speculative theology "as the surest and most commonly received doctrine"?[14]

There is no question that the steps Clement took to insure the eventual success of Thomism were suggested by Baronius. There is also no doubt on which side of the controversy Baronius stood. In the middle of the controversy, he wrote to a leading Louvain theologian, Franciscus Lamata, requesting from him a critique of Molina's assertions.[15] Accordingly, Lamata prepared a short treatise trying to establish from the Church fathers, especially from Augustine, the existence of "efficacious" grace. Evidently, Baronius was delighted about his friend's theological position because it conformed well with his own. While Lamata was preparing his critique, Baronius did some research on this matter himself, which resulted in a lengthy critique of Molina's theological teachings.[16]

Baronius' treatise begins with the declaration that the Catholic church holds the teachings of Augustine on divine grace as obligatory. Then he proceeds to describe briefly the sources—decrees of councils, writings of Church fathers and popes—in which the doctrine on grace had been further clarified. Then he gives a short treatment of the errors of Faustus (a fifth century heretic who, in refuting the Pelagian heresy, went to the other extreme and advocated predestination),[17] and defines positions held by the Jesuits and Dominicans. After this he proceeds to refute Molina's teachings. He starts with a brief historical introduction to the current controversy and then points out some fifty-five errors in Molina's book which resembled the Pelagian or semi-Pelagian heresies, and thus ran contrary to the teachings of Augustine and the traditional stand of the Church.

Baronius' treatise against Molina was not published, probably because he wanted to respect the pope's wish to de-escalate the controversy. However, he made his theological position known through private correspondence with his friends—some of whom also received manuscript copies of his critique.[18] Baronius' role in settling the controversy over Molinism may be summarized as one of secret persuasion and quiet suppression. Clement VIII's imposition of Thomism on the Jesuit *Ratio Studiorum* cannot be explained without taking into account Baronius' strongly expressed opinions. There is also undeniable evidence that Baronius personally persuaded the Jesuits to relinquish their defense of Molina.[19] His collaboration with other European theologians, openly engaged in opposing Molinism, was certainly designed to defeat Molinism.[20]

Baronius considered that the Molinist controversy had been provoked by Martin Luther's challenge to the concept of free will.[21] But the German reformer also had provoked serious discussions about the reform of the Church, which culminated in the Council of Trent. The Tridentine decrees on Church reform, though accepted with enthusiasm, had not yet been fully implemented even in the early seventeenth century, more than forty years after the council. This failure was seriously hampering the growth of the Church—which disturbed many leaders, one of whom was Cardinal Robert Bellarmine. His Jesuit colleagues, who were earnestly engaged in the reconversion of the Protestants, constantly urged him to persuade the papacy to speed up the reforms. Therefore, it was with a great sense of urgency that he took the very unusual step of submitting to the pope personally a memorandum suggesting certain important reforms within the Church.[22] "The Supreme Pontiff," he said,

> exercises a threefold personality in the Church of God. He is the pastor and rector of the universal Church, the bishop of the city of Rome, and the temporal ruler of ecclesiastical possessions. But in all these functions, the care of the whole Church has the first place; and that is the first, the most special, and the most important (function).[23]

Citing, then, the examples of Peter and his successors, the famous churchman exhorted the pontiff to apply himself to the crying needs of a long neglected Church. Indirectly, at least, Bellarmine was criticizing Clement's inordinate attention to Italian politics, particularly the temporal domains of the papacy. But submitted in a most respectful manner by such an eminent cardinal and theologian "in order to unburden my own conscience,"[24] the pope could not ignore it.

Bellarmine suggested several practical reforms which should be executed immediately in order to correct certain serious abuses—such as the elevation of unqualified persons to dignities of the Church, long delays in filling the vacancies in cathedral churches, generally prevalent absenteeism, pluralism, frequent and harmful transfer of bishops from their dioceses, and the inexcusable resignation of bishoprics. The Council of Trent had decreed the abolition of all these abuses, but the papacy had not yet gotten around to it. Worse yet, some including Clement, were still guilty of such abuses. Had not Clement raised his nephew, Pietro Aldobrandino, to the cardinalate whose only qualification was blood relation to the pope? Was not he at that time grooming still another relative, young Silvestro Aldobrandino, for the red hat?[25]

Logically, Clement assumed a defensive posture in his reply to Bellarmine.[26] In general, Clement admitted that there were some irregularities, but these were not easily corrected; he could not be held responsible for them. There were several considerations, such as the interest of the College of Cardinals, the traditional rights of temporal rulers, which made it impossible to implement some of the reforms decreed by Trent. The pope certainly could not shake the whole system without seriously disrupting everything.

Albericius, the eighteenth century biographer of Baronius, contends that Clement's reply to Bellarmine was actually prepared by

Baronius.[27] He claims to have examined the original letter of Bellarmine and the reply given by Baronius on behalf of the pope, which were kept at that time in the Vallicelliana Library, But Calenzio, who wrote the biography of Baronius in the early 1900's, could not trace these documents in that library. Nor are they available there now. It is quite possible that they have been stolen or mislaid. In any case, if Baronius did write this defensive reply to Bellarmine, we can legitimately raise a question about his interest in Church reform. On the other hand, we have to understand that he was writing on behalf of Clement whose views he had to represent, not his own. However, this letter fits into the general pattern of his writings which always defends the authority in the Church without even questioning the possibility of an error.

Whatever happened between Clement and Baronius as penitent and confessor cannot, naturally, be known. But there is no evidence that Baronius used his official position to correct the nepotism the pope was openly practicing. Was not an Oratorian, one of Baronius' own co-religionists, sent to Perugia to groom young Silvestro Aldobrandino for the cardinalate? Baronius, undoubtedly, knew about it and seems to have accepted the situation. He himself wrote to the tutor, Germanico Fedeli, that "His Holiness wishes to elevate him (Silvestro) to higher dignity."[28] Perhaps Baronius was resigning himself to a situation over which he had no control. If that was the case, he did try to make the best of it when he wrote to Germanico Fedeli to train the boy well. "Fortify the foundation as if (he is) the high pillar by which the Holy Church is supported," he said.[29]

Even though in his official capacity as confessor and theologian of the pope Baronius was ineffective in correcting Clement's nepotism, he succeeded in using his official position to recommend worthy candidates for high ecclesiastical dignities. We have already seen that he recommended Robert Bellarmine, the later critic of the pope, to the cardinalate. Paolo Aringhi relates that many others were also promoted to high positions at the Vatican through the recommendation of Baronius.[30]

His influential position at the Vatican enabled him to recommend worthy persons for ecclesiastical offices outside of the curia as well. Many such recommendations were made to personal friends whom he had met during his career in Rome and corresponded with frequently. One man in particular stands out as his closest friend and most frequent correspondent—Federico Borromeo, cardinal archbishop of Milan. The life-long friendship between these two men started when they met in Rome, probably at the Oratory in 1586, when Federico was in the Eternal City to accept the red hat and join the curia. As soon as he arrived in Rome, he went to see Philip Neri and "put himself in his hands," says his biographer Castiglioni.[31] This is not at all surprising, considering the long-standing friendship of Federico's uncle, Carlo, with Neri. Carlo was a friend of Baronius also, which was still another reason for Federico to visit the Oratory. Carlo's original efforts to bring Baronius to Milan did not succeed, but their friendship did not diminish. In fact, Carlo, found another way of using Baronius' services—by obtaining his counsel in difficult problems of Church reform.[32] Baronius' respect for Carlo also was very great, so much so that he stole the sandals Carlo wore on his pilgrimage to Rome in the Jubilee year, 1575, and always kept them as a relic.[33]

It was only natural that when Carlo's nephew and Baronius met they would fast become personal friends. First of all, they had two common sources of spiritual inspiration, Philip Neri and Carlo Borromeo. They tried to emulate their mutual heroes, though in different ways. Baronius followed the footsteps of Neri into the Oratory while maintaining a great interest in Carlo Borromeo's works of Church reform. Federico followed his uncle as archbishop of Milan and continued the reforms he started while maintaining his original devotion to Neri. There is no better document for Federico's devotion to Neri than his short treatise, *Dicta et Facta Sancti Philippi Nerii*, in which he eulogizes him.[34] Besides their common veneration for Carlo Borromeo and Philip Neri, Federico and Baronius served at the same time on various commissions of the Vatican, which helped to strengthen their friendship.[35]

The warmth and affection these two churchmen held for each other are revealed in their numerous letters. Copies of many letters they exchanged are preserved in several Vallicelliana codices.[36] In one of them, dated June 10, 1601, Baronius expressed his gratitude to Borromeo for generously leaving at his disposal the Borromeo house in Rome at Piazza Novona.[37] In this letter, Baronius also tried to cheer up his friend who at that time was lying ill. On July 21, 1601, Baronius wrote two letters to Milan, one to a certain Monsignor Seneca,[38] an official of the archdiocese, and the other to Federico Borromeo.[39] In the first, he discussed with Seneca some miracles which reportedly had occurred through the intercession of the departed Carlo Borromeo. He assured Seneca that he had already discussed the miracles with the pope, and that appropriate action would be taken in view of Carlo's canonization. In

the second letter, Baronius advised Federico on the correct procedures for the canonization, and repeated his pledge of help in this
matter. Indeed, Baronius was also caught up in the race for getting
friends canonized, as most of his contemporary churchmen were.

Both Baronius and Federico Borromeo were serious Church reformers, but they were not exceptions to the common practice of
trading favors. Their letters, put together, read like a list of favors
given and received. For example, Baronius pulled strings at the
Vatican on behalf of Borromeo so that a case between the Milan
archdiocese and the Cistercian monks might be decided in the
former's favor. Baronius did a very difficult favor for the bishop of
Evora who had been recommended by Borromeo. In return, Borromeo was asked to admit a young friend of Baronius, Giovanni
Paravicino, into the Swiss College which was under the Milan archdiocese. Still another favor: Borromeo was requested to take under
his protection the Hospital of Saint Bernard, which was being established in the Alps for the care of poor travellers.[40]

Federico Borromeo was only one, though perhaps the most important, friend with whom Baronius exchanged favors. Another
was the famous aristocrat-sage of Brescia, Alessandro Luzzago. Baronius met him in Ferrara during Clement VIII's visit of 1598.
Luzzago was one of numerous dignitaries who went to Ferrara to
pay their respects to the pope. When Clement met Luzzago, he expressed his intention of elevating him to the purple in recognition
of his many charitable works. Fearing that the pope would immediately impose this ecclesiastical dignity on him Luzzago slipped
out of Ferrara without even taking leave of his new friend, Baronius. He then wrote to Baronius at Ferrara, explaining the reason
for his abrupt departure and asking for his continued friendship.[41]
The friendship thus established was productive for both of them.
For example, Luzzago received a favor from Baronius in the form
of a recommendation to the pope. In return, Baronius requested
him to use his influence on the bishop of Brescia in restoring the
pension of a certain Bartolomeo Ciuffarini.[42] Their friendship, unfortunately, ended with Luzzago's premature death in 1602. We
have a letter which Baronius wrote at that time to Luzzago's
father, consoling him and offering many indulgences which he had
secured from the pope for his deceased friend.[43]

Baronius indeed was trading favors with his friends, but none of
these was   for personal gain. In fact, most favors they traded were
for charity or Church reform. And it was not only for friends that
Baronius did favors; even strangers who came to know of his repu-

tation as a curia cardinal with much influence and interest in Church reform wrote to him requesting his intervention in one matter or another. One such letter was from a certain Monsignor d'Alarcons who was concerned about the condition of the Spanish Church.[44] He had approached the papal nuncio to Spain, he said, but no action was taken; perhaps Baronius could do something about it. The fact that this letter came from Spain, in the ruling circles of which country Baronius was unpopular, gives added significance to it.

As a cardinal of the curia, Baronius was called on to serve the Church in many ways; for instance, as the cardinal protector of the nascent Congregation of the Religious Fathers of the Mother of God (the Luccan Fathers). This congregation had been founded in Lucca some time before for the reformation of the clergy, but internal dissension was threatening its very existence in the early 1600's. The founder, Giovanni Leonardi, was a saintly person, much favored in the Vatican but *persona non grata* to the Republic of Lucca. The members of the congregation, evidently under pressure from the Republic, were trying to oust the founder from the position of authority.

Baronius wrote several letters to these fathers, exhorting them to remain under the authority of Leonardi.[45] He spoke in the name of Pope Clement and with authority. His admonitions seem to have had the desired effect because in a contemporary letter he congratulated the fathers about their new constitution, approved by the Vatican (no doubt through his intervention), and about the inauguration of their new house in Rome.[46] Nevertheless, the congregation seems to have sunk into disorder within a few years, for Baronius was again called upon for help. In a letter dated March 28, 1607, the superior general of the congregation, Gervasio de Lairvel, decried the ignorance and impiety of his subordinates.[47] As a remedy he suggested the transfer of their monastery to Pont à Mousson, in Lorraine, where he thought a more congenial environment for learning and piety existed. Baronius was also requested by the cardinal of Lorraine to aid them in this matter.[48] Accordingly, he requested permission from the Holy See for the transfer,[49] but he did not live to see the outcome of his efforts.

Baronius was also the cardinal protector of the Oratorian congregation, which actually offered him some personal satisfaction. As we have seen from his earlier life, he had considered the Roman Oratory his home. The life in the Oratory had been much more agreeable to him than that of the papal palace. Even after he had been forcibly taken away from the Oratory, he continued to visit there whenever possible. When the oppressive problems of the papal curia tested his wits he went there for a friendly conversation and some rest. His Oratorian biographers mention this fact proudly. Aringhi's description of a particular incident illustrates the attachment Baronius felt for the Oratory.[50] Sometime in 1600 he fell ill, probably because of overwork, which sent him naturally to the Oratory for rest and recuperation. While he was lying ill there, Pope Clement passed by one day, and being anxious to know the condition of his confessor, he sent an aide to inquire. Baronius' pointed message was, as Aringhi reports: "Please thank His Holiness on behalf of me and tell him that I would be much better where I am now if His Holiness would kindly take back this beretta and let me return to stay here forever with my fathers and brothers; and tell exactly what I said to His Holiness."[51] Of course, Clement did not grant him the wish.

There is no doubt that some of Baronius' happiest moments in life were those he spent at the Oratory. It was a meeting place for churchmen, lay apostles, the intellectual and cultural elite of Rome, and all and sundry people who were interested in spiritual renovation. Philip Neri's hilarious personality pervaded the life there, even long after his death. In such an atmosphere, even a very serious natured person like Baronius came to enjoy the delights of innocent fun. There is a letter which the Oratorian Cardinal Tarugi wrote to another member of the congregation, Germanico Fedeli, with the pleasant description of a carnival-like celebration they had held at the Oratory.[52] The two cardinals of the congregation joined with other members and a great number of guests in electing a mock king for the occasion. Then they had a sumptuous supper followed by comical skits and delightful singing. The fraternal feeling displayed on this occasion would partly explain Baronius' attachment to the Oratory.

Aside from personal attachment, he was also bound by duty to work for the welfare of the Oratorians as their cardinal protector. The Roman and Neapolitan branches of the congregation had held for some time differences of opinion about the structure of the congregation, the Roman group wanting to adhere strictly to the idea of secular priesthood and the Neapolitans desiring strongly to adopt the format of a religious order. These basic differences, compounded with a great number of smaller feuds, eventually broke the two houses apart in such a way that a formal separation had to be arranged in 1602.[53]

This unfortunate turn of events must have hurt Baronius deeply, not only because he was the co-founder of the congregation, but also because of his special concern for the Neapolitan branch, having had a great share in starting it. He was also extremely close to the members of the Neapolitan house, particularly to Talpa, who proofread the *Annales* from the beginning and offered many valuable suggestions. Baronius perhaps wrote more letters to Talpa than to any other person. It was not at all surprising, therefore, that he took the initiative in finding a solution for the differences between the two houses and bringing about their eventual reunion.[54] This was to be finally accomplished in 1607, only a short time before his death.

However strife-stricken the Oratorian congregation was at this time, secular priests in many parts of Europe wanted to organize themselves in its model. This is likely because it still was able to accomplish many of the goals Neri had set for it, and because of the reputation of Neri and Baronius. Many churchmen requested the Roman Oratory to send some of their members to help establish oratories in other parts of Europe. For example, through Baronius Cardinal d'Este sent such a request in 1602 which unfortunately was denied, probably because of the shortage of men at the Oratory.[55] Another case was the Luccan Fathers who patterned their organization after the Oratory under the guidance of Baronius. The efforts of Cardinal Bérulle to establish oratories in France has already been noted, but they came to fruition only long after the death of Bérulle. The first French Oratory was founded at Aix, shortly after the death of Baronius, who was also an inspiration behind it.[56] Establishment of new oratories did not mean any direct burden on the Roman Oratory for there were no formal connections between them. However, as a founding member of the Oratory and a curia cardinal, Baronius was dragged into the expansion movement of the Oratory in many ways—a distraction he liked, no doubt, but a distraction all the same from the work of completing the *Annales*.

Another tribulation Baronius had to face as a curia cardinal, just as all the prelates of his time—indeed of any time—was the constant requests from relatives for financial aid. Early in his career at the Vatican, he had made it clear to his relatives back in southern Italy that he was not to be counted on to make them rich. But when young relatives approached him, expressing their desire to become religious, he could not turn them down—particularly in view of the shortage of vocations he saw in the Oratory itself. Accordingly, he helped a number of his young relatives to enter the

Oratory and several others to join different monasteries and convents.[57] But he admonished all of them against taking advantage of his prominent position in the curia; instead, they should be all the more humble because of it, he advised. If any of them had any ambition of ecclesiastical ladder climbing, they were disappointed for Baronius did not help promote any one of them to an ecclesiastical dignity. In only one instance did he obtain a benefice for a relative: an abbacy worth four hundred *scudi*. And that was because of the exceptional poverty of his parents who would have been forced to recall their son home were it not for this help.[58]

In spite of his many functions as a Vatican prelate, his concerns for the Oratorian congregation, and his involvements with the institutional reform of the Church, Baronius kept alive his interest in the *Annales*. His continued communication with scholars of Europe was one important source of inspiration. Some of his correspondents at this time were churchmen, like Jacques Davy du Perron (later cardinal),[59] who were interested in combating Protestants, while others were true scholars who discussed with him matters of mutual interest and sought his friendship.

Among the scholars was Papire Masson, who sought Baronius' opinion about his work on the bishops of Rome from Peter to Sixtus V.[60] The book was under censure by the Holy See for some disagreeable assertions. Baronius wrote back, therefore, requesting Masson to correct those passages that "offend good ears."[61] Another correspondent of Baronius at this time was the famous Nicolas Faber, who sent him some documents on early Church history that he had discovered.[62] Still another was the Jesuit Matthaeus Roderius, who dedicated to Baronius his book on the *Acts of the Eighth Ecumenical Council* (Constantinople), for the compilation of which he had received Baronius' help.[63] Even some Protestants, like Isaac Casaubon, famous philologist and historian of the time, wrote to Baronius in order to establish his acquaintance, and consult with him about scholarly matters.[64] For instance, Casaubon wrote to Baronius on May 7, 1603, announcing the publication of his work *Historiae Augustae* (qui Suetonium sequuntur) and requesting to review the same. Thus, stimulated by the encouragement of the learned world, Baronius completed the tenth volume of the *Annales* in the summer of 1602.

This volume was dedicated to the Holy Roman Emperor Rudolph II. In his letter to the emperor, Baronius apologized for not dedicating a volume to the emperor until then even though he realized that the emperor surpassed all other Christian kings in dignity.[65] However, he had been waiting for an appropriate time, he said, and this was one because the present volume which covered the history of the Church from 843 to 1000 contained the beginnings of the German Empire. Then he exhorted the emperor about the benefits he stood to gain from reading the *Annales*. Quoting the prophet's words: "Stand ye on the ways, and see, and ask for the old paths, which is the good way, and walk ye in it: and you shall find refreshment for your souls" (Jeremias 6: 16), Baronius urged Rudolph to emulate his saintly ancestors who had served the Church well.

In the tenth volume's prefatory letter to the reader, Baronius asserted that in the history of the ten centuries that he so far narrated, he had not found the Church deviating even slightly from the original commission Christ had given it. Thus, he made clear the main unifying theme of the *Annales*. The most important theme that ran through the ten volumes of the *Annales* was the uninterrupted evolution of the Church just as Christ had designed it. Of course, this assertion was made against the contention of the Magdeburg Centuriators that the Church had deviated somewhere between the third and seventh century from the path which had been established for it by Christ. The main reason for this deviation was the establishment of the papacy as the supreme authority in the Church, they had contended. The *Annales*, as Baronius viewed it, was an attempt to set the record straight.

When the tenth volume of the *Annales* came out in 1602, Baronius was in his sixty-fourth year. He had been working on it for the past forty-five years under very difficult conditions. What had been started as simple sermons in the Oratory became a significant work, mainly because circumstances dictated that way. He had no intention or desire to write a history of the Church. In the early stages, it had been Neri's insistence that led him to sermonize and then to write history. Certainly, in later years he enjoyed the scholarly work, but it had been his desire to defend the Church that really kept the fire alive in him. But now he came to a point where he had already accomplished what had become the main purpose of the work—refuting the Magdeburg Centuriators. The year one thousand seemed to him an appropriate year with which to conclude the *Annales*. As he mentioned later in the preface to the eleventh volume, he really intended to quit; it was his friends, and the well-wishers of the Church who urged him to continue, which he did to the last days of his life.

The cardinal's hat, too, was weighing more heavily on him at this time. On many occasions before, he had attempted to relinquish the dignity with little success. Now, though fully realizing that it was impossible, he continued to wish that he could. As his biographer Aringhi relates, Baronius once exclaimed to a priest of the Oratory: "Oh! how willingly would I, if it was in my power, exchange my purple beretta for yours!"[66] But if he felt that the red had was so terribly heavy, how much greater a burden the tiara would be, if it were to be imposed on him? This was not an idle dream, but an actual probability. Ecclesiastical circles were speculating on who would be the successor of Clement VIII. The pope was ailing and death was imminent. Speculators mostly favored Baronius as the next pope, justifiably indeed, for he was by far the most prominent cardinal at the Vatican. Future events would prove how accurate this speculation was, and how valid the fears of Baronius, who, through his earlier actions had, deliberately or not, closed forever the possibility of his own election to the papacy.

7

The Clamorous Conclaves

Soon after Baronius was elevated to the dignity of the cardinal in 1596, he wrote to King Philip II of Spain, advising him of the matter. This was in accord with a long tradition by which new cardinals informed their secular sovereigns of their elevation. Baronius technically was a subject of Philip since he came from the kingdom of Naples which at that time was under Spain. Normally, secular rulers were pleased about the selection of their subjects for this dignity, for it was in a measure a recognition of the political importance of a country as well. It was also a way of providing representation for the country at the Vatican. Philip II, however, did not even show the courtesy of answering Baronius' letter.

Baronius had taken some trouble to assure the well wishes of his sovereign. He had dedicated the third volume of the *Annales* to him—although even then Philip had neglected to show any appreciation. But he had also made a gross error: he had sent a bound copy of volume nine of the *Annales* to the viceroy of the Spanish king in Naples, soon after its publication in 1600.[1] This volume had been dedicated to Henry IV of France, who of course was considered the archenemy of Philip II and his son and successor, Philip III. Baronius, apparently, was trying to indicate to the Spanish ruler that the honor he had shown to his enemy had not been maliciously intended—indeed he was doing this as a precaution against the possible anger of Philip.

Baronius thought if the matter was sufficiently clarified to the viceroy, the king would not be angered. But even then he had known that it was a touchy matter and that his precautionary measure might backfire. Therefore, he had tried to offset the possible error by sending the book to the viceroy through the bishop of

Acerra, a mutual friend, to be presented with proper courtesies and needed explanations. Baronius also had sent a copy to the viceroy's brother, the archbishop of Taranto at that time, along with a letter of explanation. It had not been his idea, he insisted, to dedicate the volume to Henry; it had been the pope's, and hence the dedication should not be taken as an offense against the king of Spain. It does not seem that Baronius received any acknowledgement for this correspondence either.[2] The hostile attitude of the Spanish court towards him, therefore, was perfectly clear.

Why then did Baronius include in the eleventh volume of the *Annales* a treatise on the so-called *Monarchia Siciliae*—a treatise in which he categorically opposed an issue touching on the vital interests of the Spanish crown, its claim for the governance of the Church in Sicily? The inevitable outcome, as anyone could see, would be the hardening of the already existing enmity towards him. The Oratorian chronicler, Zazzara gave one explanation: that Baronius deliberately did this in view of the imminent conclave for a papal election so that he might insure the opposition of the Spanish cardinals against his own probable candidacy.[3] But the explanation is a bit pietistic. A more likely explanation is that he felt it his duty to defend his Church regardless of the consequences. Or perhaps he felt that the damage had already been done beyond repair as far as the Spanish were concerned. Why, then, not challenge them openly with the hope of galvanizing the French faction, even possibly others, in the College of Cardinals, on his side?

The second theory receives better support from Baronius' papers. On November 7, 1604, several months before the *Monarchia Siciliae* was published, Baronius wrote about it to his friend and confidant, Talpa.[4] In this letter he recounts the efforts on the part of several popes, even very recently, to correct the abuses resulting from the exercise of a falsely claimed authority over the Church in Sicily by the Spanish king. Therefore, he says, he is impelled to treat the matter at this time. He may also have been anxious to bring the issue to a head while Clement was still alive, considering the pope's zeal in preserving the temporal rights of the Church. It is probable, too, that he may have been afraid that if a Spaniard were to be elected pope, the question would be buried for a long time to come. Baronius declares, then, that he is writing with all the talent he can muster and with the dignity worthy of a cardinal of the Church. He is also writing for his own personal benefit, for the outcry he can expect from the Spaniards at the next conclave will be of no little help in stimulating his humility and furthering the salvation of his soul. But the main justification he offers is that of defending the rights of the Church. Whatever personal disadvantages of benefits might accrue to him were purely secondary.

What was known as the "Monarchia Siciliae" was the ecclesiastical tribunal erected by the secular ruler of Sicily and held under his complete control. His right to do so was based on a document which was said to have been issued by Pope Urban II, at Salerno on July 5, 1099. This document, addressed to Count Roger of Sicily, gives to that prince the right to govern the Sicilian Church as a legate of the papacy. The privilege was given, so the document says, as a gesture of the pope's gratitude towards him for saving Sicily from the Saracens and re-establishing the Church there, and it is to pass on after Roger's death to his son, Simon, other sons, and legitimate heirs thereafter. This document came to light for the first time in 1513 in a collection of the official papers of Spain prepared by one Joannes Luca Barberius for Ferdinand the Catholic. Actually, it was of little importance at the time, since Ferdinand exercised full control over the Church of Sicily anyway. But it thereafter became a point of reference in all contestations of the authority of the Spanish crown.

The control of the crown over the Sicilian Church was so complete that it reserved to itself the appointments of ecclesiastical offices; it governed ecclesiastical courts to which all clergy, even bishops, were responsible; and, it claimed the right to excommunicate or absolve persons, including clergy and religious of all ranks. In fact, the crown even refused to receive a resident papal nuncio in Sicily, citing in support a clause from the document in which Urban II had agreed not to send any papal representative to that island without the consent of Roger and his successors.

Thus by virtue of this document the Church in Sicily was deprived of all freedom and autonomy in temporal and spiritual matters. But the situation had been tolerated by the papacy until the Council of Trent. After Trent, however, probably because of the sense of responsibility it generated, several popes had attempted to free the Sicilian Church from the subjugation of the crown. The Vatican curia had compiled a great number of abuses which were said to have been perpetrated against the Sicilian Church by the secular rulers,[5] and in 1571 Pius V had sent his nephew, Cardinal Allesandrino, to Spain in order to present these grievances to the king and negotiate a settlement. The papal nuncio to Spain at that time, Cardinal Giovanni Facchinetti (later Pope Innocent IX), also tried to bring the matter to a satisfactory conclusion.

Sometime in the mid-1590's, Baronius too had made a private appeal to Philip II. In a letter addressed to Philip's confessor, Baronius had pointed out particularly the persecution of the bishops by the king's viceroy in Naples, Count Olivares.[6] What would he write in the future volumes of the *Annales*, he had exclaimed, about the current occurrences in Naples? That the bishops of the Church were exiled by a great Catholic king, as in the times of Decius? As a Neapolitan, Baronius had special reasons for deploring the conditions there, but the letter certainly had been intended to bring to the attention of the king the situation of the Church both in Sicily and Naples. None of these attempts had met with success; the Spanish court had been adamant in preserving the special privileges it claimed on the basis of Urban's letter.

Thus, the only way open to the papacy was to throw the issue into the public forum and openly challenge the authenticity and legality of the document itself. The man most eminently qualified to initiate such a debate, undoubtedly, was Baronius, by virtue of his historical erudition and of the positions he held as the librarian of the Church and the theologian of the pope. It is not clear whether or not Clement VIII commissioned him to do this, but there is no doubt that he was aware of the venture and even blessed it.[7] Therefore, the *Monarchia Siciliae,* which opened the debate, may be considered as representative of the official papal position, even though the work itself was truly Baronius', and even though by inserting it in the eleventh volume of his *Annales* he took complete responsibility for it.

This volume was published early in 1605, and was dedicated to Sigismund III of Poland in honor of his strong stand against heresies and his valiant efforts against the Turks. It contained the history of the Church from 1000 to 1099. Toward the end of the volume, under the year 1097, the long treatise on the *Monarchia Siciliae* was inserted. Baronius attempted to prove that the document attributed to Urban II was either spurious or at the very least essentially changed from the original. He considered that very probably it had been concocted by Alfonso of Aragon. It may also have been probable, he wrote, that the document had been issued by the anti-pope Anacletus II, and not by a legitimate pope. Moreover, even if the document were authentic, it contained nothing that would give the Sicilian ruler the right of governing the Church; at the most he could be a vice-legate of the Holy See, ultimately responsible to the pope. And if such a delegation of powers had been granted, it would have been only to Roger himself, his son

Simon, maybe another son, and the direct descendants of that family. After all, in the document there was no mention of the successors of the Sicilian throne from a different line. In any case, the term, "monarchia," was inappropriate to be used to describe the governance of the Church in Sicily or anywhere else. Monarchy meant sovereignty, and there was only one sovereign authority in the Church, that was the papacy; it was schismatical to claim sov" eignty outside of papal authority. Thus, Baronius attacked the claims of the Spanish king from various angles: historical, constitutional, and theological.

But in order to soften the blow Baronius included at the beginning of the treatise a declaration that his purpose was not to take away any legitimate right from the "Most Catholic Majesty," but to assure the triumph of justice and truth. Ordinarily such a treatise might cause envy and antagonism against the author, he observed, but was not the king of Spain the most ardent lover of truth, protector of justice, and defender of religion? With such faith in Philip III of Spain, and with the hope that he would be the restorer of the Church in Sicily like Zorobabel had been in the Old Testament, Baronius concluded his essay.

However politely he discussed the issue, he certainly was challenging the authority of Spain. As soon as the *Annales* volume came off the press, the Spanish ambassador in Rome rushed a letter to the viceroy of Sicily, Duke Feria.[8] In this letter, the ambassador described the gravity of Baronius' attack and insisted that measures should be taken immediately in order to preserve the ecclesiastical tribunal of Sicily, the so-called "Sicilian Monarchy." The only concession he suggested in his dispatch was a possible change in the name of the institution; monarchy may be a misleading term, he agreed.

But the ambassador's letter was only a prelude to a host of other treatises supporting one side or the other. On the Spanish side, Duke Feria, the viceroy of Sicily was the first to defend the "Sicilian Monarchy" publicly.[9] He attacked the arguments of Baronius and emphasized the legality and advisability of the institution. The president of the Royal Consistory, Mario de Gregoria, then followed with another treatise supporting his government's position.[10] These two Sicilian officials were joined by two historians, Fra Angelo Sciacca, a Franciscan,[11] and the other an anonymous author, who accused Baronius of rhetorical and declamatory treatment of the issue rather than historical.[12]

Two prominent cardinals of the Church, published critical treatises against Baronius' *Monarchia Siciliae*. One was Ascanius Cardinal Colonna, member of the famous Roman family and for a long time in the service of Spain as professor of canon law at the universities of Salamanca and Alcala. His main argument was that this was an affront to such an illustrious king, a loyal son of the Church.[13] (Considering Cardinal Colonna's important position in Rome, and the propaganda advantage Spain was getting by the wide circulation of his treatise, Baronius felt impelled to write a reply to him, the only one he published against his numerous critics.)[14]

The other cardinal who published an essay against Baronius was Maffeo Barberini who later became Pope Urban VIII.[15] Barberini argued that it was not theologically wrong to delegate ecclesiastical authority to laymen. In the case of the "Sicilian Monarchy," the long tradition and the tacit approval of many popes made it a perfectly legal institution.

Several famous scholars also came out in support of Baronius' arguments against the "Sicilian Monarchy." Among them were Pietro Strozzi, Giacomo Sismondi, and Domenico Rinaldi.[16] None of them brought forward any new arguments, but their support added strength to Baronius' position. Thus, the debate Baronius initiated flared up into a very heated controversy, with eminent men lined up on both sides.

The Spanish court instructed its diplomatic representatives around Europe to take a strong stand against the papal position for which Baronius volunteered to be the outstanding advocate. In order to curtail the circulation of Baronius' treatise, odious to the Spanish authorities, volume eleven of the *Annales* was banned from the two kingdoms of Naples and Sicily. In Antwerp, the publisher J. Moretus, who was preparing a new edition of the *Annales*, was ordered to leave out the treatise on the *Monarchia Siciliae* from Volume XI.[17] In Venice, the Spanish ambassador put pressure on the publisher, Melchior Scotus, to prevent the sale of the eleventh volume of his edition of the *Annales*.[18] In order to evade the restrictive measures Spain was resorting to, another publisher ventured to publish Baronius' *Monarchia Siciliae* separately from the *Annales* in France, a country where Spain could not exert any pressure. But it came out only in 1608, two years after the death of the author.[19] In this edition, Cardinal Colonna's criticism of the work and Baronius' reply to it were included; also a letter Baronius wrote to Philip III on June 13, 1605.[20]

In this letter to Philip III Baronius alluded to the *jus exclusivum* by which Spain had defeated his candidacy in two papal elections. But the main purpose of the letter was to explain to Philip the purity of his intentions in writing the *Monarchia Siciliae*. He had written with no malice, he professed, but with the good of the Church in mind and with the advice of the late Pope Clement VIII. But his plea did not seem to have any effect on Philip at this time, and if Philip's anger subsided somewhat a year later, it was probably just because the whole controversy had died down.

Baronius noticed this change of Philip's attitude in a letter to Talpa on May 27, 1606.[21] Cardinal Zapanda, he said, had sent a copy of his reply to Cardinal Colonna to Philip who had had it translated into Spanish and had read it personally several times. As a result, he had come to admire Baronius and was now convinced of his innocence. The matter had then been referred to the duke of Sora in the letters that came from Spain. Moreover, Baronius continued, the pope had told him that the king was going to send a legate to Rome to arrange a settlement of the issue with the Holy See, and that he would also send a new ambassador to the Vatican (probably in the hope of bettering relations).

But nothing substantial seems to have come out of these developments. Tempers flared again when the king, rightly or not, detected a political motive in Baronius' treatise soon after it was published from Paris; the French government might have been behind it, he thought. Therefore, a formal edict was published by Philip III on October 3, 1610, banning the treatise from all Spanish possessions.[22] The ire of the Spanish was also given vent through public burnings of Volume XI.[23] Thus, the angry controversy raged on for a long time after the death of the man who started it. Even as late as the eighteenth century, treatises were published against the *Monarchia Siciliae*.[24] But by then the controversy had become purely academic. The papacy was not in a position to take any meaningful steps against the powerful Spanish monarch. The so-called "Sicilian Monarchy" was to be abolished only after the unification of Italy.

Clement VIII died in the heat of this controversy, on March 3, 1605. The conclave to elect a new pope was officially convened on March 14, but in the intervening days interested parties readied their propaganda machines to insure the election of their own candidates or to guarantee the exclusion of those of their opponents. The Spanish party's clamorous demonstration against Baronius excelled all others in its anger and intense determination. They launched their attack in a general congregation of the cardinals held on March 9. The aged Spanish Cardinal d'Avila read to the congregation a letter from the viceroy of Sicily addressed to the deceased Pope Clement. It was a strong invective against Baronius for having questioned the "Sicilian Monarchy." It called on the pope and the College of Cardinals to censor Baronius for such an offense done to so important a Catholic king. This was followed by denunciations, charges, and counter charges, as if Baronius had been brought to trial for a grievous crime.

Baronius answered the Spanish charges in a subdued but forthright manner. He had not attacked the "Most Catholic Majesty," he explained, but had simply presented the truth of the matter as he saw it from historical evidences. His only purpose had been to protect the rights of the Church and to correct the abuses which were the results of the disruption of proper ecclesiastical authority. He had not done this on his own, he added, but with the encouragement and approval of the deceased pope and three other cardinals of the curia. Needless to say, these explanations did not have any effect on the Spanish party, which was bent on destroying his chances for election to the papacy.[25] Baronius was not censured, as the Spanish wanted; but he was made the object of an open attack before those who might have voted for him. And, it was under these conditions that the cardinals entered the conclave on March 14, 1605.

From the beginning it was apparent that there were at least four parties in the conclave: the French, the Spanish, and two other groups, one of which followed Cardinal Pietro Aldobrandino, nephew of Clement VIII, and the other Cardinal Peretti (Montalto), nephew of Sixtus V. The French party was led by two gifted diplomats, Cardinals Jacques Davy Du Perron and Francois de Joyeuse. Their efforts were coordinated through the French Ambassador Philippe de Béthune under the direct supervision of Henry IV and his minister, Villeroy. Their first choice was the archbishop of Florence, Cardinal Alessandro de' Medici, who was a distant relative of the uncle of the queen of France, Marie des Médicis. Furthermore Alessandro had been instrumental in negotiating Henry's treaty of Vervins with Spain (1598), which secured his position on the throne of France. He thus became the favorite candidate of the French. Their second choice was Baronius, whose efforts in the reconciliation of Henry with the Church they still gratefully remembered.

The Spanish party in the conclave was led by the aged and incompetent Cardinal d'Avila. The Spanish ambassador, Marchese di

Villena, was equally incompetent, and in addition he was "arrogant, punctilious, and ignorant."[26] They did not seem to have any strong preference, though in the beginning they seem to have favored Montalto, who was by no means a strong candidate.[27]

Cardinal Aldobrandino, on the other hand, was a strong contender by virtue of the influence of his deceased uncle, Clement VIII. Out of the sixty cardinals in the conclave, thirty-eight had been given the red hat by his uncle.[28] Such a large number of cardinals had been created by Clement at least partially in view of a future conclave and of the chances of electing another Aldobrandino. In order to strengthen his chances, Cardinal Aldobrandino had also made a pact with the previous Spanish ambassador, the duke of Sassa. But the new ambassador seemed to have ignored this fact.[29]

Some of the men whom Clement VIII had elevated to the purple would not have supported the cause of Aldobrandino because he was partially responsible for some of the abuses under the pontificate of Clement.[30] His success, therefore, depended on securing the solid support of the Spaniards. In order to accomplish this, he negotiated with the Spanish through the duke of Savoy and the Piedmontese ambassador in Rome, Filiberto Gherardo Scaglia.[31] But the Spaniards seem to have had very little sense of direction and purpose to be of any substantial help to Aldobrandino. Instead of strongly promoting his or anyone else's candidacy, they limited themselves to excluding from the race six cardinals unacceptable to them. Among these six were Medici and Baronius.[32] On the other hand, the French party resolutely held onto their original position of supporting Medici or Baronius, in that order.

According to the rules, a candidate had to obtain a two-thirds majority to be elected pope. That meant a minimum of forty votes out of sixty. But while the conflicting interests of the two major parties and the private dealings of different candidates made themselves felt, the conclave dragged on without giving the needed majority to anyone. Baronius, however, received a consistently high number of votes on every ballot, while the fortunes of the other candidates seem to have fluctuated radically. Towards the close of the conclave he received some very high scores, not far short of the needed majority. On March 27, for example, he received thirty-one votes.[33] On March 30, he received thirty-two votes, only eight short of election and the highest he ever received. This brought a barrage of public attacks and accusations against him from the Spanish side, which was obviously shaken and panicked about his

increasing popularity. The aged Cardinal d'Ávila publicly demanded that the cardinals respect the wishes of the king of Spain and
abandon their support of Baronius.[34] The Spanish government also
was thoroughly infuriated about the turn of events in Rome in favor of Baronius, as reported by the Venetian ambassador to Madrid.[35] But this did not change matters much. On the morning of
April 1, Baronius still received twenty-eight votes. Cardinal Medici
received only thirteen votes this time.[36] It became evident, however, that the Spanish were dead set against the candidacy of Baronius. They still commanded some twenty-three or twenty-five
votes, which enabled them to block his election.[37]

It was clear to the French party that the candidacy of Baronius
would not succeed. This made them throw their support back to
Medici, who was their first choice anyway. But Aldobrandino
seems to have been the spoiler of this move, and although far
from a majority, he still had considerable support. The French
were afraid that he would now move to make deals with the cardinals of their own rank, as he had done with the Spanish.[38] Cardinal Joyeuse, the chief French strategist, decided to move fast
and push the candidacy of Medici. He also made an arrangement
with Baronius to lend his support, which he was only too glad to
do.[39] Accordingly, a ballot was taken immediately on the evening
of April 1. The Spanish and Aldobrandino were caught unguarded,
while Medici, who had received only thirteen votes that morning,
obtained more than a two-thirds majority and was elected pope.
He took the name of Leo XI.

The consistent support Baronius received from a good number
of cardinals in the conclave was a reflection, it seems, of the favor
he enjoyed from the French party and of his own reputation as a
scholarly and saintly prelate. Of course, the good relations he
maintained with important cardinals like Borromeo and Medici
was also a factor to be counted. But there is no indication that he
actively sought the position. The report of Cardinal Joyeuse, which
appears to be frank and accurate, pictures him at the best as a reluctant candidate. Nor does any other contemporary record indicate any activity on his part to win the election.

There are several contemporary reports which show Baronius'
disinclination. Zazzara relates in his *Memoirs* that Baronius told
him about his ardent prayers during the conclaves so that he might
be spared election to the papacy.[40] During the two conclaves in
which he participated he was so nervous about the possibility of
being elected pope that he even had nightmares—dreaming that he

was falling from narrow bridges and precipices. The two attendants of Baronius during the conclave, one Reginaldo and one Ottavio Vestrio, reported his agony when his candidacy was on the rise, and his elation and gratitude when another cardinal was elected.[41] Pateri's *Memoirs*, too, recorded the same kind of attitude and behavior on the part of Baronius.[42] There is only an indirect reference to suggest that he may have wanted to become pope. In a conversation between Cardinals Spinelli and Verona reported by the anonymous historian of the conclave, Spinelli supposedly made a devastating attack on Baronius.

> He is inept for this position: he is not a theologian or jurist; he has copied four histories; he is a prickly writer; he lacks so much to govern well the universal church.[43]

Spinelli concluded with the sarcastic exclamation:

> Oh! God, Father Baronius wants to be pope? I am getting the death pains!

But in the absence of any supporting evidence, this story must probably be discounted as a piece of the kind of gossip that was rife during the conclave.

The election of Leo XI, of course, was a great victory for the French, and it was celebrated as such.[44] But the Spanish were infuriated about it, and Aldobrandino was glum, to put it mildly. But this situation did not last for too long because the new pope died after a reign of only twenty-five days. Another conclave was convened even before some of the cardinals had a chance to leave Rome.

The new conclave was a restaging of the same scene with the same actors. But the Spanish party was determined, this time, that another French victory should not happen. They still did not have a candidate of their own, however. The French party did not have one either, though they still maintained their interest in Baronius. But he did not have a chance because of the resolute opposition of the Spanish party. Aldobrandino, having no decisive support for his own candidacy, played the role of king-maker and promoted the cause of Cardinal Tosco, a Lombard who had the support of the grand duke of Tuscany, the duke of Savoy, and the House of Este.[45]

Tosco was a respected jurist and had published eight tomes on canon law,[46] and he seems to have been unpolitical enough to be acceptable both to the French and the Spanish.[47] For one reason

or another, Baronius alone came out openly and vigorously against
Tosco. When the other cardinals responded to the call of Aldobrandino and went to perform the symbolic adoratio to Tosco as
a sign of their approval, Baronius and his Oratorian co-religionist,
Tarugi, stood alone, resisting Aldobrandino's repeated invitation.[48]
According to Joyeuse's·report to Henry IV, Baronius stood there
exclaiming that he did not want to create a schism, but he would
be the last to perform such an adoratio because the man was un-
worthy of it.[49] Quoting the Psalmist, "These will be written in the
next generation," he defiantly refused to hop on the bandwagon.

The anonymous historian of the conclave provides a plausible
reason for Baronius' opposition: his conviction that Tosco was
very irresponsible about his pastoral duties.[50] Tosco had been the
bishop of Tivoli for many years but had never even bothered to
visit his diocese. Teodoro Amideno, who wrote an *Elogia Pontifi-*
cum et Cardinalium suo aevo defunctorum, gives still another reason for Baronius' objection. Tosco, according to him, was in the
habit of using obscene language and vulgar expressions common
in Lombardy.[51] These vulgarities were the talk of the town, so to
speak, and they made him an improper choice for so high an office. Baronius' strong feeling against Tosco was recorded by still
another contemporary, Oratorian Pietro Consolini.[52] According to
him, Baronius invoked the help of the miracle working saint, Gregory Thaumaturgus, to stem the tide that was rising in favor of
Tosco.

Whatever the role of the saint may have been, Baronius' resolute
stand seemed to have had a miraculous effect. The cardinals who
were rushing to perform the adoratio to Tosco suddenly stopped,
stunned and shocked. Then Cardinal Montalto, himself a disappointed candidate, cried out "Let us make him pope, this holy
man who speaks with such zeal!" Suddenly an outcry broke out
from among the conclavists: "Baronio, Baronio!" an Equally loud
cry echoed: "Tosco, Tosco!" Those who cried for Baronius, mainly
French, caught hold of him and dragged him to the Pauline chapel.
He put up a big fight, kicking them, and holding onto pillars and
doors, shouting "I don't want to be pope, make another man who
will be worthy of the Holy See"; but to no avail. The others led
Tosco to the Sistine chapel. The two parties, then, began to pro-
claim loudly their allegiance to the respective candidates, and to
perform the adoratio.[53] The resulting noise and confusion was so
great that rumors spread in Rome that the cardinals had elected
two popes.[54]

The frenzy of the small crowd in both halls was such that there was a real possibility of schism. The tense and vibrant atmosphere was something similar to a modern political convention. The sudden surge of support that both sides expected from their steam roller tactics materialized, but it did not amount to a decisive victory for either side. It took some time before the steam ran out and both sides came to the realization that neither was going to get a two-thirds majority, however loud they might shout. Compromise was the only way open to them, outside of open schism. Therefore, the leaders of the two camps, Aldobrandino and Montalto, negotiated a settlement through the mediation of Cardinal Joyeuse. They picked Camillo Borghese, a man acceptable to both sides. Baronius expressed his assent with a sigh of relief: "Yes, that my son is much better than me."[55] Thus, Borghese became Pope Paul V on May 16, 1605.[56]

One thing that was very evident in these two conclaves was the openly professed antagonism of the Spanish party towards Baronius. Inside and outside the conclaves, they campaigned against him. In doing so, they were exercising what was known in those days as the *jus exclusivum*. This was a custom which became prevalent at the time of Charles V by which the Catholic secular powers interfered in a formal manner in the election of the popes.[57] Intervention by secular powers in papal elections was not new at all to this time, but the formal manner in which one candidate's election was checked in the name of national interest, through the express demand of a ruler who claimed a right to do so was a new phenomenon.

The three main Catholic powers with a great stake in the papal elections of the mid-sixteenth century were Spain, France, and Austria. They interfered in the conduct of the conclaves in two different ways, depending on their relative strengths within the College of Cardinals. If they commanded a two-thirds majority, they exercised an "inclusive," which meant that they worked for the election of one of their favorite candidates. The list of chosen names was given to all the cardinals from their country and arrangements were made to vote en bloc for their men. If they did not have the hope of controlling a two-thirds majority, they concentrated on checking the election of the candidates unacceptable to them for one reason or another. Objectionable names were given to their own cardinals, with proper instructions. In either case, the secular authority interfered indirectly, through the voting rights of the cardinals. In no way, therefore, did a secular power exercise a veto over the election.[58]

In elections of any sort, it is only natural that participants with common interests group together in favor of a candidate or against him. When such a spontaneous grouping occurs, without an express purpose or express direction from another source, it amounts to a "material" exclusion or inclusion, as Ruffini terms it. But when a group is formed for or against a candidate, in a well-thought out plan, and with the direction of an outside source, it is designated "formal."[59] Ruffini's thesis is that the Spanish exercised a "formal exclusive" in the case of Baronius, with the explicit direction of their government. He convincingly argues the point, with supporting evidence from the archives of the Vatican, Torino, and various other sources.[60] Sofia Vaccaro, who was until lately the librarian at Vallicella, also supports the same thesis.[61] Gaetano Catalano who recently made a study of the "Sicilian Monarchy" is also in basic agreement with this thesis.[62] The many sources these two authorities draw upon are strongly supported by still another contemporary report. Zazzara's *Memoirs* record that the Spanish ambassador at the time of the two conclaves went to see Baronius before he left Rome in November, 1606, and apologized for the dirty work he had to do under obligation of his office—a clear indication of the official intervention of Spain against Baronius' candidacy.[63]

Even though the so-called *jus exclusivum* did not have a juridical basis, it was generally practiced by secular authorities in the late sixteenth and early seventeenth centuries as a more or less accepted custom. Needless to say, this resulted in confusion, scandal, and a general detriment to Church government. Paul V, who experienced some of this confusion personally, was the first one to establish some regulations against this practice, through his bull *Decet Romanum Pontificem.* Gregory XV established further restrictions through his bull *Aeterni Patris Filius* in 1621. He limited the electoral procedures to three categories: scrutiny, which meant secret balloting; compromise, by which the delegates gave the elective power by general consent to a small committee of cardinals; acclamation, which meant the unanimous agreement upon a candidate. But it was only in our own century that all loopholes of secular interference were closed by the new rules established by Pius X in his bull *Vacante Sede Apostolica* of December 25, 1904. These rules decreed that the cardinals in the conclave should be completely cut off from outside intervention, and that they not engage in active campaigning within the conclave.

8

The Final Years

Once the tumultous events of the two papal elections were over, Baronius retired to the Oratorians' country home in Frascati. There, finally, he enjoyed a long deserved rest, and gradually returned to his normal way of life. The new pope was a healthy man of only fifty-five years, and there was no fear of another conclave in the near future. Indeed, Paul V was to live for another sixteen years. It was with considerable relief, therefore, that Baronius went back to his studies.

But this did not mean that he was freed from his work in the curia. Recognizing Baronius' scholarship and experience, Paul V even imposed new tasks on him. One of the first things Paul did after his elevation was to appoint a commission for the revision of the *Rituale Romanum,* which served as a handbook for all the liturgical ceremonies of the Church, and Baronius was appointed a member.

Liturgical reform, of course, had been one of the prescriptions of the Council of Trent which had been undertaken piecemeal by several previous popes, such as Pius V, Gregory XIII, and Clement VIII. But the *Rituale Romanum* still remained to be updated. The immediate attention the pope gave to this matter was an indication of his interest in complying with the prescriptions of Trent, just as it was a reflection of his own training and lifelong occupation as a canon lawyer—dealing with details of rules and protocol. The commission started its work immediately, but its task was not completed until 1614, seven years after the death of Baronius.[1] But his participation in the early stages of the work left an imprint on the *Rituale Romanum.* This was the last of the number of major liturgical books, which included such important works as the *Roman Martyrology*, *Roman Missal*, and *Roman Breviary*, that he helped to revise.

Another, and perhaps the greatest, service Baronius rendered to Paul V was his counsel regarding the punitive measures the pope was contemplating against the Republic of Venice and his public defense of it, once the interdict against Venice had become a matter of great public controversy. How enthusiastic a supporter of the interdict Baronius was is not an open question as William J. Bouwsma suggests in his brilliant treatise on Venetian republicanism.[2] In view of his speech at the consistory of April 17, 1606, in which Baronius urged the pope in the strongest possible terms to act sternly against the defiant Venetians,[3] and in view of still another letter wrote to Paul further encouraging such actions,one can hardly imagine him to be a hesitant recruit.[4]

In his speech at the consistory Baronius stated that "Peter's ministry is to feed and to kill, as the Lord commanded him," and urged Paul V, the current holder of Peter's office, to fulfill the function that was required of him, in this instance, the latter. Making allusions to Christ's words to Peter "feed my lambs" (John 21:15), and Peter's vision of the basketful of animals lowered from heaven with the accompanying command to "kill and eat" (Acts 10:13), Baronius put together an argument strongly favoring an interdict against Venice, which in his view would satisfy the Petrine functions of spiritual feeding and temporal killing. He further compared Paul V with Gregory VII and Alexander III, strong defenders of ecclesiastical rights and privileges, and expressed his hope that Paul would be as resolute as these, his predecessors. In his letter to the pope (which is undated, but, clearly from the contents, was written after the promulgation of the interdict), he compared the present conflict with the struggle of Moses and Aaron to liberate the Israelites from the pharaoh of Egypt. He urged the pope to strike hard as the Old Testament leaders had because as the vicar of Christ he had the right and authority to do so. His enemies would eventually be overcome, he reminded the pontiff, because the power of God was on his side.

Baronius was by no means the only curia cardinal who urged the pope to punish Venice. Almost every member of the college, except the Venetian cardinals, and perhaps Cardinal Du Perron (the French prelate who by reasons of special Venetian-French relationship was obligated to remain neutral), supported the pope;[5] and some, for example Cardinal Colonna, even formally urged the pope to impose the interdict. The gist of Colonna's argument was that it was better to correct those who persist in error by severe punishment than to spoil them by leniency.[6] Thus the papal imposition of the interdict on all of Venetian territory and the excommunication of the Doge, Leonardo Donà, and the Senate of the republic was no arbitrary or impulsive action by Paul V. The personal reaction of Paul to a series of events that transpired in Venice was to figure prominently, however, as the pope's lifelong career as a jurist had made him especially sensitive to any infractions of the law, which offense in this case was magnified by his vision of the laws of the Church as divinely sanctioned and consequently any infraction of them an offense against Christ himself.

Paul's deep feelings, important as they were, would not have resulted in such a serious confrontation with Venice, had not both the papacy and the republic been moved by conflicting historic and ideological forces. The nature and influence of these forces have been most ably discussed by Bouwsma, and for that reason a detailed analysis of them is not necessary. Bouwsma's conception of the Rome-Venice conflict of 1605-7 as the classic confrontation of two world views—one, that of the Renaissance and the other that of the Counter-Reformation—is disputable, however.[8] Although polemicists of both sides have, once the interdict had become a volatile issue, resorted to broad philosophical principles to support their respective positions, the conflict itself was quite limited in its scope. It had its roots in the historic tensions between church and state that had to do more with concrete issues of traditional and canonical privileges of the church and the clerics than with any cosmic view; and these tensions dated far beyond the Renaissance and the Counter-Reformation.[7]

Why the conflict broke out at the time it did, the way it did, and took the course it did, may be understood in the light of a variety of factors, among them were the following: On the part of the papacy, its relative freedom from difficult diplomatic problems elsewhere, the confident attitude of the papacy as a result of the successes of the Counter-Reformation, the ascendance of a pope who was particularly sensitive to juridical issues—Paul V, and the general feeling in the curia that recent Venetian legislations and other actions constituted a defiance beyond the point of toleration; on the part of Venice, her sagging commerce and consequent dependence on an alternate source of revenue, namely land— large portions of which was controlled by the Church, her eagerness to protect her dignity at a time when her position as a major power in Europe was seriously threatened by a multitude of adverse circumstances, and the need for freedom of activity, especially in international commerce, unhampered by religious considerations. The events that precipitated the confrontation, serious though they were, would not have assumed such ominous proportions had it not been for these factors.

These events, although they are not the concern of this study, may be briefly recounted here in order to show the involvement of Baronius in them. Even before doing that, it should be noted that Rome-Venice relations had been in a state of considerable tension for nearly a century for reasons of differences in religious or juridical issues as well as for the territorial or other temporal ambitions of one party or the other. Julius II's confrontation with Venice in the early sixteenth century (1509-10) is all too well known. But as the century grew, many long-standing differences between the two powers became major irritants for a variety of reasons.

Rome's annoyance with Venice about her relations with the Turks became intense after the Christian victory at Lepanto had made a complete defeat of the historic enemy a clear possibility. [9] Rome's apprehensions about Venice's associations with heretics became serious accusations in the wake of the republic's disregard for the jurisdictional sanctions of Trent, her taxations of the clergy for special purposes, her reluctance to allow her patriarchs and bishops to submit to the examinations and visitations required by Rome, her flirtation with excommunicated Henry IV of France, and various other disputed issues.[10] On the other hand, Rome's aggressive mood of territorial consolidation in late sixteenth century, especially in the wake of her repossession of Ferrara, and her attempts to end Venice's monopoly on Adriatic trade by opening Ancona as a free port and supporting freedom of shipping on the Po, became intolerable offenses to Venice when coupled with the steady enlargement of the landed possessions of the Church in Venetian territories.

It is in view of these circumstances that the first piece of Venetian legislation that became the subject of the papal censure should be examined—the law of 1602 which prohibited the return to the Church of ecclesiastical lands on long-term leases to laymen.[12] Two subsequent laws, which also aimed at restricting landholdings by the Church, should also be considered in view of the general state of tension that existed between Rome and Venice. The first of these, a law of 1603, prohibited construction of new churches in Venetian territories without prior permission of the government. The other, a law of 1605, prohibited alienation of landholdings by laymen to the Church, except for temporary transfer of up to two years. But these laws, offensive as they were to Rome, did not elicit any angry reactions from Rome. What broke the camel's back was the rather tactless violation by Venice of a long-standing ecclesiastical law that provided immunity of clerics from secular courts.

Two clerics, one a canon of Vicenza who was accused of public scorn of a government announcement bearing the seal of Saint Mark and of general moral turpitude, and the other, Abbot Brandolino of Nerveso who was accused of sorcery, incest, and murder, were imprisoned by Venice in 1605 without any consultation with ecclesiastical authorities. Given the atmosphere of tension, this was taken as an act of defiance to which Rome reacted angrily. Negotiations were to follow, in which the question of the arrest of the two clerics as well as the recent legislation were discussed. But neither side being in a mood to yield, the matter came to a head by the end of 1605. On Christmas day of that year, Paul V's ultimatum was presented to the Senate of Venice, which needless to say, was rejected,[13] and the pope's bull which excommunicated the Doge, Leonardo Donà, and the Senate, and which imposed an interdict on all Venetian territories, was signed and promulgated on April 17, 1606.[14]

The public debate that this action prompted and the polemical literature that grew out of the ensuing controversy are all well described by Bouwsma.[15] But a brief survey of the major participants in the debate and their works may be in order so that Baronius' involvement in the Venetian affair is understood in proper perspective.

Venetian reaction to the papal bull was, as must have been expected, one of defiance. The Doge and the Senate replied to it with an order requiring all clergy to disregard the interdict and to take an oath of allegiance to the government.[16] Their action was explained and defended publicly by a senator, Antonio Quirini, in a treatise on the rights of the sovereign Republic of Venice.[17] His main argument was that the temporal welfare of the people of the republic was entrusted to its legitimately established secular government which possessed the right to administer justice regardless of vocational status. The papacy's interference on behalf of the clerics guilty of criminal acts was deemed an unjustifiable intrusion. So also, he continued, the pope's claim that religious orders and pious organizations did not need to get the permission of the government in building edifices violated the rights of the republic.

Quirini's treatise was published with the endorsement of several

important churchmen and jurists, who gave their attestation that
it contained no theological or legal error. The following were the
men who endorsed the treatise: Pietro Antonio Ribetti, archdeacon and vicar general of Venice; Fra Paolo Sarpi, superior of the
Servites and the official theologian of the republic; Fra Bernardo
Giordani, theologian of the Franciscan Order; Fra Michael Angelo
Bonicelli, theologian of the Friars Minor Observants; Fra Marco
Antonio Capelli, theologian of Friars Minor Conventuals; Fra Camillo, theologian of the Augustinian Order; Marco Aurelio Pellegrini, Marco Antonio Ottelio, Giovachino Scanio, professors of law
at the University of Padua. This was an impressive group, one
which represented a cross-section of the religious orders and the
law profession and one which was purposely put together by the
government in order to bear on the debate maximum weight of
legal and theological opinion.

Following the treatise of Quirini, Paolo Sarpi published a long
essay, entitled *Consideratio supra censuris Sanctitatis Papae Pauli
V contra Serenissimam Venetiarum Rempublicam.*[18] Sarpi concentrated on theological arguments against the right the papacy
claimed of imposing censures against Venice. He said that the Venetian republic considered always that the basis of all power and
right was true religion and piety. The great number of churches,
monasteries, and religious congregations in Venice were a testimony to this fact. But he contended that their religiosity did not
oblige them to be submissive to the papacy in temporal matters in
which they had full autonomy. Citing passages from both the Old
and New Testaments and from the provisions of canon law, Sarpi
concluded that in refusing to submit to the censures of Paul V, the
Venetians were not in any way questioning legitimate papal authority. "Peter's privilege remains," he said, "wherever it is upheld
with right judgment, without excessive severity or leniency; nothing would be bound or absolved unless Blessed Peter himself had
absolved or bound."[19]

The order to take an oath of allegiance to the government and
to disregard the interdict was obeyed by a majority of the clergy in
Venice. But many scrupulous priests and religious still seem to
have been puzzled and bewildered by the extraordinary situation.
It must have been for their benefit that a battery of eminent theologians put together a treatise, explaining why, in good conscience,
the pope's order could be disobeyed.[20] The treatise was prepared
jointly by Sarpi, Pietro Antonio Ribetti, Bernardo Giordani, Michael Angelo Bonicelli, Marco Antonio Capelli, Camillo (Augus-

tiniano), and Fra Fulgentio of the Servite Order. The pope should be obeyed, they said; but so should the secular authorities. The Church and state have their own jurisdictions, they said, but one should not encroach upon the other's authority.

Then were offered several reasons for considering Paul's censures null and void. First of all, the interdict was not published properly; it was published only in Rome and not in Venice. This was a curious argument indeed, given the fact that the Venetian government took every measure to prevent the publication of the papal bull in its territories.[21] Moreover, compliance to the pope's order would cause much scandal and confusion in the Church, particularly in Venice, for it might result in punishment by the secular authority involving the loss of life and property of private and public persons, under which severe circumstances no law need to be obeyed.

Furthermore, the pope's authority was valid only in the strictly religious sphere; and even there it was probably subject to that of the councils and the canons. Until a decision was made on this matter, those papal orders which were apparently not in accordance with the councils and canons were not to be heeded. In any case, the faithful had the right to examine the legitimacy of any order and to decide whether or not to obey. In this particular case, it was clear that the pope exceeded the powers given him by Christ. Since he was abusing his authority, he was guilty of sin and therefore, his order should be defied. The authors also pointed out many examples from history where the secular rulers and ecclesiastical leaders defied papal pronouncements; for which they needed to look only into their own recent history. Within the previous four centuries, Venice had been placed under interdict by popes four times, once as close as a century before, all of which she defied.[22]

It is at this juncture that Baronius came out with his famous *Paraenesis ad Rempublicam Venetam.*[23] After his initial counsels to the pope Baronius became even more deeply involved in the controversy. A group of clergymen and faithful who had accepted the interdict, some of whom were Venetian citizens under the spiritual care of the Milan diocese, approached him through his friend, Federico Borromeo, so that he might make special provisions for their spiritual needs. Accordingly, he represented their case before the pope, and on January 27, 1607, he wrote to Borromeo a detailed description of the concessions the pope had authorized.[24] These included faculties for qualified priests to absolve the secular and religious clergy who had violated the interdict; permission to absolve from excommunication those who had written or read literature against the interdict condemned by the Holy Office; faculties for monks who had observed the interdict to hear confessions, even without permission from the ordinary of the diocese, should religious or secular priests who had violated the interdict approach them for that purpose; a plenary indulgence for all those who observed the interdict; and an indulgence of seven years every time someone tried to persuade others to observe the interdict. These and many other concessions were intended as a reward for the few priests and religious who obeyed the interdict and as an inducement for others to do the same.

But such measures seem to have had little effect at the moment. Much more important was Baronius' *Paraenesis*. As the title indicated, it was an exhortation to the Venetians, and it was composed more like a sermon than a scholarly treatise. It pained him immensely, he said, to address them as gentiles, as people outside the Church. But as a cardinal of the Church he could not help but break the silence and openly defend the vicar of Christ. He still cherished the pleasant memories of his visit to Venice, when he had had the opportunity to meet with so many of the senators and magistrates of the republic, and when he had had the privilege of preaching before them. They had listened to him, he remembered, "as an angel of God, even as Jesus Christ" (Gal. 4:14). Then he expressed his shock, again using the words of Saint Paul, "Till now, you had been shaping your course well; who is it that has come between you and your loyalty to the truth?" (Gal. 5:7).

He warned them in the words of the Proverbs (18:3), "Little the godless man reeks of it, when he falls into sin's mire, but shame and reproach go with him." Therefore, they should ponder over their grievous sins of usurping the divinely established authority of the Church. Follow the example of the holy emperors, who dared not presume to have any authority in ecclesiastical matters, he exhorted, and follow the teachings of the holy councils.

He then reminded the Venetians of the Christian alliance under Pius V which brought the victory over the Turks at Lepanto, and berated them for being ungrateful. He referred to the order to disregard the interdict, and chided them for being haughty and disobedient. "Unlooked-for humiliation the Lord has in store," he warned with the words of Ecclesiasticus (10:17), "Vanished utterly in yonder confederacy; proud thrones cast down, to make room for the oppressed, proud nations withered from the root, and a humbled race of exiles planted anew!"

He then addressed himself to the bishops and other clergymen who had obeyed the republic's orders—who were the majority of the ecclesiastics in Venice. Only the Jesuits, the Theatines, and the Capuchins had refused to obey, and they had been forced to vacate their churches and relinquish their properties.[25] Baronius contemptuously described those who complied with the government's orders as mercenaries and pastors destroying their own sheep like wolves. The offense was great, he concluded; but he had great hopes for a quick repentance. "Is it ever possible for Mark (the patron of Venice) to be separated from Peter by schism?", he asked. He thus exhorted the republic again to return to Holy Mother Church as a loyal daughter, and he closed his treatise with the words of Saint Augustine to the Donatists: "Let this (*Paraenesis*) be a correction if you wish, a testimony (against you) if you do not."[26]

Baronius' *Paraenesis*, as well as his earlier speech in the consistory, were widely circulated in Italy and in Europe by the advocates of papal authority. Both of them met with rebuttals from the other side. As soon as his speech was published, Fra Giovanni Marsilio, a Neapolitan Franciscan residing in Venice, came out with a refutation.[27] Baronius' justification of the interdict had been based on the command Peter received from heaven, "Kill and eat." Marsilio pointed out that this divine command was not at all applicable in this case. Instead, he cited a seemingly more appropriate command given by Christ to Peter, "Put thy sword back into its sheath" (John 18:11), and argued in the light of this command that the punitive measures taken by the pope were improper for the successor of Peter. But Marsilio's arguments were challenged immediately by a friend of Baronius, Gerardus Loppersius, who reaffirmed his interpretation of the biblical text "Kill and eat."[28] He also accused Marsilio of using barbaric language and techniques in trying to refute Baronius' argument.

Marsilio also published a rebuttal of the *Paraenesis* under the pseudonym, Nicholaus Crassus.[29] Addressing Baronius directly he wrote that the two-fold function of exhortation and refutation he professedly undertook in the *Paraenesis* were nothing but misguided attempts of censure and invective. As for Baronius' references to history, they were either torn out of context or improperly interpreted. Exemption from the judicial procedures of the state, which Baronius claimed for the clergy, had no basis in divine and natural law for the clergy were still subjects of the state even after their ordination. Had not Baronius heard about the teaching of Christ: "Render therefore to Caesar the things that are

Caesar's" (Mat. 22:21), he asked. Thus, he concluded that Baronius' exhortation ran contrary to the precepts of Christ and the
Church fathers.

However, a friend of Baronius soon came out with a pamphlet
in defense of the *Paraenesis*.[30] It was published under the pseudonym, Nicodemus Macrus, just as Marsilio's treatise had been, but
the real author probably was Caspar Schopp, friend and convert of
Baronius.[31] Written in a satirical vein, Macrus accused Crassus of
indulging in impudence, lies, and invectives. Spiced with numerous
citations from the Greek philosophers, his treatise concentrated on
a critique of the method, style, and the intent of Crassus' work. In
summary, he described the *Antiparaenesis* as an "asinine" and
"ostentatious" attempt by an "adolescent" to wrestle with the
eminent scholar and holy cardinal, Baronius. There were other
works, too, which were published against Baronius' position on
the interdict, but for one reason or another they were not re-
butted.[32]

At the heighth of the controversy, Baronius had also written a
small essay entitled *Quod haeretici sint habiti qui obstinate jura
ecclesiae labefectant*. It was intended to show that the Church always held the right to censure secular rulers who encroached upon
its rights. Citing many historical precedents, particularly Gregory
VII's censures against Emperor Henry IV, he tried to provide justification for the interdict of Venice. Somehow or other this essay
was not published during the controversy. So many other polemical works were coming out at the time that he must have thought
another would be superfluous. In 1861 Rocco Baronio, a descen-
dant of Baronius' family, and a student at the Vatican Seminary,
discovered the Latin manuscript in the Vallicelliana Library and
had it published with an Italian translation.[33]

Baronius' *Paraenesis* undoubtedly contributed to the fury of the
debate between Rome and Venice, which increased in intensity
every time a new polemical treatise was published by either side.
That this debate had gone down to the level of polemics and personal invectives was clear from the "open letters" published by
two Venetian jurists addressed to Paul V.[34] The first jurist opened
his letter with the questions, "Most Holy Father, are your eyes
carnal? Do you see like a man?"—obviously suggesting that Paul's
position was blind and irrational. He argued further from the Bible
that it was also against divine precepts. Referring to Peter's teaching (First Epistle 2:13-15) to obey secular authorities, he accused
Paul V of disobeying the prince of the apostles and his own prede-

cessor. Paul also departed, he said, from the teachings and practices of his other predecessors, such as Leo IV and Gelasius, who taught the importance of obeying secular authorities. The second jurist used the same line of argument, but he added an exhortation to Paul V to be prudent like the ancient Roman and Greek rulers, who had realized the futility of using force on people. Only an atmosphere of freedom would set matters right, he advised.

Soon after the jurists' letters were published, an anonymous theologian brought out an open letter to a priest who had requested his advice about whether or not to honor the interdict.[35] He advised the inquirer, obviously vexed by scruples, that he did not need to have any qualms of conscience about disobeying the papal censures because they were null and void. Then he proceeded to explain through theological reasoning under eight headings, the reasons for the nullity of the interdict—which argument provoked Rome's foremost theologian, Cardinal Bellarmine, to write a vehement rebuttal.[36]

Bellarmine started his critique with a condemnation of the excessive freedom the Venetians were taking in publishing theological treatises without ecclesiastical approval and often without the names of the authors and the places and dates of publication, a practice clearly forbidden under penalty of excommunication by the Council of Trent.[37] Then he contradicted the author's first argument that the power of secular rulers was given directly to them by God and that everyone, without exception, should be subject to them. He held the position that whatever the source of secular authority, the clergy was not subject to it.

The Venetian contended that Aaron, who had been the priest of the Israelites, recognized the superior authority of Moses, who had been the secular leader. Bellarmine countered that both Moses and Aaron were priests and that Moses' superior authority had been based on special divine disposition, not upon his secular authority. The Venetian suggested that historically the Church had never enjoyed authority over its members in temporal matters. True, Emperor Justinian had, at the request of the bishops of Constantinople, given the Church the privilege of judging the clergy in civil cases, but this never extended to criminal cases. Bellarmine argued that the Scriptures and the decrees of the councils upheld the exclusive right of the Church to judge its clergy in all matters. In support, he cited the teaching of Saint Paul (I Timothy 5:17-20) and Canon 9 of the Council of Chalcedon, which forbade clerics to take their cases to secular authorities. In short, the arguments of

the two authors hinged on one main question, whether or not secular authorities had the right to bring the clergy to justice, the Venetian strongly affirming and Bellarmine resolutely denying the
thesis.

Soon after Bellarmine's critical treatise was published, Giovanni
Marsilio came out with a work in defense of the eight-point argument of the anonymous theologian.[38] Scripture and divine law
were the basis of his arguments, he contended, and he brought
forth still more citations from the Bible and Church fathers to
back them up. Furthermore, he accused Bellarmine of skirting the
real issues by well-worn theological jargon and of arguing around
scriptural passages that had no bearing on the questions at hand.

It was obvious from Bellarmine's references to the excesses of
the Venetians and from the customs of the Roman Curia that the
Holy Office and the Inquisition would look into the controversy—
which they did. They did not have to investigate much to find
heretical ideas nor did they have to look hard to identify the most
volatile Venetian polemicists. Paolo Sarpi, Giovanni Marsilio, and
Fulgenzio Manfredi, who was an influential preacher against the
interdict, were found guilty of heretical pronouncements and were
ordered to appear personally before the tribunal of the Roman Inquisition.[39] Their response was one of defiance as was typified by
Marsilio's answer.

In a letter transmitted on his behalf by the Tribunal of the Inquisition in Venice to the inquisitor general in Rome, dated September 9, 1606, Marsilio talked about a document involving him
published in Rome by the inquisitor general.[40] Obviously the Venetian government did not allow the summons to be served in
Venice. The document, he thought, was either a warning or a summons to appear before the Roman Inquisition in order to answer
charges brought against him. But he could not appear before the
Roman Inquisition, he declared, for he was forbidden under penalty of death to leave Venice. Besides, he did not have a safe conduct, nor did he think that the Roman Inquisition would judge
him impartially.

It was public knowledge, Marsilio said, that he had defended the
eight-point argument of the anonymous theologian against which
Cardinal Bellarmine argued publicly; certainly this must have prejudiced the judges against him. His suspicion was confirmed, he
added, by the unusual step taken by the Roman Inquisition, when
it overrode the Venetian tribunal. That tribunal had always con-
ducted investigations of all heresy charges made in the city of

Venice and had always pronounced appropriate judgments. There was thus no apparent reason to call him to Rome, except for the purpose of imposing an unfair judgment. He was ready to appear anywhere, before any tribunal which was not prejudiced against him, and he was willing even to shed his blood for the true Catholic faith; but he did not intend to appear before the Roman Inquisition. If, however, the Roman Inquisition chose to judge him in absentia, without giving him an opportunity to answer the charges, he would consider the judgment null and void. Sarpi and Manfredi also published similar responses to the order of Rome upon which they were all formally excommunicated.[41]

The next round of polemics was inaugurated by the publication of a new pamphlet edited by someone in Paris.[42] Bouwsma contends that the editor was none other than Paolo Sarpi, which seems to be very probable from the way Sarpi came to its defense once it came under attack from the Roman side.[43] This pamphlet contained a short treatise on the validity of excommunication taken from the works of the fourteenth century theologian, Jean Gerson. In a prefatory letter to the reader, the editor said that it was incredible to hear about the severe censures imposed on the Venetian republic by the pope. In his opinion, the censures were contrary to all norms of justice. In order to determine their validity, he had searched the works of many respected authors and had finally come across one which threw ample light on the matter.

Gerson's short treatise dealt with the nature and meaning of excommunication and of ecclesiastical punishments resulting from the exercise of religious functions by persons forbidden to do so by Church law or by virtue of a censure. The focus of the treatise, however, was the *contemptus clavium*, or contempt of the ecclesiastical authority, as a result of the abuse of power. If a subordinate disobeyed his bishop, it might constitute contempt of authority, he said, but it would be much worse if the prelate abused his power. Worst of all would be the pope's abuse of power, for there was no superior authority to appeal to except a general council. The idea of the superiority of the general councils over the pope had once been considered heretical, he agreed, but he added that it was no longer true after the Councils of Pisa and Constance.

The pope's orders or censures need not be obeyed, Gerson contended, if they proved to be extremely burdensome or if they caused scandal in the Church. If the secular authorities objected, he said, the people need not honor the excommunication imposed by the pope. Often such excommunications were not based on any

right but on force and violence, and the law of nature was to repel
force by force.

Again, it was Bellarmine who came out with a rebuttal of Gerson's treatise.[44] He started by announcing that he did not believe
that Gerson's treatise had been really published in Paris, and he
chided the editor about remaining anonymous and omitting the
name of the publisher. Then he went on to distinguish between
various kinds of freedoms a person or a republic could aspire to.
He listed six, some of them desirable and others either undesirable
or unobtainable: freedom as opposed to the necessities of nature;
Christian freedom as opposed to the servitude of sin; civil liberty
as opposed to slavery; liberty of a republic as opposed to monarchy; liberty of an absolute ruler in temporal matters as opposed
to the interference by subordinates; and liberty to do evil against
justice. The last was the same as servitude to sin, and that was exactly what Venice wanted, he said. As for Gerson's treatise, it was
not by any means applicable to the interdict of Venice; the circumstances under which the pope imposed the interdict clearly
justified his actions. Gerson himself had been a pious and learned
theologian, but the unfortunate times and the deplorable events
had misled his thinking about the rights of the papacy, he concluded.

Bellarmine was challenged immediately by Paolo Sarpi, whose
apology for Gerson's treatise was published shortly afterwards.[45]
First of all, referring to Bellarmine's doubt about whether or not
Gerson's treatise really had been edited and published in Paris,
Sarpi said that the Roman cardinal was trying to confuse the issue.
What difference did it make where it had been published, he asked.
It was a common practice that works of well-known authors were
translated, edited, and published without any mention of the
names of the translator or editor. Gerson's works were so well-
known that the name of the editor could easily be omitted. As for
Bellarmine's main argument that Gerson had been a well-intentioned but misguided scholar, Sarpi answered that he had been not
only a pious and learned theologian, but also a prophetic one to
speak so relevantly of future events. He added further that the
bull *Unam Sanctam* of Boniface VIII and similar papal documents
against the claims of secular rulers and provincial churches had no
relevance at all, because they had been extravagant, one-sided,
and invalid papal claims.

Thus went on the polemics of the controversy, increasing the
heat of the tension with every pamphlet and further separating the

two sides. Both sides, but particularly Venice, looked for the support of public opinion. For that reason, many of the tracts were
published in Italian, and thus accessible to all ranks of the people,
who after all were equally affected by the interdict. In order to
strike a patriotic note to an issue already filled with emotion, the
Venetians also circulated popular songs.[46] Reminiscing over the
many instances when the papal power had been successfully resisted in the past by secular rulers and their subjects, these songs
called on the Venetians for a strong and unified stand against the
interdict.

Thus the situation deteriorated to such a level that there was a
real threat of the pamphlet warfare turning into an armed conflict
between the papacy and the Venetian republic.[47] Besides the fear
or war, which both sides shared, Rome also was concerned about
the possibility of Venice becoming Protestant if pushed too far, a
concern which Venetian writers and diplomats consciously encouraged for obvious reasons, although the real possibility of Venice going that route was very slim.[48] Serious disagreements about
major policies also started to weaken Venetian resolve to stand
firm. Both sides were thus moving toward a position of relative
flexibility in early 1607 when Henry IV of France offered to me-
diate between the two parties. Both sides agreed, and Henry's representative, the skillful diplomat Cardinal Francois Joyeuse, was
on the scene in March, traveling between Rome and Venice. The
Spanish ambassador to Venice, Cardinal Francisco de Castro, also
seems to have taken part in the negotiations. The road to reconciliation certainly was not easy but an agreement was finally reached
and the interdict was lifted on April 21, 1607, a little more than a
year after it was imposed.

The records of the Consistorial Congregation for April 30, 1607,
shows an entry to the effect that the pope received reports from
Cardinals Joyeuse and Castro that an agreement was reached with
the republic.[49] The records also show the conditions under which
Joyeuse had been authorized to lift the interdict and excommunications. They were: (1) the immediate and unconditional release
of the two imprisoned ecclesiastics, (2) restoration of the confis-
cated properties and re-admission of the expelled clerics, (3) re-
traction of the pronouncements made by the Doge against the censures and a disavowal on his part of all the other literature published against the papacy in this regard, and (4) a solemn promise
on the part of the republic not to enforce the laws of 1604 and
1605 against ecclesiastical immunity.

According to the records, the two cardinals had reported to the pope that these conditions had already been met. But in actuality, Venice had not met even one of the conditions in full, nor did it have any intention to do so. It seems that the only thing Venice agreed to was to hand over the imprisoned clerics to a third party, namely French authorities. Furthermore, Venetian authorities even refused to receive an absolution from the interdict and excommunications, thus once again disclaiming the validity of the papal censures. It is most probable that the papacy would not have taken any other course even if the full extent of Venetian intransigence at the final phase of the settlement was made known in Rome, but it seems that Joyeuse, brilliant diplomat as he was, had given a much rosier picture of the settlement to Rome than it really was. In any case, at the conclusion of the whole affair, Rome won none of the issues on which she quarrelled with Venice, although publicists on both sides claimed victory.[50]

Baronius was in the middle of the controversy from the very beginning. He was, as we have seen, at least in part, responsible for the stern action taken by the pope. He was also responsible for a good part of the polemical literature that came out during the controversy, either by direct involvement or by provocation. On the other hand, he was also very much involved in the efforts of Cardinal Joyeuse in bringing about a reconciliation. Joyeuse seems to have been in contact with Baronius during the negotiations, not only because he had known Baronius' deep interest in the matter, but also because he realized the weight of his opinion in the papal court.[51] Finally, when Joyeuse arrived in Rome after concluding the negotiations with Venice, it was Baronius who went to the pope, together with the French Cardinal Du Perron, in order to persuade him to accept the settlement.[52]

Thus, Baronius played a leading role in the Venetian affair from beginning to end, and this role seems to have been generally recognized at the time. He was congratulated for it by the sympathizers of Rome. The Spanish ambassador to Rome, Gian Farrante Pacecco, Marchese de Villena, for instance, congratulated him, and Cardinal Aldobrandino praised him in a letter of August 12, 1606.[53]

Baronius' role in the Venetian controversy clearly demonstrated that he still had a great deal of influence at the Vatican, even after the death of Clement VIII. True, he was no longer the theologian or the confessor of the pope. Nevertheless, he still had the ear of Paul V, who certainly could not forget his support at the conclave. Besides, he still held an important position as the librarian of the Church, and he still enjoyed the friendships of many of the other important members of the curia.

The main reason he had always been reluctant to accept ecclesiastical dignities was his belief, justifiable indeed, that they would expose him to the temptations of worldliness, nepotism, and benefice hunting. When these dignities had been forced upon him, he had always decided resolutely not to succumb to these temptations. He was generally successful in resisting them by means of an austere personal life and a severe detachment from material possessions. But as his years at the Vatican progressed, he seems to have been drawn into situations where he had to compromise. The positions he held were so close to the seat of supreme power in the Church that they inevitably exposed him to all kinds of requests for favors. Some of them were indeed legitimate requests which no conscientious churchman could turn down, and none that he was instrumental in granting seems to have violated the principles of justice or the reformatory prescriptions of the Council of Trent.

There are not many instances when Baronius used his influential position in the Vatican to secure ecclesiastical benefices for his friends. Once he obtained a modest benefice for a relative, and that was for a justifiable reason, namely to help him pursue a religious life without having the worry of supporting his destitute parents. On another occasion, Baronius was asked by his friend, Antonius Hierat, to obtain a benefice for a mutual friend, Severinus Binius. Binius was a Catholic writer who had published in 1606 a collection of the acts and decrees of the general councils, the purpose of which was the refutation of many Protestant arguments related to doctrine and Church practices. Hierat recommended him for a canonicate at the church of Saint Cunibert in Cologne that had been recently vacated.[54] Baronius obtained the benefice; and in doing so he seems to have been falling back on the Renaissance practice of using ecclesiastical benefices for patronizing arts and letters. But there is a difference: he did not do it for the sake of art and letters, nor for the sake of friendship, but for the service of the Church as he saw it—a patronage more in tune with the Counter-Reformation than with the Renaissance. After all, the beneficiary in this case was a writer who used his talents in defense of the Church. At least in Baronius' mind, this was not an abuse of the ecclesiastical benefice; he had acted in good conscience.

But obtaining benefices for friends, for whatever high purposes they may have been, certainly was not one of the main uses Baronius found for his influence in Rome. As an outstanding leader of the Counter-Reformation, he directed his intellectual labors and his other activities towards the confrontation and defeat of the movements which the institutional Church considered to be heretical. That was the primary purpose of the *Annales*, his lifelong work. His involvement in the absolution of Henry IV and in the two great controversies about the "Sicilian Monarchy" and the interdict of Venice all had one underlying purpose: the preservation and strengthening of the institutional Church. Thus, he proved himself to be a Counter-Reformation prelate in the strongest sense of the word. It was not surprising, therefore, that men involved in Counter-Reformation activities were his most frequent correspondents; for he was, indeed, recognized as a most important leader of that movement.

Two letters he received from Ireland during 1606 bear testimony to his unique leadership. They were from Jacobus Vitus, vicar-apostolic of the Dioceses of Lismore and Waterford.[55] Vitus talked about some other letters, since lost, that he had previously written to Baronius. But the two that survived give a good idea of the nature of the whole correspondence. Vitus described in detail the persecutions that the Catholics of Ireland, particularly the priests and religious, were subjected to, and he wrote about the several royal edicts banning Jesuits and other priests from Ireland. He deplored the scarcity of priests and requested Baronius to get the general of the Jesuits, Claudio Aquaviva, to send some men to relieve the situation. Vitus, being the ordinary of the two dioceses, could certainly have approached Aquaviva directly, or have appealed to the pope himself. Instead, he chose to write to Baronius, thus recognizing Baronius' special interest in combating heresy as well as his influence in Rome.

* * * * * *

Baronius' involvement in the Sicilian and Venetian controversies cost him a great deal of time and energy. Needless to say, the two noisome conclaves were also disturbing experiences. But these did not seem to have distracted him considerably from his work on the *Annales*. He was constantly reminded of his major vocation, even in the midst of his other obligations, by fellow scholars and writers from all over Europe, who either wrote to him directly or honored him in some manner such as dedicating their works to him.

For example, Laurentius Pignorius, famous archaeologist and specialist in interpreting ancient medallions, wrote Baronius in 1605, announcing the dedication of his forthcoming book on Egyptian mythology.[56] It had been an ancient custom, he said, to offer the first fruits to kings, but he would be doing the same thing if he dedicated his work to a man of the greatest dignity such as Baronius. Similarly, M. Antonius Bonicarius dedicated to him a book of songs in honor of Francis of Assisi.[57] Federico Mezio dedicated to Baronius a work on the life of Saint Mary of Egypt, which he had translated from Greek into Latin. This work allegedly had been authorized by Saint Sophronius, the seventh century patriarch of Jerusalem. Mezio's translation was never printed, but his manuscript is still in the Vallicelliana Library, which makes it very probable that the translation was inspired by Baronius himself.[58]

Vittorio Filippini dedicated to him, most appropriately, his work entitled *Considerazioni appartenenti alla dignita et officio de' Sommi Pontifici, loro virtù, e norma di ben reggere i popoli a se soggeti,* of which the manuscript is still preserved in the Vallicelliana Library.[59] The work dealt mainly with the bad effects of the quarrels and bickerings on the Church during the two conclaves in which Baronius' election to the papacy had been successfully blocked by the Spaniards. These and many other works that were dedicated to Baronius at this time testify to his continued renown and popularity as a scholar and as a leader of the reformation in his Church.[60]

Among those who wrote to Baronius in 1606 expressing their esteem and appreciation for his work were many scholars and Church leaders. The most famous of them was Francis de Sales, who had recently (1603) been appointed bishop of Geneva. When Francis visited Rome late in 1606, Baronius had extended to him many courtesies and had presented him with a set of the *Annales.* On his way back to Geneva, Francis wrote to thank Baronius for his prayers and moral support in the difficult work in his new see which he termed "the daughter of Babylon." In particular, he asked Baronius to "stand for me before the Holy See against those workers of iniquity."[61] Francis expressed his deep admiration for Baronius' historical work as well.

Another letter came from the Jesuit Benedictus Pereius, the famous biblical scholar who had just published the third volume of his work on selected problems in the scriptures.[62] "Baronius walks

day by day, enriching the Church of Christ by the inestimable treasure of the *Annales*," he said. Then, lavishing more praises upon
him, he concluded with the prayer that God might enable the author of the *Annales* to complete a work "of so great labor, of so
great utility, full of erudition, written with serious judgment, and
accomplished with total diligence." From Paris, R. Viseur, a famous theologian, wrote to express his appreciation for the *Annales*
and for Baronius' work on the *Martyrology*.[63] Calling Baronius
"the most splendid light of our century," Viseur also submitted to
his judgment one of his own works, a commentary on the life and
relics of John the Baptist.

Severinus Binius wrote from Cologne soon after the publication
of his collection of the canons and decrees of the councils, confessing how great a help the *Annales* had been to him.[64] He called it a
"most brilliant" work. From Portugal, Fra Emmanuel, a member
of the Reformed Augustinian order, wrote to express his admiration for the *Annales* and enclosed two epigrams in his praise.[65] One
song went like this: "You win like Caesar, but your victory is different; he destroyed the enemies by sword, you by the pen."

Thus, Baronius had been encouraged constantly by frineds and
fellow scholars to continue with his important work on the *Annales*, even in the midst of the clamor of conclaves and curial activities. These testimonies also reveal the immense impact of the
Annales on the Catholic literary world, and the widespread use of
it by Counter-Reformation writers as an arsenal of historic arguments in defense of the Church.

The continued popular interest in the *Annales* also must have
been a source of added incentive to him. In 1606 several requests
came to him for permission to reduce the *Annales* into a compendium for popular use. Two such compendiums were already in
preparation: one by a Jesuit and another by a Parisian scholar. But
now one more was proposed by his fellow Oratorians at Napels,
who had been reading the proofs of the *Annales* from the beginning; and still another was proposed by Henri de Sponde, an ex-
Calvinist and now the bishop of Pamiers.[66] Baronius refused permission to the Oratorians, but later he granted it to Sponde.

In response to such great public interest, Baronius worked hard
to bring to light the twelfth volume of the *Annales*. It came off the
Vatican Press during the second half of 1607, a little after Baronius' death. It was dedicated to Paul V with a letter dated May 22.
It covered the years 1100–1193, nearly a century, and it was one
of the bulkiest volumes of the series.

As he had done in previous volumes, Baronius included a short note to the reader. Usually the note was an exhortation to Catholic readers that they might be confirmed in their faith by reading the *Annales*, or to non-Catholics that they might learn about the truth of the Catholic church. In this note, however, he told the reader that any edification he or anyone else might obtain from reading the *Annales* should be considered above all as a gift from God. As for himself, he requested the reader to pray for his soul, especially at Mass, after his death.[67] He added also a note of thanksgiving to the Virgin, as had been his usual practice. In this, too, the dominating theme was his death and appearance before God. He prayed to the Virgin that he might be able to participate in the "celestial kingdom and the eternal heredity." At the end of the volume he attached an appendix in which he included numerous additions to the previous volumes which normally he would have added in a later edition of those volumes. Obviously he was feeling like a man already spent, and he had no intention of pursuing the *Annales* any further.

Indeed, Baronius had a premonition of impending death. This had come to him in a vision several years before, at a time when he had been intensely involved in the work of the *Annales*. A few months before his death, when he was living in the convent of Sant' Onofrio, he described this vision in detail to Agostino Manni, a fellow Oratorian priest who was his confessor during the last years of his life. Manni recorded this revelation and left it among the memorabilia of Baronius at Vallicella.[68] Supposedly, Baronius had awakened from sleep one night and had seen on the wall facing him in broad black letters the Roman numerals LXIX. Pondering over the significance of it, he could come to only one conclusion: that the numerals indicated something about the course of his life. Not wishing to take it seriously, he tried to ignore the vision when it occurred still another time, though the numerals were white instead of black this time. On reflection, however, he became ever more certain that they meant the length of his lifetime, sixty-nine years.

However, he did not seem to have completely given up his work on the *Annales* even at the end. After all, this was his way of serving the Church, and a good religious was bound by duty to work for the glory of God and his Church as long as he could. Baronius intended to do exactly that. He made a good start on Volume XIII, covering the first year of the reign of Innocent III, a pontificate he would have particularly wished to write about because of its contribution to the strengthening of papal power. The unfinished manuscript of his Volume XIII, which is still preserved in the Vallicelliana Library, contains a broad outline of the history of the Church down to as far as the fifteenth century.[69] But unfortunately, his visions proved to be right: death overtook him before he could proceed beyond the first year of Innocent's pontificate.

* * * * * *

Baronius had fallen ill several times in his later years, often because of overexhaustion. Keeping an unusually strict regimen, he accomplished a prodigious amount of work, and work inevitably took its toll. Early in 1607, his health deteriorated so much that he began to complain about it, an unusual thing for him to do. In a letter to his close friend, Talpa, he talked about ailments which destroyed his appetite.[70] For the past eight months he had been mostly on a liquid diet, he said. Talpa counseled his friend to take care of his health, and he even seems to have suggested that he go to his native Sora for some rest. By this time Baronius must have been extremely weak, for the answer to Talpa's letter was written by his secretary, with only a few lines added at the end in his own hand.[71] He thanked Talpa for the good advice, but he asserted his own wish to prepare well for his imminent death. Zazzara's *Memoirs* also record a conversation between Baronius and one of his friends, Abbot Crescenzo, in which he once again expressed his wish to die, and to die as a simple priest, rather than as a cardinal.[72] Though of course, this wish could not be fulfilled.

Constant intestinal ailment and consequent deterioration of his health must have been what led Baronius to change his residence in May, 1606, from the papal palace to the convent of Sant' Onofrio on the Gianicolo hill overlooking the Vatican. It was here that the famous poet, Torquato Tasso, had spent his last days nearly eleven years before. (The stump of the tree under the shade of which once Tasso wrote some of his famous lyrics still stands there.) Baronius spent nearly a year at Sant' Onofrio and then moved once again to the Borromeo palace in Piazza Navona, which Cardinal Federico put at his disposal.[73] But worsening ailments, the awareness of imminent death, and his enduring affection for his co-religionists then induced him to move back to the Oratory at Vallicella. He must have made this move sometime early in May, 1607, for there is a letter to him from Borromeo of May 22, 1607, expressing his regret that his friend had to leave the palace and urging him to modify his usual austerities.[74]

Baronius returned to Vallicella with great joy, and with the hope of dying there peacefully. He expressed his sentiments in the words of Job "I shall die in my nest" (Job, 29:18). But his physicians advised him to change his residence to the country house at Frascati in the hope of improving his condition. He followed their advice, but in vain: the intestinal ailments only became worse. It seems to have been clear to him as to everybody else that death was imminent. "Let us go," he said, "let me die in Rome. It is not proper for a cardinal to die on a farm. And I wish more than anything else to close my days and my eyes in my Congregation, among my fathers."[75] Thus, he returned to Vallicella on June 19, 1607, bedridden and in severe pain.

The last days of Baronius, as graphically described by Barnabeus, were typical of his early pious upbringing in Sora and of his lifelong practice of austerity and devotion.[76] He insisted on being brought to the chapel every day so that he could attend Mass and receive the Eucharist with ardor. He filled the days with ejaculatory prayers and meditation on death. He declared again his deep regret in having had to accept the cardinalate, which, he said, brought him the greatest sufferings in life. He was not worthy of being a simple priest; that was the reason God imposed this burden on him! Friends and fellow churchmen came to visit him, among them Bellarmine, who made a request, using the words of the good thief who was crucified with Christ: "Remember me when thou comest into thy kingdom" (Luke 23:42). Whenever a priest came to see him, Baronius insisted on receiving his blessing. When a lay person visited, he asked him to say a prayer and sprinkle him with holy water. Finally, when the gravity of the sickness became extreme, he was given the last rites by Flamminio Ricci, the superior of the Oratory at Vallicella. Then he lay in bed, constantly fixing his eyes on the statues of Christ, the Virgin Mary, and the Apostles Peter and Paul, which had been placed before him at his request. He frequently kissed the statuette of the Virgin and a reliquary full of relics of different saints. Then on Saturday, June 30, 1607, the feast of Saint Paul, he died.

He had instructed his physicians not to perform a post-mortem operation on him, but they did it anyway and found three gaping ulcers in the stomach—obvious signs of tension and overwork. The next day his body was laid in state in the Church of Santa Maria at Vallicella where a throng of people, including thirty cardinals, came to pay homage to him. He had wanted to be buried in his titular Church of Saints Nereus and Achilleus, but respecting the wish of the Oratorians to keep his remains in their church he had consented to be entombed at Vallicella.[77] Accordingly, a grave was prepared on the left side of the main altar of the church. A year later, his friend and co-religionist, Cardinal Tarugi, also died and was buried in a grave beside his. Today only one marble slab marks both their graves, with the appropriate inscriptions of their names and titles.

July 13 was the date chosen to pay tributes to Baronius. Accordingly, prominent Romans, including several cardinals, participated in the ceremonies at Vallicella, and heard an eloquent eulogy by the learned Oratorian Michelangelo Bucci.[78] Similar ceremonies were held in the Naples Oratory with a funeral oration by Giovanni Battista Mucanzio, which the cardinal archbishop and other prominent religious and civic leaders attended.[79] The Jesuit College in Rome also held ceremonies in his honor. Diverse eulogies in prose and in verse were prepared by members of the college and presented to the Oratorians.[80] Henry IV personally attended the services held in Paris. Numerous other eulogies were sent to Vallicella by friends and admirers which are still kept in the Vallicelliana Library.[81]

Invariably, all these eulogies contained prominent references to the various services Baronius had rendered to the Church, particularly the *Annales*. All of them extolled his humility, charity, devotion to the Church, love of poverty, and many other so-called Christian virtues. One virtue that was played up was his spirit of poverty. This virtue, scarcely practiced by the higher clergy of that time or of any other time was amply justified by his last will.[82] All he had left to distribute among his numerous relatives he had helped to enter various religious institutions were pious articles which had been donated to him by his countless admirers. The more valuable of them were left to his titular church of Saints Nereus and Achilleus and to the Oratorians' church at Vallicella. The only landed property he owned, a small estate at Frascati, was left to the Luccan fathers in order to establish a monastery there. His house at Sora was given to a poor relative. Very little money was left in his possession, and that was distributed among his servants and some needy relatives. Thus at the time of his death practically nothing was left of his estate, and the Oratorians had to dig into their own treasury to defray the cost of his funeral.[83]

Soon after Baronius' death, the Oratorians collected a good number of testimonies from his friends, servants, fellow religious, and acquaintances about his various virtues.[84] Anecdotes relating to his many virtues were recorded in a manner that they may appear extraordinary and even heroic. Evidently this was done for the possible use in a future canonization procedure. Steps had already been taken to canonize Philip Neri, the founder. Another saint would have enhanced the prestige of the congregation still further. Indeed it was then, as it is even today, one of the ways religious orders obtained popularity and even wealth, for Saints attracted pilgrims and their offerings.

One of the virtues mentioned prominently among these testimonies was Baronius' purity. This seems to be particularly interesting, for his relationship with women is seldom mentioned by any of his biographers. Curiously enough, this testimony comes from a nun who had been Baronius' penitent for over twenty years when he was at Vallicella as an ordinary priest. The nun, Maria Francesca Checchi of the Convent of Purification in Rome, alludes to the many visits he had made to the convent.[85] The last of these visits was made a short time before his death. During this visit, Baronius told her "Dearest Sister, let us be gratified and be grateful to the Madonna for the gift of purity." Being curious about what he meant, she asked him whether he was a virgin. Then he raised his eyes towards heaven and extending his hands to a nearby statue of the Virgin, said with great fervor and devotion "By the grace of God and the Virgin Mary, Our Lady, I am a virgin and no worldly person has ever touched my flesh."[86]

Sister Checchi also mentioned a vision Baronius had had soon after his elevation to the cardinalate. The Blessed Virgin had supposedly offered him a gold tray full of various kinds of fruits. However, some of them were rotten; and Baronius had decided that they represented the insidious temptations of life.[87]

The same nun reported two apparitions of Baronius to her after his death.[88] In the first, he appeared in very rich clothes, bearing ten necklaces of most beautiful jewels. He had told her the significance of the necklaces, she said, but she forgot it. The second time he appeared was in 1634, and he came to announce her impending death. Baronius' intimate personal revelations to this nun and her vision of him would indicate that their relationship was more than that of just a confessor and penitent. However, it is difficult to visualize a close relationship between them like that of Abelard and Heloise, because Baronius seems to have been successful in suppressing all normal impulses of a romantic nature. His occasional visits to the convent certainly consisted of nothing more than spiritual counseling or pious conversations.

Baronius, indeed, had given extremely great importance to virginity. In his testimony on behalf of the canonization of Philip Neri, he emphasized Neri's virginity more than any other virtue. Neri revealed to him, he said, that he had always been a virgin. For many years he had been freed, by the special grace of God, even from natural ejaculation. One incident which Neri had related to Baronius many times, he said, was about a narrow escape from a severe temptation. One time in his early youth, Neri had been left alone in the house with a maid. When she began to seduce him forcibly, he ran towards the staircase, but the woman being very angry threw a stool at him. Fortunately, he escaped without injury. Neri had considered this a miracle, and Baronius reported this as such to the commission.[89]

Baronius' own celibacy had been well protected by his innate seriousness and his total lack of a sense of humor. His writings and his correspondence were all in a very serious vein. Philip Neri, a man with a very pleasant nature, had worried about his disciple's severity and moroseness and his constant preoccupation with the ultimate things. For these reasons Neri ordered him very early not to preach on death, hell, and subjects of that sort. On several occasions, even in his later years, Neri humiliated him publicly, calling him a "barbarian". These reproaches may have been intended to strengthen Baronius' humility, but it is even more probable that Neri was referring to Baronius' inability to smile. Neri's prediction about his chances of becoming pope also reflects a disapproval of the seriousness of Baronius' nature and comportment. "You will become a cardinal, but you will not become pope because of your fierce and rigid nature," Neri told him once.[90]

However, absence of humor had never been considered a disqualification for sainthood in the Catholic church. In fact, very few of the canonized saints seem to have possessed any. Until very recently, austerity, retreat from the world, chastisement of the flesh, and such other negative qualities were considered the main marks of holiness. Baronius, evidently possessed all these qualities, and the Oratorians were anxious to have him canonized. They, therefore, began to negotiate with the bishop of Sora in order to start the procedure of beatification as the canonical prescirptions called for the procedure to be initiated by the ordinary of the diocese to which the holy person had belonged.

Usually, a bishop would initiate such a procedure if large numbers of the faithful expressed their extraordinary esteem for the holiness of a deceased person by praying to him or paying him homage such as lighting candles at his grave. Reports of miraculous favors rendered through the intercession of the holy person would facilitate the matter. There is no indication that great numbers of people expressed their devotion to Baronius. During his lifetime he did not seem to have had anything like the close rapport with people that Philip Neri had enjoyed. His reputation had been mainly among the higher clergy and the elite in the Church.

As for miraculous favors, several were reported which the Oratorians carefully recorded for future use. One of them was reported by a certain Capuchin, Fra Francesco.[91] While passing by a village near Naples, he saw a boy fall into a well. Suddenly he called on Baronius saying "soul of Cardinal Baronius, help this poor child." Reportedly, a man dressed in red appeared and held the boy by his hand above the water until others came and pulled him out of the well. Another of the alleged miracles happened in 1620 to a Roman woman, Vittoria del Bufalo.[92] She had been bedridden with a fever and a throat infection which suffocated her. When she prayed to Baronius, the ailments miraculously left her and she became perfectly well.

Perhaps the insistence of the Oratorians, more than the alleged miracles or popular demand, induced the bishop of Sora in 1624 to initiate an investigation of the life and virtues of Baronius as the first step towards his beatification and canonization.[93] But the procedure was not carried out with any enthusiasm. Baronius had made too many enemies and had involved himself in too many controversies. The Spanish authorities particularly held a grudge against him, and Sora after all was within the dominions of the king of Spain. Thus, a damper was put on his beatification procedures, and eventually it was abandoned.[94] Now that the old enmities are long forgotten and conditions have changed, the Oratorians are trying to reopen the cause of Baronius: and they may be impeded this time only by the growing lack of interest in the whole matter of canonization.

9

Baronius the Historian
His Contributions to
Modern Historiography

Baronius first started work on the *Annales* for one very simple reason: Philip Neri asked him to do so.[1] But after many years of working from sheer obedience, he discovered another motive: not a love of learning, nor a curiosity about the past, nor a view of history, but the defense of the Catholic church against all critics, external and internal. As he indicated in the preface of the *Annales*, "The door opened to us is wide and visible, but the adversaries are many."[2] As his work progressed he saw the Magdeburg Centuriators and their successors more clearly as his chief adversaries who, in his view, defiled the face of the Church through their writings against her. He believed that in the pages of his historical work ". . . the ancient image of the Church should be restored to its original form."[3] He also said, "I consider it enough and more if the genuine and undefiled image of the face of the Church can be shown in its original and beautiful form," in order to defeat all the critics of the Church and convince all the non-believers and heretics about her authenticity.[4]

In carrying out these objectives with maximum effectiveness, Baronius sought to employ what he thought was the most suitable historical methodology. He looked far and wide, among ancients and moderns, for a model, but almost naturally chose Eusebius, the first historian of the Church, as his chief guide, because of the identity of his theme and because of the affinity of his goals and purposes with those of his own.

The notion of the orthodoxy of the Church as opposed to the heretical departures in doctrine and practice and the persecutions of inimical powers was the central theme of his work, as it had been of Eusebius'. He also separated ecclesiastical history from political history, as Eusebius had done, for he looked upon the

Church as an institution standing apart, perhaps above, political in-stitutions. At the same time, he took inspiration from the early Christian hagiographers, most particularly from Athanasius, whose life of Saint Antony had inaugurated the trend of treating the lives of saints apart from military heroes and political leaders.[5] In fact, Baronius combined the history of the Church and the lives of the saints in such a manner that they became the integral parts of a continuing story.

As Arnaldo Momigliano has shown, one of the important differ-ences between classical historians and early Christian historians was that the latter rejected free judgment as the basis of argument and put argument from authority in its place.[6] The elaborate use of documents thus became necessary, for the only way to substantiate the authority of the Church fathers in support of one argument or another was through documents. But this particular characteristic of Christian historiography had largely vanished in the Middle Ages, probably because a relative absence of theological and historical controversies made simple narration of events adequate for the faithful. Thus ecclesiastical historians from Cassiodorus to Bede and from Adam of Bremen to John of Salisbury were noted more for their chronological narration of history than for their employ-ment of documents. However, their successors of the sixteenth century once again turned to the extensive use of documents with great care of accuracy and authenticity.[7] The Madgeburg Centuria-tors and Baronius were the culmination and supreme examples of this revival. Undoubtedly, their work was stimulated by conflict, which obliged both Catholics and Protestants to support their op-posing views with authoritative historical evidence.

The great reformers had rested their principal case on a histor-ical argument—namely, that Christ's teachings had been distorted by an unlawfully organized hierarchy. This argument ran through all the writings of Luther.[8] It was also given prominent mention by Calvin.[9] The only way, then, that the Catholics could oppose the Protestant position was by employing historical arguments. In other words, they had to prove that Catholicism had always been and still was the same as it had been in the beginning. If Christian-ity had been born a religion with a sense of history, as Herbert Butterfield contends, the Reformation and the debates that re-sulted from it once again brought this sense in to sharp focus.[10]

But the Reformation was not alone in directing attention to the documents of the past. The historical outlook engendered by Re-naissance humanism was equally important; and indeed it is this outlook that was predominant in the first period of what Hubert

Jedin calls the "Catholic Reform"—before the start of the Protestant secession.[11] However, with regard to the method which they used in examining their sources, the humanist historians on one hand and Baronius and Magdeburg Centuriators on the other, do not seem to have much in common. The former were more analytical and interpretive, and the latter more intent on presenting the largest number of authorities possible. Nonetheless, the Reformation and Counter-Reformation historians avidly adopted the humanists' interest in history based on documents. And they were facilitated in this task by the preparatory work of the humanists, who provided them with many carefully annotated, printed editions and with neatly copied manuscripts kept in well-organized libraries.

This is particularly true of Baronius, who had the unique opportunity of using the most valuable manuscript collections of the Vatican, which popes from Nicolas V on had entrusted to the care of some of the best humanist scholars of the day. Strangely enough, however, Baronius did not choose to imitate the methodology and style of those who provided him with the documents, the humanists. Take, for example, one of the chief characteristics of humanist historiography from its early beginnings, namely philological analysis of texts for establishing their authenticity. From the time of Petrarch on, textual criticism had become an important method of historical investigation.[12] With the advanced techniques of philological and stylistic examinations perfected by humanist scholars such as Valla, this method was widely used by historians and literary critics. Some of Baronius' own contemporaries, particularly M. Antonius Muretus, were famous for it.[13]

Baronius, however, did not engage this method at all, even though on many occasions he should have resorted to it simply to be effective. One such occasion was the Sicilian controversy where he was confronted with the bull of Urban II on which the Spanish party rested their case. Baronius simply reproduced the bull in his *Monarchia Siciliae* and analyzed its theological implications. His argument seems to have been that the document was theologically unsound, and that, therefore, it could not be authentic. He cited circumstantial evidence, such as the decrees and pronouncements of subsequent popes which ran contrary to the privileges of the Sicilian rulers mentioned in Urban's bull.[14] However, he did not even make an attempt to analyze the document philologically—anymore than he had in the case of the Donation of Constantine. In treating this document, too, Baronius was satisfied with weak circumstantial evidence, namely the generosity of Constantine to the Church, while his humanist predecessor Valla had most effectively shown through a philological critique the unauthenticity of the document.[15]

Another characteristic of humanist historiography which Baronius consciously rejected was its concern for form—that is elegance of style—as opposed to content, a characteristic which was more true of the earlier humanists such as Valla and Bruni. But, the late quatrocento humanist trend of putting accuracy of facts and truthfulness of content above form, the chief initiators of which were perhaps Bernardo Rucellai and Giovanni Pontano, appealed to him.[16] Yet the real inspiration for Baronius to adopt an arid style, marked by simplicity and clarity, seems to have come not from his humanist contemporaries or predecessors, but from classical writers, especially Aristotle. Aristotle's works in Latin translations were known to Baronius and the Aristotelian philosophical system still undergirded the theological writings of the Church, despite the strong influence of Platonism in late fifteenth and early sixteenth centuries.

The Aristotelian distinction between what is permitted in poetry and history seems to have been the central point. According to Aristotle, a poet, when he deals with historical events, should be guided by the principle of thematic unity. A historian, in contrast, is expected to adhere to strict chronological sequence and to describe everything as they happened, without any freedom to choose what material to include. Not only did Aristotle deny the historian any right to interpret historical events philosophically (as that role was left to the poet-philosopher), but he also deprived him of the opportunity to show the interrelationship between events, causal or otherwise, as he assigned to the historian only the simple role of describing truthfully what had been.[17]

Baronius seems to have been influenced also by similar precepts on historiography laid down by Polybius whose *The Histories* was very familiar to him. Polybius advocated above all objectivity, a personal non-involvement of the historian in the events he dealt with. But he held, too, the view that a historian should do more than a mere narration of events, that is, he should explain their causes, underlying forces, and the motives of the characters. Without this, history would be only of ephemeral value, he contended. In all this Polybius has assigned a didactic role for the historian, a role as a guide and judge of what course of action men should undertake, which view Baronius seems to have accepted as his own.[18]

In adopting simplicity of style Baronius may also have been influenced by fellow ecclesiastics in Rome. Many of these colleagues,
although they had been deeply involved in the humanistic tradition, had, in the wake of the Counter-Reformation, become somewhat contemptuous of the humanistic preoccupation with the Ciceronian style. They seem to have identified this style with the
worldliness of an earlier era when, among other things, elegance of
arts and letters took precedence over religion.[19] What may have
been particularly objectionable to Baronius was Cicero's concept
of history as a handmaiden of rhetoric and his license to "manip-
ulate historical material in order to make a point convincingly."[20]
These views seem to have had currency among some medieval and
early humanist historians as Beatrice Reynolds pointed out: "Italian historiography of the humanistic school, influenced by the medieval preoccupation with rhetoric and more thoroughly versed in
the oratorical art of Cicero, made form its first objective."[21] Thus
in rejecting the Ciceronian concept of historical writing, Baronius
was in a sense eschewing some of the values of the humanist tradition which, as current scholarship has it, came under suspicion of
the Counter-Reformation.

That contemporary trend in historical writing was attentive to
the Ciceronian precept of elegance was certainly clear to Baronius.
But it should have also been equally clear to him that humanist
historians, at least from Bruni onward, did pay as much attention
to the truth of the historical narrative as to its style. "The rhet-
oricians, however, had used history as illustrative material, and had
not scrupled to distort it for their purpose. Bruni was an innovator
in that his emphasis was on truth rather than entertainment; his
goal was to inform, in Ciceronian Latin, within the limits of Florentine patriotism."[22] In this, Bruni and his successors were following the precepts of some later theorists of the antiquity than
Cicero, notably Quintilian, Dionysian, and Lucian, who progres-
sively moved away from the Ciceronian concept of the primacy
of rhetoric over history. Lucian in particular had established a
clear distinction between rhetorician and historian, "advising a
vocabulary suitable for exposition (of historical material), a lucid
demonstration of truth,"[23] as well as a set of guidelines for historians to follow in the collection and critical selection of data and
the organization and compilation of the historical work as "a picture of the past reflecting the truth."[24]

Contemporary humanist historians were not only aware of these
precepts governing the content of historical works but also were

faithful followers of them. This should have been evident to Baronius, at least from so many published treatises of his time on historical writing. For example, Giovanni Pontano, a respected authority on historiography at that time, concluded his work on historical writing, *Actius: Poetic numbers and law of history*, by pointing out four major guidelines, namely brevity, diligence for the whole truth, gravity worthy of the matter in hand, and elegance.[25]

Equally emphatic on the necessity of truthfulness and clarity in historical writing were other important theorists of the time such as Robertello, Sebastian Fox-Morcillo, Francis Patrizzi, François Baudouin, Jean Bodin, Giovanni Antonio Viperano, and Uberto Foglietta. In fact, according to Beatrice Reynolds, these theorists considered authenticity of the content more essential to historical writing than form and went as far as to assert that "if the account was based on truth, the *fundamentum, firmamentum, spiritus, et anima* of the art, then even without elegance, it would be history."[26]

The question, then, why Baronius eschewed an established tradition of historical writing, that is the refined style of the humanists, and opted for the arid style of the medieval chroniclers should be answered not by his stated reason of faithfulness to historical veracity, but by his adoption of an apostolic goal for his work.[27] He indicated this in many places in the *Annales*, for example in the "ad lectorem" of Volume X and in the letter to non-Catholic readers which prefaced Volume II.[28] In all cases his contention was that a simple narration of the historical facts would convince the reader of the authenticity of the Catholic church. The implicit argument here is this: historical events being primarily the work of God (according to the Scholastic conception of the world which Baronius followed), and in this case, historical events that concern the Church being a special kind of work of God, if related as they occurred, without any arguments one way or the other and without any means of persuasion such as rhetoric, would serve as a proclamation of the authenticity of the Catholic church. In other words, by merely reviewing the events of ecclesiastical history chronologically, the reader would clearly see how God built his Church from its earliest foundations up to its present status.

This apostolic goal that he set for the *Annales* and his conviction that an annalistic narrative would be the most effective didactic tool precluded any possibility of his ever considering a system or a style other than this, although historiographers of his time had established a formula by which the form of historical writing could be variously chosen to suit the content. This formula, which was predicated on a balance between form and content, was established mainly through the efforts of Bernardo Rucellai, under whose auspices many formal discussions on historiography were held in which historians of such significance as Giovanni Pontano participated.[29] This formula, even though perhaps acceptable in principle to Baronius, was tainted by an overriding concern for patriotism which practitioners of history exhibited in his time.[30] It must have been evident to Baronius that in a larger Renaissance heritage the discriminating use of historical sources and bias reporting of historical events for nationalistic and religious reasons were common, as Beatrice Reynolds has shown, despite the historians' professions otherwise.[31] Baronius perceived this patriotic or nationalistic concern of contemporary humanist historians as essentially a danger to his own goal of obtaining universal acceptance of the Church, and thus he rejected it outright.

When Baronius contemptuously called a certain type of historical narrative "long winded, round about, and drawn out in a round about fashion," and a certain type of speech as "contrived with the greatest skill and invented and composed according to the opinion of each individual and displayed according to what the author seems fit," and attributed them to "ethnic" historians, he was indeed pointing his finger at the patriotic historian who wrote history with a nationalistic point of view.[32] Baronius considered this nationalistic view of history totally inappropriate to his subject matter, because the history of the whole Church was above nationalistic concerns.

Apart from these considerations, there were reasons that seemed to Baronius intrinsic to his subject matter which prompted him to adopt the kind of simple style he used. One such reason was the sacred character of the institution that he was dealing with, the Church; the sacredness of her beliefs, sacraments, laws, ceremonies, and dependent institutions, in his estimation at least, were to be held above controversy. The way he proposed to do this was by keeping ecclesiastical history separate from subjects that would yield to controversy, such as secular history, and by employing the type of language and style that are suitable to the description of self-evident truths, as opposed to those that are suitable to discussion or argument. Church history had a quality of self-evident veracity, in his view, and the Church historian, therefore, was expected to hold it a class above other histories which are subject to doubt and controversy.

Thus Baronius tied ecclesiastical historiography with the dogmas of the Church, and claimed for the ecclesiastical historian a credibility that is unique, not for reasons of the weight of his arguments or the persuasion of his language, but for the simple reason that he was repeating in his book what God has done in the Church. Thus in a sense, Baronius removed the burden of proof from the ecclesiastical historian and placed a burden of belief on the reader. The well-intentioned reader would unquestionably arrive at one conclusion after reading his Church history, he wrote to his friend Talpa, that is the authenticity of the Church.[33]

His eagerness to hold Church history above controversy may have been, at least in part, caused by the sad experiences of some contemporary secular histories which came under severe attack by critics. A good case in point was the *Historia sui temporis* of Baronius' fellow Roman ecclesiastic Paolo Giovio (d. 1552) which was vilified savagely, one critic going as far as to say that "when he put a history on sale he reaped a richer reward from lies than any other man from telling the truth."[34] Obviously Giovio fell prey to such criticism because of the controversial character of the subject matter he dealt with, namely, the recent warfares between the French king and the emperor, a matter fraught with emotion to start with, which he made even worse by his anti-French slant.

But there were other secular histories, written about the same time and in the same type of literary style, which were not vilified to any serious extent, for example, Carlo Sigonio's *Historia de occidentali imperio* and the *Historia de regno Italiae*, works well known to Baronius as the author was a close friend.

Thus it should have been clear to Baronius that the mere fact that a historical work dealt with secular matters did not invite controversy. And it should have been even more clear that a work such as he was contemplating could not even hope to be spared of controversy in the age of the Reformation and Counter-Reformation merely because it dealt with ecclesiastical history. If anything, ecclesiastical history was the point of controversy in the sixteenth century. The best he could do was to use a simple narrative to avoid at least disputations on linguistic or stylistic grounds.

The exclusiveness Baronius claimed for ecclesiastical historiography was not an innovation, however, although his reasons for doing so were new. The concept of separateness was embedded in the tradition of ecclesiastical historiography from its early beginnings in the fourth century, and a similar concept also existed in the tradition of secular historiography of the time, as Momigliano suggested.[35] This separation between sacred and profane was largely respected by medieval chroniclers of both traditions, a practice which was strengthened, at least on the secular side, by the rediscovery of pagan histories by the humanists, which prepared the "conditions which made Machiavelli and Guicciardini possible."[36] Thus, when Baronius set ecclesiastical history apart from secular history, he was in conformity with an established tradition of humanist historiography, although their reasons for doing so were worlds apart.

The simple chronological narrative without literary embellishments and even without any real analysis of the causes and effects of historical events which Baronius advocated had precedence only in medieval chronicles, however. The absence of such elaborations in the medieval works as well as in Baronius' was not the result of a lack of historical consciousness, but that of a typically Christian concept of history as the work of Providence in which scheme subordinate or particular causes of historical events needed not to be seriously considered as they were totally dependent on the all-encompassing causality of God. Thus, Baronius and the medieval chroniclers narrated their story "as a single line of action" and as if historical events were not causally related to one another, but somehow linked to a common outside force.[37] Events thus follow one after another without any visible precipitating cause, a chronological sequence with no forces intrinsic to the events themselves at work. It stands to logic, then, that an annalistic narrative is most suited to this view of history.

Despite Baronius' aversion to the rhetorical style of humanist historiography, he did in fact adopt the humanist practice of inserting speeches in direct discourse (examples abound in the pages of the *Annales*), a practice which was made popular by Bruni and one that was clearly a rhetorical device aimed at didactic effectiveness.[38] Certainly it was the didactic usefulness of the practice that prompted Baronius to use this device rather than a concern for rhetorical elegance. Such direct citations of speeches were also justified by his promise of reporting everything as they occurred, although the accuracy of the speeches he quoted was a matter he should have had ascertained at first in order to make that promise entirely true. This was something Baronius failed to do as we shall see later in this chapter.

The providential guidance Baronius and the medieval ecclesiastical chroniclers attribute to human events betrays a universalistic view. Some humanist historians of Baronius' day also betrayed a universalistic view when they called for an "integral history" or a history that encompassed all human events and institutions, François Baudouin and Jean Bodin for example.[39] But Baronius and the medieval chroniclers fell short of true universalism in their actual writing of history, as they focused mainly on one institution, the Church, and dealt only secondarily with other human events and institutions. Humanist historiography also fell short of universalism as they excluded natural history and divine (ecclesiastical) history. Bodin's scheme of historical writing is a case in point.[40] Thus the seeming universalism of these two historiographical schools are not only mutually exclusive but also essentially unreal.

By rejecting the Ciceronian and humanist historiographical precepts and accepting the Aristotelian and medieval concepts of history, Baronius established his own rules of writing history that suited his own religious and didactic goals. He explained in the preface of the *Annales*:

> First of all, as far as the title is concerned, I give the following reason for preferring to call this my work ecclesiastical annals rather than history: for by this distinction the ancients separated history from the annals (Gall. lib. 5, c. 18; Isid. Orig. li, I in fin) in that the former deals appropriately with contemporary affairs which the author has either seen or could have seen, and he points out not only what has happened but also how it happened and by what design. The writer of the annals, on the other hand, entrusts to memory most of all what his own age does not know, and he does this in a year by year account, by documentation. I am, however, dealing not only with ancient affairs but also, and most of all, with ecclesiastical matters in which not only, as in the rest of history, truth must claim the first place for itself but also it is almost a religious sanction not to depart even a fingernail from the truth. For this reason, lest I be influenced even by the slightest suspicion of betraying the truth, and being obedient to the Christian laws that teach (Matt. 5), "Your speech be yes, yes or no, no; whatever is beyond this is evil," I will leave to the ethnic historians those narratives that are long winded, round about, and drawn out in a round about fashion, and those speeches contrived with the greatest skill and invented and composed according to the opinion of each individual and displayed according to what the author seems fit. I will, therefore, write annals rather than history. And I will follow the kind of speech that is most appropriate to the majesty and dignity of the Church. And I shall narrate the things that have to be discussed in a way that is wholly pure and sincere, and free from any kind of invention or

figment, just as they happened, taking them year by year. For
Arnobius—the most weighty proclaimer of our affairs—says (Ad-
versit. Gent. li, I): "Never did truth follow invention, nor does
anything which is explored and which is certain allow itself to
be led around through a round about way of speech, through re-
capitulations, arguments, definitions, and all those ornamenta-
tions of speech for which trustworthiness is required in the
very nature of their composition; while they give food for those
who suspect, they do not show the features of truth. There was
a time, says Gregory Nazianzen (Gregor. Naz. orat. in laud.
Athanasii), when a type of history was flourishing, and very
much distinguished, when those things were considered very superfluous, and the type of writing that was contaminated with
the beauty of words and art did not even have access to the holy
entrances." In addition to this, in the writing of the annals one
ought to make little use of the customary embellishments of
phrases and words, for the author of the *Dialogus de Oratoribus*,
whether it was Tacitus or someone else, testifies this and dem-
onstrates this clearly (Apud Tacit. de Orator, dialog.). Therefore, in retracing ecclesiastical history to its beginnings I shall
review the affairs in such a way that I will deal with ecclesiastical things in an ecclesiastical fashion. While I rely on the testimony of the ancients in all things, I should give consideration to
the truth. Therefore, I have decided to record as much as possible the exact words of the ancients, no matter how uncouth and
rugged they may seem to be at times, rather than replace or
describe them by my own. And in order that the same truth
may shine forth more and more, I shall nowhere leave anything
that is ambiguous or that we have felt to be contrary to the
truth uninvestigated.[41]

Baronius first of all defined history, following the example of
ancients, as the record of events by eyewitnesses and contemporaries who were directly involved with the events they recorded.[42]
He defined annals, then, as the work of subsequent writers who
tried to arrange the records in a chronological perspective. Thus,
chronology was the key to a clear understanding of what happened
in the past; and Baronius made it the basis of the guidelines he set
up for himself during the planning stages of the *Annales*. As he put
it in a note to himself:

First of all, one rule should be observed in all these (historical
research and writing). That is the chronological sequence. If this
is violated, insurmountable difficulties will arise and errors will

occur. Let the chronicles written by diverse authors for diverse times guide you in this. Such chronicles could be the annals compiled year by year during the reign of an emperor or events jotted down for some other reason.[43]

Therefore, at the very outset Baronius indicated his adherence to a chronological arrangement of historical data as opposed to a topical arrangement used by his humanist predecessors. He declared a preference for a simplicity of style following the biblical precept of "Let your word be yes for yes, and no for no; whatever goes beyond this comes of evil" (Matt. 5:37). And he established a distinction between ecclesiastical history and secular history with a promise to treat "ecclesiastical matters ecclesiastically," using the style "most appropriate to the majesty and dignity of the Church," thus claiming for ecclesiastical history some special dignity and veracity.

A practical consideration for using the chronological narrative may have been, for him, the need to refute the *Magdeburg Centuries*. Only a chronological treatment of events would demonstrate the uninterrupted evolution of Christian dogmas and Church practices from earliest times and disprove the thesis of a hiatus sometime between the fourth and sixth centuries. That is precisely what he said in his letter to the non-Catholic readers attached to the second volume of the *Annales*.[44] He asked them to examine the course of events he narrated so simply in the *Annales* and then to form a dispassionate judgment. He was not treating the heretics with hate or acrimony, but with utmost liberality and love, he said. If they would understand how the doctrine was gradually unfolded, they would return willingly to the Church to which the doctrine was entrusted. Baronius repeated the same argument in the "ad lectorem" of the tenth volume.[45] What he was attempting to do in the *Annales* was nothing more than to narrate the facts as simply as possible. The facts themselves would attest to the ever-present holiness of the Church, its unity, catholicity, and apostolicity. It indeed was this fact that was particularly emphasized by his translators, summarizers, and continuators that followed him; for example Antoin Pagi, who prepared a new edition of the *Annales* in the eighteenth century, and purged it of many historical errors.[46]

Thus, Baronius borrowed the annalistic form of the medieval chroniclers, for he believed it was the simplest and the clearest way of establishing the authenticity of the Catholic church. He borrowed the use of documents from the early Christian historians because it most effectively substantiated his narrative.[47] Indeed, he included an extraordinary number of sources in his text—so many that they give the work what is perhaps its most notable characteristic. But what may have been a novelty in Baronius soon became common to all historical writings of the sixteenth and the seventeenth centuries, as Momigliano has pointed out.[48] Not only the number, but also the kind of documents considered appropriate for extensive quotations multiplied; and theorists of history soon felt obliged to divide them into categories. So did the French historiographer, Louis Ellis du Pin, abbot of Claraval, in his *The Universal Library of Historians*, which established the following list: festivals, columns, inscriptions, trophies, tombs, coins, seals, tradition, songs, registers, memoirs, and histories.[49]

For all these categories, Du Pin could well have looked in the *Annales* alone. Baronius searched far and wide for historical documents and sought the aid of his scholarly friends in all parts of Europe in locating them. He collected materials from various libraries in Rome, particularly from the Vatican Library, and from the archives of the Dominicans, the Augustinians, the Lateran palace, the Capitoline in Aracoeli, and the Sforziana, as indicated from one of his notebooks in which he copied down relevant information.[50] Of these notes, those which were used in the *Annales*, either by Baronius or his continuator Odoricus Reynaldus, are crossed out. Another Baronian codex in the Vallicelliana Library contains a complete list which Baronius prepared of all the documents and historical works available at that time in and around Rome.[51] Still another contains copies of the letters exchanged between the schismatic patriarch of Constantinople, Photius, and Popes Adrian II, John VIII, Nicolas I, and others with regard to the controversy about the Procession of the Holy Spirit.[52] This theological argument, of course, had been one of the causes of the schism between East and West. Baronius obtained these letters from the very library of Photius, for the seventeenth century copyist of the codex entered the following note at its beginning (p. iii): "Photii Epistolae transmissae e Rmo Episcopo Bellunesi Romam ad Card. Baronium anno D. 1598." Some of Photius' Greek letters were translated into Latin by Federicus Metius, at Baronius' request, since Baronius did not have much facility in the Greek language.[53] Some of the numerous errors that crept into the *Annales*, then, may have been the result of poor translations.

Baronius was also fortunate in benefiting from the wide ranging researches of an Oratorian colleague, Antonio Gallonio. While Baronius was writing the *Annales*, Gallonio attempted to write a multivolume work on the lives of saints, for which he collected materials from all parts of Europe. His great collection of documents relating to the lives of saints are still kept in twenty Vallicelliana codices.[54] However, he was able to compose only two volumes of his proposed work, containing the lives of saints until the year 271.[55] And these were never published, very probably because the *Annales* of Baronius totally consumed the interest of the Catholic public and that of the Oratorians, and no encouragement was given to Gallonio.[56] There is no doubt that Baronius profited by the researches of Gallonio, for the two scholars lived in the same house and both of them, Baronius from 1584 to 1587 and Gallonio from 1590 to 1593, were librarians at Vallicella.[57]

Another scholar whose researches were helpful to Baronius was Tommaso Bozzio, again a fellow Oratorian at Vallicella. Bozzio's interest was, like Gallonio's, the lives of saints. He collected *Vitae* from many ancient manuscripts in and around Rome, and the collection still remains in manuscript form in the Vallicelliana Library.[58] There are numerous other codices too, at Vallicella containing lives of saints. Though most of them were collected after the time of Baronius, they reflect an Oratorian dream of Baronius' time: the publication of the complete *Vitae Sanctorum*. But this dream was not to be fulfilled until a century later when the Bollandists published their *Acta Sanctorum*.

Besides his scholarly Oratorian colleagues, Baronius maintained a circle of friends in many parts of Europe who aided him in his search for historical documents. As early as 1579, nine years before the first volume of the *Annales* was published, the famous scholar Carlo Sigonio sent him a manuscript entitled *Historia Ecclesiastica*.[59] Sigonio had prepared this work as an answer to the *Magdeburg Centuries*, as commissioned by Pope Gregory XIII. He sent this to Baronius, as he stated in his letter, for a review and possible corrections because Baronius had already established a reputation for historical learning through his nightly talks on Church history in the Oratory. It seems, however, that Sigonio's real intention was to stimulate Baronius' study of Church history, and eventually to leave him the task of refuting the Centuriators, for he never tried to reclaim the manuscript or publish it in his lifetime. About one hundred and fifty years later, it would be published,[60] but for the time being it served Baronius as a model and a source of information.

Fulvio Orsini, famous classicist of that time, was another friend and collaborator. He allowed Baronius to use his valuable private library and gave him expert advice in archeological questions. One such service Orsini rendered was identifying the coins with the inscriptions of Crispus that Baronius used in the *Annales* to prove Crispus' Christian affiliation.[61]

The famous French scholar, Nicolas Faber, was another valuable collaborator. On August 23, 1592, for example, Faber sent copies of two documents: one contained excerpts from the life of Saint Ambrose written by Paulinus, and the other was a letter written by the Roman synod to Pope Julius I.[62] On March 1, 1603, he sent a letter of Pope Sylvester II and two letters of Nestorius, copies from an ancient codex containing the documents of the Council of Ephesus.[63] On December 1, 1602, he sent a copy of the complete text of a rescript of Emperors Theodosius and Valentinian taken from an ancient codex.[64] Baronius had quoted in the *Annales* part of this edict, establishing Christian feast days, but Faber thought that the complete text of the edict should be included in a future edition.[65] In the middle of the controversy over the so-called "Sicilian Monarchy," Faber sent an ancient codex containing many documents about the Church's rights in Sicily.[66] He also enclosed a copy of the donation of Otto III to Pope Sylvester II, with the warning that the Protestants, who already had knowledge of this document, might claim that this was the document which the papacy contended to be the donation of Constantine to Sylvester I. These were only the more important of the documents Faber made available to Baronius.

There were many other scholars, too, who sent historical documents to Baronius. Among them was the French Jesuit Fronto Ducaeus, who on August 23, 1592, sent a number of documents collected from various archives in France.[67] Another was Aloysius Lollinus, bishop of Belluno, who supplied Baronius with many documents concerning the fourteenth-century monk Barlaamus. Many of these documents were in Greek; and Baronius had them translated by Lollinus.[68] Still another was Carlo Glussano, bishop of Novara, who sent a copy of the document concerning certain donations made by Emperor Otto I to the bishop of Novara.[69] This document was transmitted with the request that Baronius make appropriate reference to these donations in the *Annales*.

While Baronius sought the aid of many scholars in collecting documents, he solicited the help of still others in solving difficult historical problems. For instance, he consulted with Dionisius Petavius, chancellor of the Sorbonne, regarding the exact date of the birth of Christ.[70]

Aside from the contemporary scholars with whom Baronius corresponded directly or who sent materials to him for inclusion in the *Annales*, his indebtedness also extended to many early modern and near contemporary historians whose works he merely consulted or borrowed heavily from. This was particularly true in the case of national histories. A great number of histories were composed in practically every country in Europe during the previous two centuries in the wake of the rise of national monarchies. These works grew also because of the historical consciousness of the Italian humanist tradition permeating in trans-Alpine lands, in many cases through the instrumentality, at least in part, of the Italian humanist authors. Thus for the history of Spain, Baronius leaned heavily (aside from the obvious classical authors and the medieval ecclesiastical chroniclers, Lucas of Tuy and Roderick of Toledo) on the works of near contemporaries such as the *Anacephaleosis* of Alfonso of Carthagena (d. 1456) which was no more than a brief account of the kings of Spain and France and of the popes and Roman emperors; the *Historia Hispanica* of Ruy Sánchez de Arévalo (d. 1470); the *Paralipomenon* of Juan Margarit y Pau (d. 1484) which dealt especially with the ancient history of Spain; *De regibus Hispanorum* and *De regibus Siciliae* of Michael Riccio (d. 1515); *De rebus Hispaniae memorabilibus* of Lucio Marineo (d. 1533); and the historical works of contemporary Jesuit theologian Mariana (d. 1607).

For the history of France, Baronius used the medieval *Historia regnum Francorum* of the monks of Saint Denis; the *Oratorio historialis* of Robert Blondel (d. 1460); the *Compendium* of Robert Gaguin (d. 1501); the *De rebus Francorum gestis* of fellow Italian Paolo Emilio (d. 1529); and the works of his near contemporaries Guillaume Du Bellay (d. 1543) and Jacques Auguste de Thou. For the history of Germanic lands he consulted the Augsburg and Nuremberg chronicles of Sigismund Meistertin (d. 1489); Abbot Trithemius' (d. 1516) *Catalogus illustrium virorum germanorum* which was styled along the lines of Platina's *Vitae* and his *Compendium* which traced the history of the Franks to the legendary kingdom that existed beyond the period of the Roman Empire; *Rerum germanicarum libri III* of Beatus Rhenanus (d. 1547), the translator of Tacitus' works; *Liber chronicarum* of Hartman Schedel (d. 1514); the *Respublica Romana in exteris provinciis* of Austrian historian Wolfgang Lazius (d. 1565); and the *Chronica regnorum aquilonarium* of the Saxon writer Albert Krantz (d. 1517).

For the Slavic countries Baronius' modern sources were John Turoczi's *Chronicon regnum Hungariae; Decades rerum Hungaricarum* of the Italian humanist writer Antonio Bonfani (d. 1505); *Reges Hungariae* of Michael Riccio; the *Historiae Polonicae a Slavorum Polonorumque originibus libri XIII* by Polish humanist Johannes Dlugosz; the *Life of Attila* and the *Deeds of King Vladislaus* by Callimachus (Filippo Buonaccorsi, d. 1496); *Chronica Polonorum* of Matthias Miechovius (d. 1523); *De origine et rebus gestis Polonorum* of official Polish archivist Martin Kromer (d. 1589); and the *Historia regni Bohemie* of John Skala Dubravius (d. 1553). For the Low Countries he consulted the *Annales Belgici* of Aegidius of Roya (d. 1478); the *Rerum gestarum a Brabantiae ducibus historia* of Adrian Barland (d. 1539); the *Historia Batavica* of Gerard Geldenhauer (d. 1542); the *Flandicarum rerum annales* by Jacob Meyer (d. 1552), which was written in the style of Baronius' own work; and the major works of the Catholic apologist Pontus de Huyter (d. 1602), namely *Historiae rerum Burgundicarum libri VI* and *Rerum Belgicarum sive Austricarum libri XVI*.

For the history of England his modern sources were, aside from the chronicles of the monks of Saint Albans which were updated and elaborated in early fifteenth century by Thomas Walsingham, the *Anglia historia* of Polydore Vergil (d. 1555) and *Historia Majoris Britanniae tam Angliae quam Scotiae* of John Major (d. 1549). For the history of Scotland he consulted Hector Boece's (d. 1536) *Historia gentis Scotorum*, a work noted more for its classical style in imitation of Livy than for the historicity of its contents, and his contemporary John Leslie's (d. 1596) *Libri decem de origine, moribus, et rebus gestis Scotorum* while conspicuously ignoring the much more widely read *Rerum Scoticarum Historia* of the Protestant George Buchanan (d. 1582).

While references to these and many other works of early modern writers are found on the pages of the *Annales*, they are by far outnumbered by references to classical, early Christian, and medieval writers who apparently were far more important to Baronius for their proximity to the times he discussed, if for nothing else. A partial list of his ancient and medieval sources are included in an early chapter of this book.[71] But he also considered many of them, especially medieval chroniclers, more acceptable for their chronological narration of history without literary embellishments.

To be sure, Baronius' research was not limited to written documents and personal consultations. Archaeology was one of his chief sources of historical information. For this he had the brilliant example of Flavio Biondo of Forli (d. 1463) who undertook a massive study of Italian cities and Roman institutions and published his findings in his renowned works *Italia illustrata* and *Roma instaurata*. Over a century earlier Biondo's patron Pius II also had done similar work in his *Cosmographia*.[72] But what inspired Baronius most was the relics of the early Church in the newly discovered catacombs.[73] The accidental discovery of the first one in 1578, by workmen who were digging a well in Bartolomeo Sanchez's farm, caused great excitement in Rome, and subsequent discoveries of still more catacombs attracted the pious and the scholarly alike to Rome.

Both as a pious pilgrim and as a scholarly researcher, Baronius marvelled at the sudden unfolding of early Christian history in the catacombs. His frequent visits to the catacombs and to other historical monuments brought him numerous dividends in historical data as well as in spiritual benefits. For example, he was able to substantiate his argument that the veneration of saints and their images had been a common practice in the early Church from the evidence he gathered from the catacombs. He could now support Spartianus' description of how the Jews in Jerusalem used subterranean passages to hide during Hadrian's persecution by pointing out that Christians used the same means during persecutions against them.[75] His arguments that the early Christians buried their dead, unlike the gentiles who cremated dead bodies, and that the Christians frequently visited their cemeteries to pray for the dead, were almost totally based on the inscriptions and other evidences from the catacombs.[76] He supported the contention that Constantine built the first Vatican basilica by the inscriptions he read on the marble slabs excavated from the site of that church.[77]

Ancient coins were another source he used extensively for historical information. For example, he substantiated his argument that Trajan adopted Hadrian as consul and tribune by the silver coins struck for that occasion, which he discovered in a collection of Laelius Pasqualinus, a Roman canon.[78] Similarly, he backed up his contention that Hadrian returned from Syria to Rome to assume the office of Augustus by using the coins minted for that occasion.[79] Then, in order to prove that Constantine had been a faithful Christian from his early Roman days, Baronius reproduced the picture of a coin attached to the Emperor's throne in the Lateran palace.[80] On one side of the coin there was an image of

Christ sitting on a throne, and on the other side there was the likeness of Constantine's son Crispus who, as Baronius contended, had been baptized together with his father. The inscription over the image of Christ reads "Salus et Spes Reipublicae." Thus from the same coin he argued the case for the Christian faith of both Constantine and Crispus.

Again Baronius used the gold coin minted during the time of Galla Placidia and her son Valentinian III in order to prove their Christian orthodoxy.[81] On one side of the coin there was the image of Valentinian with something like a roll in his right hand (Baronius considered this to be the Bible) and a globe crowned with a cross on the left. On the other side, there was the image of Galla Placidia wearing a cross-topped crown and holding in her left hand a gemmed cross, which Baronius explained as the symbol of authority in the Western empire. With her right hand Galla Placidia was raising a woman from a kneeling position. Baronius interpreted this as a symbol of Italy being raised from the oppression of the usurper Johannes, who had been defeated and executed with the aid of Theodosius.

Baronius therefore exhausted every source of historical information available in his time. One thing that immediately impresses anyone who opens the *Annales* is the plenitude of historical references. For example, Baronius cited some twenty-five authors in order to establish the year of Christ's birth. He cited thirty authorities to prove that Peter established his see in Rome.[82]

Considering, therefore, the amount of historical data used by Baronius in the *Annales*, the following statement of a modern reviewer may not be an exaggeration.

> Baronius found himself as it were on a beach overlooking an immense ocean of pages, of parchments, of documents, piled up without order and without limit.[83]

The same writer also commented on the assiduous and careful manner with which Baronius used this material:

> With a frightening calmness he took them one by one just as they came, and he began to read, to make notes, to catalogue. From the age of twenty until he died, he was always bent over documents of the past.[84]

So great was the historical erudition of Baronius that even a most vigorous adversary, none other than the greatest Protestant scholar of his time, Isaac Casaubon, started his criticism of the *Annales* with the following praise:

> He is the first one to deal with the history of the whole Christian world, especially as it pertains to the Church, in a continuous year by year account in such a way as if he were writing the annals of a single city. He is the first to bring into light from unknown hiding places so many things which were certainly unknown before. He is the first who explained the successions of ancient bishops in great cities; the origin, progress, and end of old heresies; the eras of the Church, whether they were tranquil or turbulent, with such unfailing diligence. Finally, if he had not spoiled his services for the Church by an unbridled bias, he would have been worthy, without question, to receive the applause and the submission of all, both ancients and moderns, who have attained only a portion of his learning.[85]

Baronius' erudition was thus recognized by contemporaries and successors alike, and the abundance of historical data he collected and compiled in the *Annales* similarly appreciated. The enormity of his undertaking itself may have been a reason for some weaknesses in the critical handling of the data he collected. It may also have been caused by Baronius' obvious adherence to some principles of early Christian historiography, particularly the emphasis on the authority of documents, previous writers, and historical figures, which was noted earlier. Such an emphasis on authoritarianism was logical for a historical tradition that was dependent on, and was, in a sense, meant as a support to a religious ethos in which authority or tradition enjoyed the same status as revealed truth. Although an imitation of early Christian historians, like Eusebius, suited well with his own stated goals for the *Annales*—the edification of Christians—it did put him on a course alien to contemporary historiography.

The dominant historiographical trend in Baronius' time initiated earlier by Bruni, Valla, and other humanists and perpetuated by their successors, held that the critical scrutiny of the documents in support of a historical argument was more important than the number of documents cited. Thus a skeptical and cautious handling of ancient authorities and documents, especially those making patriotic, religious, or other particularist claims, became necessary.

Examples abound among the humanists who have employed or advocated such caution in using documents, but two such historians whom Baronius followed in other instances may be men-

tioned here in order to place in clearer perspective the difference
in this point between the humanistic and Baronian historiography.
They were Pius II and Flavio Biondo. Pius II's openly skeptical
treatment of the Bohemian chronicles as "written by the ignorant, containing many foolish things, many lies, no ornaments of
style"[86] and his no less skeptical outlook on popular claims of the
legendary origins of the Germans (from Romans), Romans (from
the Trojans) and Britons (from Brutus)[87] stand in stark contrast
with Baronius' blind acceptance of the Donation of Constantine.
Similarly the "method of detachment, weighing of sources, elim-
inating the obviously fictitious" which Biondo employed was used
by Baronius only in a limited way.[88] Thus an objective which
Biondo and many other humanists of the fifteenth and sixteenth
centuries sought to achieve, and one which modern historians consider as a responsibility, that is, the elimination of authoritarianism, was not fully achieved by Baronius.[89]

Yet it was also clear that Baronius did not use his sources totally
uncritically. He thus wrote in the preface of the *Annales* about his
system of selection of sources and their use in his text:

> All these things, therefore, and most of the other things which
> can hardly be summarized briefly, we shall deal with in such a
> way that we shall say nothing lightly or thoughtlessly, nothing
> vainly, nothing that cannot be backed by most tested witnesses
> or shown by reason or proved by analogies, and finally nothing
> that cannot be confirmed as much as possible by clear and firm
> truth. For in writing these things—I say this confidently—we did
> not follow learned fables but made use of the most trustworthy
> witnesses, which the margin of my pages will easily show. (I am
> doing this lest integrating the list of individual authors in the
> text may be annoying because of its excessive length.) In the in-
> vestigation of these authors, I am disposed in such a way that I
> have decided with a certain obstinacy of mind by no means to
> follow them in every respect, no matter how weighty, no matter
> how erudite they may be, as if they could never go wrong, and
> giving more credit to their name than to the truth. I am dis-
> posed, on the other hand, not to despise altogether any author,
> no matter how low a rank he may have, for I am mindful of the
> opinion of Plini which I often experienced to be true: "There
> is no book so bad that it cannot be useful in some part." (Plini
> ad Marc.). And thus I collected everything in such a way that I
> have not even refrained from the untested and apocryphal au-
> thors (with the permission of my superiors). And just as the
> Apostle admonishes (I Thess. 5), "Test everything and keep
> what is good," whatever I have found to be true and certain in

any writer, that I have vindicated in such a way that I have rescued it from darkness into light. Concerning this, we have the opinion of Gelasius the Roman Pontiff, which is worthy of such a pope, expressed in the following words: "Do we not find many things which pertain to truth, contained in the works of the heretics themselves? Must truth be rejected simply because their books which contain perverseness are rejected?" (Gelas. de Anathem.)[90]

True to this profession of critical judgment, Baronius differed with many of the authorities he quoted. For example, he disagreed with Saint John Damascene's statement that Trajan's soul had been liberated from hell as a special consideration for his kindness to the Christians.[91] He disputed the authority of Eusebius in many instances, particularly when Eusebius seemed to be sympathetic to the Arians. In the preface of the *Annales*, Baronius stated:

> Take for example Eusebius who seems to be the first (in this case). Once he was tainted with Arianism, no matter how trustworthy he can be considered in everything else, he lied about many things, both in those things which pertain to the dogmas of the Arians and even in the history of the Christian emperor, whose life he wrote in order to favor the emperor Constantius, the patron of the Arians. I will show this more appropriately, God willing, in due course.[92]

He accused Eusebius of purposely giving a slanted report of the Arian controversy, and of Constantine's intervention in it, in order to make it look as if Arius' opponent, the orthodox Bishop Alexander, had been more at fault. He also accused Eusebius of purposely leaving out the Arians in his reproduction of Constantine's edict against the Oriental heretics.[93] Similarly, he questioned the statements of many other great historians, such as Socrates, Sozomen, Orosius, Sulpizius, Vincent of Beauvais, and Petronius of Bologna. In doing so, he followed his own stated principle that "the authority of a person does not prejudge the truth,"[94] and his belief that "Blessed is he who is never deceived."[95] Accordingly, he attempted to guard himself against misleading authorities.

His scrupulosity about clear documentation sometimes tested his courage as in some cases he had to object to dearly cherished beliefs, thus running the risk of offending large numbers of people. One such case was his denial of the Saint James legend of Spain. The legend held that Saint James the Elder had been the apostle of Spain, and that his mortal remains were miraculously brought to Santiago de Compestella some time after his martyrdom in Judea

(Acts, 12:2). But Baronius gave no recognition of the legend in his description of the martyrdom of James either in the *Martyrology* (July 25) or in the *Annales*.[96] Needless to say, the pride of the Spanish was hurt, and they never forgave him for the affront.

Baronius' many errors of fact, therefore, are not to be attributed to a faulty methodology entirely. They were in many cases caused by a lack of facility in the Greek language, and to the erroneous chronology of the Christian era, which he, like almost everyone else at the time, accepted as valid.[97] His lack of facility in Greek caused an imbalance in his treatment of the Oriental Church. His adherence to the contemporary computation of the Christian era resulted in many chronological errors, including a two year anticipation of Christ's birth.[98]

On the other hand, many other errors certainly had their origin in his conception of history as a handmaiden of dogma, a weapon against heretics. This conception is made dramatic in a frontispiece that adorned Volume I of the *Annales*: an image of the Virgin Mary towering between Peter and Paul with the inscription "in petra exaltavit me et nunc exaltavit caput mecum super inimicos meos."[99] The "ad lectorem" to Volume X indicates that this picture had become actual.[100] Whoever reads the *Annales*, Baronius pointed out, could not but be convinced of the unity, sanctity, catholicity, and apostolicity of the Catholic church.

Yet Baronius claimed to be perfectly impartial in writing history. As he wrote to his intimate friend, Talpa, a short time after the publication of Volume I,

> The profession of a historian is different from that of a defender of the dogmas. In such a way should history demonstrate the dogmas through tradition and truth that the historian should not appear to have intended this, but instead it should be left to the reader, whether Catholic or heretic, to extract the certainty of the truth from what is said and well-authenticated, and from that to form arguments for the destruction of heresy.[101]

Here he seems to advocate a role for historians which is different only in method from that of the defender of dogmas. Both work for the same purpose: the defense of the truth, which is, to Baronius, synonymous with Catholicism. Honesty, moreover, is a moral obligation of Catholics; and honesty is prudent as well, since it will inevitably support the truth which the Church maintains. If the historians follow the straight and narrow path of honest investigation, he should, according to Baronius, end up with conclusions that are totally acceptable to the Catholic church. There is nothing unhistorical or dishonest, then, in starting historical investigation by assuming the validity of Catholic dogma. Therefore, it seems that in his opinion, a historical fact should conform to the Church's doctrine and practice in order to be true. In other words, he held that he was engaging in a perfectly honest and impartial investigation of historical fact while holding a strong faith in the historical validity of Catholicism.

Nevertheless, this faith had its dangers; and in spite of what he professed, Baronius did indeed make historical judgments that were unwarranted, even in his time, solely for the purpose of supporting the Church. The most blatant case was his reaffirmation of the authenticity of the Donation of Constantine.[102] He held this unhistorical position tenaciously in spite of the advice of friends and fellow scholars to the contrary. It would be inconceivable, he said, that the good Christian Emperor Constantine, who had given so many gifts to so many basilicas and churches throughout the Empire, would not have given something special to the head of the universal Church. The documents disproving the Donation notwithstanding, he concluded that the bountiful gifts mentioned in the Donation, (which all educated men knew to be a forgery) must actually have been given to the pope.[103] Even his close friend, Talpa, questioned this argument; but Baronius refused to yield. Indeed, his reaction to the criticism of his friend was so violent that he had to add an apology at the end of his letter: "Perdonatemi se vi pare se parli troppo resentitamente, Veritas Christi urget nos."[104]

Baronius seems to have had some doubts about the validity of the "donation," but the consideration for the welfare of the Church helped him to overcome such doubts. The following letter of Bellarmine to Baronius, dated April 9, 1607, will illustrate this fact. The letter deals with what happened in a consistory held by Paul V during the height of the Venetian controversy. It should be noted that during the controversy the whole question of papal authority was contested by Venetian scholars and, naturally, the Donation was also attacked, for the papacy rested many of its claims for privileges on this document. The letter which specifically deals with the wording of a papal bull follows:

Illus. et rev. sign. mio Oss.

If Your Lordship have the approval of the pope, I would be of the opinion that you should change nothing. Undoubtedly,

Cardinal Perrone will tell you the same thing. When the pope talked to me in the consistory, he told me that he understood that Your Lordship questioned the Donation of Constantine. I told him that there was no basis for the Donation, but that nevertheless by rejecting the diploma of Otto Your Lordship defended rather than disproved the Donation; but that at the end of this exposition Your Lordship blamed those who make so much of this edict of Constantine as if the Church would have had to perish if that Donation had not taken place. Then His Holiness said that all the canon lawyers consider the Donation as valid, and, therefore, he wished that it not be questioned.

Then Don Constantino the Benedictine came to me and presented me with a pamphlet which he had written in support of the Donation. And when I had read it, I told him that this did not prove anything.

His Lordship, Cardinal Monreale, made note of these words: "We have a prophetic speech which is more firm," and he said that this had nothing to do with the temporal state of the papacy which the pope does not claim to have by divine right; and therefore, he would like to take out these words. I told him that these words had been spoken to prove the spiritual authority, which the pope does not have from Constantine, as the edict indicates, but from the words of the Gospel. At first I was of the opinion that the four last lines should be deleted: "Haec dixisse et aperuisse voluimus, etc." in order to please the pope and the canonists, but since His Holiness has already spoken and since Cardinal Monreale left them to the pope, marked with a line, and they do not displease him, I would not do otherwise since I had no other motive for changing or deleting anything but to not annoy the pope.

This is my opinion, which I put below yours in this case as in every other matter. With this I kiss your hand and recommend myself to your prayers.

Di Casa, etc.[105]

It was clear from this letter what had been the strongest motivation behind Baronius' upholding the Donation; certainly it was not faithfulness to historical evidence. The world of learning did not forgive Baronius for this error for a long time. As late as 1745, scholars were writing critiques devastating Baronius' arguments in favor of the Donation, Hieronymus Fuscus for example.[106]

Another instance in which Baronius argued from faith rather than from evidence, was the circumstances of the baptism of Constantine. He contended that Constantine had been baptized in Rome by Pope Sylvester, and that he made many donations to the baptistry where he received the sacrament. His opinion was based on circumstantial evidence, such as Constantine's fervent confession of faith at the Council of Nicea and a few questionable documents like the *Acts of Pope Sylvester I.* In doing so, he discarded the testimony of Eusebius and he overlooked the opinions of many near contemporaries like Theodoretus, Sozomen, and Saint Jerome. In this case too, as in many other instances, Baronius called Eusebius a malicious liar.[107] Obviously, he could not bring himself, as a militant defender of the papacy, to admit that the first Christian emperor may have been baptized at Constantinople, not at Rome, and by Eusebius of Nicomedia whom he considered an Arian heretic.

There are many more cases in which Baronius supported the belief of the Church or her temporal rights against clear historical evidence. For example, he arbitrarily rejected the unquestionable documents of the Sixth Ecumenical Council held in Constantinople in 680–81 A.D., which condemned Pope Honorius I for the heresy of Monergism—a doctrine according to which Christ had only one will, though he had two natures. His only historical justification for this rejection was the statement of Honorius' successor, Leo II, that he had not actually been condemned for being a heretic himself, but for not taking prompt action in order to suppress heresy.[108] But at a time when the very institution of the papacy had come under attack, Baronius could not bring himself to admit the condemnation of a pope for heresy—no matter what the documents, which he professed to follow faithfully, said in support of it.

Similarly, Baronius' attempt to disprove the authenticity of the bull of Urban II, dated July 5, 1098, which the Spanish kings had produced as the basis of their so-called *Monarchia Siciliae*, was also an exercise in futile apologetics. True, he did not have all the documents that Giesebrecht had when he definitively proved that Urban's bull had been authentic.[109] Giesebrecht discovered a manuscript, a letter of October 1, 1117, by Pope Pasqual II to Roger II of Sicily, in which the bull was mentioned and the privileges it conferred on the ruler of Sicily confirmed. However, Baronius' passionate arguments were based on the theological prerogatives claimed by the papacy, not on the documents he had at his disposal.

Still another example of Baronius' tenacious adherence to what was good for the papacy concerned the contention that the institution of the electors of Germany had been established by Gregory

V in 996. Baronius unequivocably asserted that this was a fact. [110]
But already in 1558 Onofrio Panvinio, a Roman priest as well as a
famous historian, had established that the documents on which
this claim had been based were spurious. [111] Panvinio pointed out
that there had been no "king" of Bohemia in 996 but only a duke.
As the document in question cited the "king" of Bohemia as one
of the persons on whom the office of electorship had been conferred, it should have been of a date later than 996. But this did
not prevent Baronius from defending the so-called papal institution. In this matter he was backed up by Bellarmine. [112] But Bellarmine never claimed to be a historian; and his support did little
good to Baronius' reputation for objectivity.

Nor, for that matter, did the adjectives he used to describe heretics of all ages, bolster his reputation for objectivity. The reference to the Magdeburg Centuriators in the preface of Volume I
leaves no doubt about his attitude:

> Among the more recent writers, there are quite a few who
> are exiles from the Catholic church, who, while they claim to
> collect the history of ancient times, have attempted nothing else
> but by heaping up lies to obstruct for us an open road and to
> block the royal highway. And then, as if they had sworn to
> wage war with joined weapons against truth, they have piled up
> every falsehood. They have changed everything and turned
> everything upside down, striving for no other goal than to con-
> struct a new tower of confusion, reaching up to heaven, if it
> were possible, with which they might fight against God and His
> saints, driven by blind fury. [113]

He did not have the occasion to refer to Protestants directly, since
the *Annales* did not reach the period of the Reformation. But
when he dealt with earlier heretics, he made it clear that he was
condemning those of his own age as well. The adjectives he used
were not very kind; "miserrimi nostri temporis . . . levissimi et
sordidissimi Novatores," for example. [114] And the observation was
hardly called for by his immediate subject, namely, the schism of
Photius, which he had already termed "diabolic." But he could
not resist the opportunity of condemning *en bloc* the "Novatores
audacissimi omnium haereticorum." [115] Polemics were rampant in
the sixteenth century, and in the historical setting of the *Annales,*
that is, *vis à vis* the Reformation and Counter-Reformation, he
could even be excused for engaging in them. As a historian, however, he is out of tune not only with modern historiography but

also with the style and techniques of his immediate predecessors, the Renaissance historians.

Even though Baronius was not very careful in determining the authenticity of the documents he used, he was extremely scrupulous in quoting them correctly. In fact, he was so scrupulous about it that he would not even allow the language of his citations to be updated—which is clear from what he wrote to his friend, Talpa, regarding the corrections in a text made by Gian Giovenale Ancina, an Oratorian whom he had charged with proofreading and linguistic emendations.

> The Reverend Father Giuvenale has used great diligence in the emendation. But he causes great annoyance to me with his exaggerated scrupulosity since in many places he has committed violence to the text with his pen by correcting and changing at his pleasure, according to his latinity, many texts cited from various authors. Thus he forces me to go over those texts again and to restore them to their former state. It is considered almost a sacrilege to lay hands on the cited texts by correcting them unless there is an obvious error of print or different readings, in which case one of them must be placed in the margin. Please ask him to refrain from this in the future. Let him take care only of the correction of my phrases and words.[116]

In a subsequent letter to Ancina, Baronius said:

> With regard to what you write concerning corrections, it is most important to observe the following. If it concerns the text of the Holy Scripture, nothing should be touched: it is sacrosanct, beware. If it concerns the Latin Fathers, nothing ought to be touched unless it is certain that the text has been distorted: otherwise, it would be boldness. If it concerns the translation of a Greek text into Latin, some liberty may be taken: as long as the sense of the author is preserved. Let it be preserved in such a way that this be the goal; lest I have to deal with you according to the Cornelian law. Let it not be longer because we have no time for such shows.[117]

In compiling the *Annales* Baronius followed a variety of traditions, classical, humanistic, and scholastic, but the scope and magnitude of his work was such that it cannot be compared to any other up to his time. Yet several works of the humanistic school may be considered as prototypes of the *Annales*, most notably Sabellico's *Enneades* and Platina's *Vitae Pontificum*, a fact which Baronius at least by implication confirms through repeated references.[118] Apart from the annalistic arrangement of historical events, their similarities lie also in their employment of seemingly endless sources. Although both Baronius and his models took pains to identify their sources in marginal notes, they remained somewhat unreliable for the mere fact that the enormity of their number limited their critical scrutiny. The works are also comparable in their attempt to present history as a gradually unfolding drama— which failed as the historical reports they borrowed to compile their works remained largely a mass of data due to the lack of a cohesive argument and a smooth literary style. And they are similar in their emphasis of the interdependence of man and Providence in the actualization of history—which remained no more than a pious proposition due to the lack of any convincing philosophical or historical argument.

The *Annales* holds also some similarity with the works of a universalist school of historians emerging in France in the late sixteenth century, such as the *Bibliotheque historiale* of Nicolas Vignier, first published in 1588, and the *Idea of Perfect History* of Henri Voisin de la Popelinière, first published in 1598. The former resembled the *Annales* chiefly in the enormity and variety of historical data it contained and the latter in its ambitious blueprint for a truly universal history.[119] But the similarities seem to be purely coincidental as there is no evidence of mutual influence.

Perhaps the difficulty of classifying Baronius' work into any one genre of historical writing, notwithstanding the *Annales'* obvious affiliation to ecclesiastical historiography, lies in the fact that Baronius combined in his work at least three kinds of historical writings that were prevalent in his time. They were universal history, national history, and biography. For the first of these his near contemporary models were the *Chronicles* of Archbishop Antonine (d. 1459) which followed the four monarchies theory; the continuation of Prosper's *Chronicles* by Matteo Palmieri; the *Chronicle* of Jacopo Filippo of Bergamo (d. 1493), which gave some consideration to a topical arrangement of events; the *De bello a Christianis contra barbaros gesto* of Benedetto Accolti of Arezzo (d. 1466); and of course the *Compendium* of Pomponio Leto (d. 1497) and the *Enneades* of Sabellico. For national history his modern examples were, apart from the works of Flavio Biondo, Leonardo Bruni, and Pius II; the *Historia rerum Venetarum* of Sabellico; the *De bello italico* of Bernardo Rucellai; and the continuation of Sabellico's history of Venice by Cardinal Pietro Bembo. For biography, Baronius' Renaissance models were, aside from the obvious *Vitae pontificorum* of Platina, the life of Francesco Sforza by Giovanni Simonetta (d. 1491); the *De claris Genuensibus* of Jacopo Bracellai (d. 1466), the life of King Ferdinando of Naples by Lorenzo Valla; and the life of King Alfonzo of Naples by Giovanni Pontano.

The genius of Baronius was in his ability to combine all three kinds of historical writings into one single work, but here also lay his reason for failure because he mixed national and local chronicles, and biographies of national heroes, local saints and popes with his obvious theme of the universal history of Christendom. This resulted in a potpourri of historical information loosely kept beneath a veneer of universalism. Thus the *Annales* was devoid of a thematic scheme that would have helped to tie all these data into some cohesive form and devoid of a literary style that would have at least in part made up for a lack of thematic cohesion. So the *Annales* remained a work unique to itself, a massive depository of historical information, a reference book par excellant, but beyond the comprehension of the unlettered and beyond the tolerance of the lettered. Only its value as a reference work for arguments against enemies of Catholicism made it an immensely popular work for some time. But as the religious climate of Europe changed and as the Counter-Reformation waned, both the work and the author gradually yielded to their more critical and more refined successors.

Yet it must be said that Baronius put together an immense array of historical documents, and that he did so with a historical sense and faithfulness to chronology exceptional in his time. But when it came to an over-all view of history and a synthesis of all the historical data he collected, his contribution was minimal. He seems to have left this task to the reader. The role of an annalist was apparently only that of narrating the story as it really happened, but not interpreting it. The truth would be so evident from the simple narration, he contended, that no further analysis would be necessary.[120] Therefore, he did not offer any summary at the end of any volume, nor did he write elaborate introductions. His prefaces were mostly exhortations to the readers to see the truth of the Church for themselves by reading the recorded facts. For example, in his preface to the tenth volume he advised the readers to follow the events of the tenth century cautiously in order not to be misled by the tumultuous happenings.[121] As if to set the view straight for his readers, if any of them were pussillanimous and easily scandalized, Baronius added that the quarrels and schisms which occurred in that century were mainly the result of the inordinate ambitions of secular rulers, not the fault of the Church.

In the same way, Baronius showed his eagerness to point out to his readers, sometimes even in the course of his narration, the lessons to be learned from history. This is what he said after quoting a long speech of Photius, the schismatic patriarch, which was an attack against his orthodox opponent Ignatius: "Reader, here you have seen the old device of the devil: how those who have been deceived by the most shameless marks make a laughing stock out of holy men, friends of God, worshipers of justice, holy servants of God."[122] Such running comments, so frequent in the *Annales* in places where controversial issues are discussed, can only be understood in the light of Baronius' supreme didactic goal. This goal had plenty of precedents in contemporary and near contemporary historical writing, for example the Spanish historian Ruy Sánchez de Arévalo who inserted such exhortations in the guise of "greater decoration of history." He wrote in Book III of his *Historia Hispanica*: "For the greater decoration of history, we shall include some famous deeds and comparisons, memorable acts and words, from the Scriptures as well as from the annals of Romans and Greeks, adding . . . certain moral teachings suited to the matter under discussion."[123] Such exhortations and moral conclusions, however, did not constitute a historical synthesis, nor did Baronius attempt any other synthesis, summary, analysis, or interpretation of the events he discussed.

Nevertheless, the *Annales* as a whole is permeated by certain general assumptions concerning the course of history. There is no doubt that he upheld the Judeo-Christian concept of history as the work of an ever-present and all-powerful God who intervenes in every event in the universe according to his preconceived plan, the ultimate purpose of which is his own glory.[124] In the *Annales*, the God of history always acts and activates other things. His benevolent providence protects the believer and the good, while his wrath is directed against unbelievers and evildoers. The Church, of course, is the vehicle of God's grace. It is charged with the realization of his will and the exercise of his justice. As such, it is above all other institutions, and its triumph is assured because of its very mission.

Like the Magdeburg Centuriators, Baronius also depicted the course of history as a constant struggle between the forces of good and evil, but his narrative was characterized more by a sustained optimism. This optimism found its most vibrant expression when he described the triumphs of the Church after periods of schisms and persecutions. As an example, his narrative of the events after the accession of Emperor Justin (518–527) which led to the triumph of Catholicism in the East, should be termed at the least as jubilant.[125] Such triumphs of the Church, in fact, were Baronius' most favorite theme, and that is followed by the defeat and punishment of the Church's enemies. For example, after describing the failure of the schism of Photius, he devoted a page to describe how God had punished the enemies of true religion throughout history.[126] Thus, in the *Annales* Providence and Church worked together for the salvation of the world, a providentialism which was undoubtedly influenced by the scholastic concept of divine providence, particularly that of Thomas Aquinas.

The *Annales* indeed reflect a world view, but this world view is based on the catholicity of the Church, which invites all segments of the human race to its fold. Baronius did not see the world divided into separate civilizations which rise and fall in the ebbs and flows of history in time, as Arnold Toynbee does, nor did he observe the shift of the centers of more dominant cultures from one part of the globe to another, as William McNeill does.[127] For him, there was only one steady and uninterrupted flow of history, leading to the end of everything, the godhead. There was only one mainstream of history, the Church; all other currents of civilizations were auxiliary streams that would necessarily merge with it before it reached the ultimate destination.

Beyond these general characteristics, that is the providentialism and the catholicity which Baronius imposed on his treatment of history, and his strict adherence to chronological narration, the *Annales* does not represent any philosophy of history, nor does the author articulate any. We can only speculate, then, as to how he would have reacted to the various schools of historical thought that arose immediately prior to his time and in subsequent centuries. Certainly he did not consider the historical discipline as an art or a science. He distrusted the refinement of art, the fine language, attractive presentation, and colorful narrative. For him history was plain talk, forthright presentation, accurate recording of facts. Similarly, he disliked the detachment of science, the objectivity of which he considered affected and even insincere. How can anyone be sincere, Baronius might have thought, when he does not openly profess the only truth, the Church? Thus, he would have disagreed with his countryman, Vico, in his subsequent attempt to establish a *New Science* centered around "a rational civil theology of divine providence," or "a history of human ideas" devoid of ecclesiological significance.[128]

Baronius admitted a kind of historical inevitability, a certain type of determinism; but it is one which differed quite radically from the determinism, say, of Marx. It encompassed everything (even minute changes followed God's blueprint); while that of his successors touched only on some aspects of human development, Marxian determinism based on economies, for example.[129] In the light of his cosmic determinism, Baronius could hardly be expected to agree with the classical historians in whose scheme human heroes determined the course of history more than gods; and he certainly would not have agreed with Machiavelli, who sometimes explained the course of history by the influence of fortune.[130] Whatever happened in history, whether it be the rise and fall of the Roman Empire, the triumph of Christianity in the Empire, or even the schisms and heresies that shook the Church, they all fitted well into the over-all plan of God for the good of the faithful. There was nothing fortuitous about any of these historical developments. On the other hand, Baronius would also disagree with the concept, ably expounded by Collingwood, of causality in history, that is, history as caused by "conscious and responsible" agents.[131] Baronius would be willing only to grant a role of secondary causality to human agents. Ultimate causality rested with the all-pervading Divine Providence.

Baronius would go part of the way with the positivist school in their emphasis on empirical laws in order to establish conclusions about the past. But to him, empirical observations were of little help in establishing the meaning of history. For that, one would have to fall back on faith, which alone casts light on the meaning of historical realities. It is clear, then, that Baronius was a perfect example of the biased historian described by Trevelyan.[132] In this respect, the following observation of Ernest Nagel about the influence of the ingrained values scheme of a historian fits Baronius well; it is "not only casually influential upon his inquiry, but is *logically* involved, both in his standards of validity as well as in the meaning of his statements."[133]

The philosophical failings of Baronius should not minimize his contributions to history, however. His singular status as the collector and codifier of the largest amount of historical data ever gathered by one man until his time, perhaps in any time, may not earn him the title of father of modern historiography. But without his efforts, the tools of historians may have been perfected just a bit slower. His faith in history as the fountain of truth, although conditioned by his pre-conviction of the authenticity of his Church, nonetheless provided a stimulation for historical investigation for several centuries. His use of history to demonstrate the validity of an old but ongoing institution, the Catholic church, helped make history itself a living discipline. By confidently opening the vistas of history and courageously assuring that history would always support the theological and temporal claims of his Church, he laid the foundations for the work of many generations of Church historians, for example the Bollandists and the Maurists, who plunged into a minute investigation of the past, completely free from fear of encountering any danger. Thus Baronius left a legacy for Church historians of at least the next three centuries, and he was certainly the chief inspiration of Catholic historians through the nineteenth century.

Notes

1. EARLY YEARS

1. In Caesar's letters written to his uncle (Vallicelliana Library, Codex, Q. 46, p. 44) on June 5, 1558, and to his father (ibid., p. 60) on November 8, 1581, the family name is given as Barone. Also the list of the Oratorian Fathers and Brothers, printed when Baronius was the superior, shows his last name as Barone. As Calenzio suggests, Baronius must have Latinized his name (Generoso Calenzio, *La Vita e gli Scritti del Cardinale Cesare Baronio della Congregatione dell' Oratorio Bibliotecario di Santa Romana Chiesa* [Rome: Tipographia Vaticana, 1907], chap. i, p. 8) during the course of his stay in Rome. Barnabeus relates that Caesar preferred to be called by the Latinized version of Baronius rather than Barone (Hieronimus Barnabeus, *Vita Purpurati S.R.E. Principis Caesaris Baronii* [Vienna: Johannes Jacobus Wolrab, 1718], p. 2). When Baronius was translated into Italian, it became Baronio.

2. Copies of the diploma of nobility given to the Barone family can be seen in two codices of the Vallicelliana Library, Q. 50, Q. 74. The Vallicelliana Library had been the library of the Oratorians which was taken over by the state after the Napoleonic invasion of Italy.

3. There are two letters of Baronius, one to his father written on November 8, 1581 (*Vall. Cod.* Q. 46, p. 60), and the other written to his uncle on June 5, 1558 (ibid., p. 44), which deal with the misfortune of the family.

4. He thus described her to Francesco Zazzara, a fellow Oratorian. Zazzara's *Memoirs*, which had been kept in manuscript form in the archives of the Oratory of Rome, cannot be located now. But Calenzio, who consulted the manuscript, makes reference to it (Calenzio, chap. i, p. 8).

5. Barnabeus, Book I, chap. i, p. 2.

6. Marzia Baronio, Caesar's aunt, related this in her testimony about him to her confessor, Father Pompeo Pateri (Calenzio, chap. i, p. 9).

7. This incident was also taken from the testimony of Marzia Baronio (ibid.).

8. Ibid.

9. For the foregoing, I follow Benedetto Croce in his *Storia del Regno di Napoli* (Bari: Giue. Laterza et Figle, 1925), pp. 11–155.

10. Hans Baron, *The Crisis of the Early Itailan Renaissance* (Princeton: Princeton University Press, 1966), pp. 140–45, 417–21.

11. *Laurentii Vallensis viri tam graecae quam latinae linguae peritissimi in Latinam Novi Testamenti interpretationem ex collatione Graecorum exemp-*

179

180 NOTES TO CHAPTER 1

larium Adnotationes apprime utiles. The first edition of this was published in Paris in 1506 and the second edition, prepared by Erasmus came out from Basel in 1526.

12. For the foregoing, I follow P. Pietro Tacchi-Venturi, *Storia della Compagnia di Gesu in Italia* (Rome: Edizioni "La Civilta Cattolica," 1950), I, Part I, pp. 137-49.

13. For a biographical study of Sadoleto, see S. Ritter, *Jacopo Sadoleto* (Rome: Editrice Francesco Ferrara, 1912) and Richard M. Douglas, *Jacopo Sadoleto* (Cambridge, Mass.: Harvard University Press, 1959). For Sadoleto's theological debate with Calvin, see John Calvin and Jacopo Sadoleto, *A Reformation Debate*, ed. by John C. Olin (New York: Harper Torchbooks, 1966).

14. For his role in the development of the Theatine congregation, see Paul H. Hallet, *Catholic Reformer: A Life of St. Cajetan of Thiene* (Westminster, Md.: Newman Press, 1959).

15. For the reforms of Paul IV, see Leopold von Ranke, *History of the Popes* (New York: Frederick Ungar Publishing Co., 1966), I, 192-212.

16. For more information about his reforming activities, see Orestes Ferrara, *El Cardenal Contarini* (Madrid: Collection "La Nave," 1959).

17. For further information about the origin of the Capuchins, see H. Cuthbert, *The Capuchins* (New York: Sheed and Ward, 1929).

18. For Savonarola's reformation of the Dominican order, see Roberto Ridolfi, *The Life of Girolamo Savonarola* (New York: Alfred A. Knopf, 1959), pp. 66-77.

19. Croce, p. 146.

20. Barnabeus, Book I, chap. ii, p. 4.

21. A brief description of Caesar's stay in Naples and the reasons for the subsequent decision to leave the city are contained in the excerpts of his letters to his parents. Three of such letters, only one autographed, are contained in *Vall. Cod.*, Q. 46, pp. 1-50.

22. Giovanni Marciano, *Memorie historische della Congregatione dell' Oratorio* (Naples, 1693), I, Book III, chap. ix, pp. 281, 282.

23. Caesar's letter to his father, dated October 23, 1557, describes his arrival in Rome and the meeting with the cardinal (*Vall. Cod.*, Q. 46, p. 2).

24. So he wrote to his father on that date (Letter, ibid.).

25. Ibid., p. 3.

26. Louis Ponnelle and Louis Bordet, *Saint Philippe Neri* (Paris: La Colombe, 1958), p. 9.

27. Ibid., pp. 9ff; also in Meriol Trevor, *Apostle of Rome* (London: Macmillan, 1966), p. 15.

28. Ibid.

29. Ibid., p. 23.

30. Marcel Touhandeau, *St. Philip Neri* (London: Longmans, 1960), p. 47.

31. Ponnelle and Bordet, pp. 156-57.

32. Calenzio, p. 15.

33. *De Vita, virtutibus et gestis B. Philippi Nerii et instituto Congregationis Oratorii, libri VIII; scripti ab auctore coevo et ejus discipulo, opus autographum multis in locis correctum et emendatum a Caesare Cardinale Baronio et aliis. Vall. Cod.*, Q. 7, lib. I, chap. xxvii, p. 51.

34. Calenzio, p. 17.

35. Barnabeus, Book I, chap. ii, p. 4.

36. For further details about the revival of humanism after the Sack of Rome, see Pio Pecchiai, *Roma nel Cinquocento*, Vol. XIII: *Storia di Roma* (Bologna: Licinio Cappelli Editore, 1948), Part III, pp. 391ff. Also see Jean Delumeau, *Vie Economique et Sociale de Rome dans la Second Moitie du XVIe Siècle* (Paris: E. DeBoccara, 1957), I, 197.

37. Trevor, p. 35.

38. Barnabeus, Book I, chap. ii, p. 5.

39. Calenzio, p. 18.

40. Vatican Library, Lat. Cod. N. 3798, Part I, pp. 111–12.

41. Zazzara's *Memoirs* (Calenzio, pp. 18–20).

42. Calenzio, pp. 21–22.

43. Baronius' letter to his father on March 18, 1558 (a copy of it in *Vall. Cod.*, Q. 46, pp. 5–6), is the only clear indication of the date of his change of residence.

44. There are several testimonies concerning this fact, for example: (1) Cardinal Ottavio Paravicino's testimony reported in the *Memoirs* of Pompeo Pateri (ibid., Q. 57, p. 44); (2) Barnabeus, Book I, chap. vi, pp. 12–16.

45. In one of those letters, dated March 18, 1558, Caesar chides his father about his lack of religious devotion, appreciates his mother's prayers, and confirms his own decision to lead a religious life (*Vall. Cod.*, Q. 46, pp. 5-6).

46. Barnabeus, Book I, chap. vii, p. 18.

47. Calenzio, p. 30.

48 Zazzara claimed that Baronius revealed this to him (ibid., p. 28).

49. Letter in *Vall. Cod.*, Q. 46, p. 6.

50. Calenzio, p. 31.

51. Letter quoted by Pio Pachini, "La Riforma Gregoriana del Martirologio Romano," *Scuola Catholica* (March, 1923), p. 5.

52. Caesar Baronius, *Annalium Ecclesiasticorum Caesaris Baronii . . . Apparatus* (Luca: Typis Leonardi Venturini, 1740), p. 414.

53. Vatican Library, Lat. Cod., N. 3798, Part I, p. 110.

54. Baronius, *Annalium Apparatus*, pp. 422–24.

55. Zazzara's *Memoirs* (Calenzio, pp. 33–34).

56. *Vall. Cod.*, Q. 7, p. 52.

2: THE PHILIPINE CIRCLE

1. Giuseppe De Libero, *Cesare Baronio Padre della Storia Ecclesiastica* (Rome: Pia Societa San Paolo, 1939), p. 72.

2. *Vall. Cod.*, Q. 46, p. 4.

3. Ibid., p. 5.

4. Ibid., p. 6.

5. Baronius' own testimony, see chap. i, p. 30.

6. Zazzara's *Memoirs* (Calenzio, pp. 40–41).

7. Ibid.

8. *Vall. Cod.*, Q. 46, pp. 6–8.

9. Ibid., pp. 8–10.

10. The *Memoirs* of Zazzara and Pateri, both Oratorians and contemporary

co-religionists of Baronius, make mention of these vows (Calenzio, pp. 53–54).

11. Ibid.

12. *Vall. Cod.*, Q. 46, pp. 10–11.

13. Baronius to his father on May 7, 1561 (ibid., p. 11).

14. Baronius' letter to Paul on April 1, 1561, indicates this (ibid., p. 10) .

15. Letter of May 21, 1561 (ibid., p. 11).

16. Francesco Zazzara in his *Memoirs* (Calenzio, p. 60) and Paolo Aringhi in his unpublished biography of Baronius (*Vall. Cod.*, Q. 56, p. 64) testify to this fact. A contemporary biographer and disciple of Philip Neri also left his testimony (ibid., O. 7, p. 51).

17. Ibid., Q. 46, p. 33.

18. Ibid., pp. 10–15.

19. Baronius discussed this in his letter to his parents, dated January 22, 1564 (ibid., p. 35).

20. Baronius to his father on July 7, 1562 (ibid., p. 34).

21. In his letter, dated December 3, 1562 (ibid., pp. 34, 35).

22. Several of these letters are in ibid., pp. 35ff.

23. Letter of July 4, 1563 (ibid., p. 36).

24. Letter of August 11, 1563 (ibid., p. 37).

25. Letter dated December 10, 1563 (ibid., pp. 38–39).

26. Ibid., p. 38.

27. Letter of November 3, 1563 (ibid.).

28. Ibid., p. 39.

29. Ibid., p. 43.

30. Calenzio, p. 83.

31. Two of Caesar's letters to his mother, dated October 27 and November 4, 1561, testify to this fact (*Vall. Cod.*, Q. 46, p. 17).

32. Calenzio, p. 81.

33. *Ex Scriptis Patris Joannis Mattaei Ancinae* (unpublished manuscript), *Vall. Cod.*, Q. 56, p. 60; *Baronii Caesaris Vita* (unpublished manuscript), ibid., O. 58, pp. 61ff; and *Fatti della vita del Baronio* (unpublished manuscript), ibid., Q. 57, pp. 42–54.

34. Aringhi, loc. cit.

35. *Vall. Cod.*, Q. 46, pp. 40-42.

36. Ibid.

37. In a letter to his parents around this time (undated) Baronius describes the joy of having such "spiritual children" (ibid., p. 43).

38. His letter dated November 19, 1565 (ibid., p. 42).

39. The testimonies of Giovanni Matteo Ancina and Pompeo Pateri are recorded ibid., Q. 56, pp. 48–65. The testimony of Paolo Aringhi is in ibid., O. 58, p. 61.

40. There is a common belief that Baronius was the originator of the popular custom of kissing the feet of this statue of Saint Peter. But Calenzio quotes Cardinal Bartolini, an authority on the history of this statue, who contends that this custom existed before Baronius, but he popularized it (Calenzio, p. 102).

41. Paolo Aringhi, among others, describes the ceaseless hard work by Baronius (loc. cit.); and Calenzio, p. 106.

42. Calenzio cites this document and Zazzara's report about this miraculous "cure" (p. 106).

43. Baronius testified so during the canonization proceedings of Neri (Vatican Library, Latin Codex, No. 3798, Part I, pp. 110-11); Calenzio, pp. 125-29; Barnabeus, Book I, chap. xiv, pp. 36-38; and Raymundus Albericius, *Venerabilis Caesaris Baronii . . . Epistolae et Opuscula* (Rome:Tipographia Komarek, 1759-1770), I, 16-17).

44. *Vall. Cod.*, O. 58, p. 77. This codex contains a collection of memoirs by Paolo Aringhi and several other Oratorian chroniclers about the lives and deeds of the members of their congregation.

45. Ibid., Q. 46, p. 44.

46. Baronius discussed this matter in a letter to his father, dated February 4, 1568 (ibid., p. 46).

47. Calenzio, pp. 115-16.

48. Baronius' letter of February 25, 1568, to his father makes mention of this invitation (*Vall. Cod.*, Q. 46, pp. 45-46).

3: FORMATION OF A HISTORIAN

1. Pompeo Pateri reported so in his memoirs (ibid., Q. 56, p. 48).

2. Ibid., Q. 46, p. 47. This letter is dated 1578, but does not include the day or month. Calenzio, however, considers it to have been written in August or September of that year.

3. Ibid.

4. Ibid., Q. 8, n. 1.

5. Ibid.

6. Calenzio, pp. 916-22.

7. *Vall. Cod.*, Q. 46, p. 47.

8. Ibid., pp. 47-48; Q. 57, p. 26.

9. The report of this vision comes from the Oratorian chronicler, Pompeo Pateri (ibid., Q. 56, p. 45).

10. Letter dated August 18, 1580 (ibid., Q. 46, p. 48).

11. The Gregorian Calendar was inaugurated by the papal bull dated February 13, 1582. The new calendar year, however, was to start on October 5, 1582.

12. Letter dated December 6, 1580 (ibid., p. 49).

13. Ibid., Q. 56, p. 48; Barnabeus, Book XIX, p. 54.

14. *Vall. Cod.*, Q. 46, p. 60.

15. Benedict XIV in his *De Beatificatione Servorum Dei* cites Silvio Antoniano, Ludovico de Torres, Giambattista Bandino, Michele Ghisileri, Bartolomeo Gavanto, Roberto Bellarmino, and Cesare Baronio as the revisers of the Gregorian *Martyrology*. But this statement is historically incorrect (cf. Pio Paschini, "La Riforma Gregoriana del Martirologio Romano," *Sculola Cattolica*, March, 1923, p. 3).

16. Several of Baronius' letters indicate this fact (e.g., his letters to his father dated December 6, 1580, and June 28, 1583, *Vall. Cod.*, Q. 46, pp. 49-50). Several of Curzio Franchi's letters, another member of the commission, also proves this (Paschini, pp. 7, 13-14).

17. Ibid., p. 4.

18. Letter dated August 17, 1581 (*Vall. Cod.*, Q. 47, p. 33).

19. Calenzio, pp. 200–201.

20. Paschini, p. 16.

21. Henri Daniel-Rops, *The Church of Apostles and Martyrs* (Garden City, N.Y.: Image Books, 1962), II, 260.

22. Baronius himself describes this incident. Caesar Baronius, *Annales Ecclesiastici* (Luca: Typis Leonardi Venturini, 1739), iv, 613.

23. In the letter to his father, dated June 28, 1583, Baronius describes the purpose of this commission (*Vall. Cod.*, Q. 46, p. 50). This is confirmed by the letter Baronius wrote, dedicating his new edition of the *Martyrology* to Sixtus V, in which he says: "I have completed, with great labor and diligence, Most Holy Father, the annotations to the *Roman Martyrology*, revised in the last few years. It is timely to illustrate all the aspects of the Christian antiquity contained in it. With my little ability I was compelled to solve the many difficulties, often wrapped around in great obscurity. I was commanded to do this by Cardinal Guglielmo Sirleto. . . ." (Dedicatory letter to Sixtus V, in *Martyrologium Romanum* [Rome: Ex Typographia Dominici Basae, 1586]).

24. Baronius' own testimony in a note in *Vall. Cod.*, Q. 63, p. 291.

25. In his commentaries Baronius critically evaluated the historicity of the different saints mentioned in the previous Latin and Greek *Martyrologies* as well as in the new, revised edition. He pointed out which narrations were certainly unhistorical, which were undoubtedly historical, and which were doubtful. But several errors still remained unnoticed. An example is the description of Saint Sulpicius Severus of Bourges as a bishop (under the date January 29 in the *Martyrology*). But he never was a bishop (Paschini, p. 18). It must be added, however, that Baronius continued to make more corrections, as a result of his subsequent research. Two new editions (besides several reprints) with many corrections and additions were made by him, one in 1587, and the other in 1598. A copy of this third edition is kept in the Vallicelliana Library with many marginal notes by Baronius (*Vall. Cod.*, Q. 31) which indicates that he intended even further emendations.

26. In a letter to Giacomo Pamelio, the editor of the works of Tertullian, dated December 1, 1586 (Latino Latini, *Lucubrationes* [Rome, 1659], I, 312).

27. Lindano had examined Baronius' *Notationes* before publication. This was done by order of Sixtus V as a prerequisite to ecclesiastical approbation of the work. His opinion of the work was expressed in a letter to Baronius dated December 20, 1586 (Letter in Raymundus Albericius, ed., *Caesar Baronius: Epistolae et opuscula; pleraque nunc primum ex archetypis in lucem eruta. Novam ejusdem Baronii vitam operi praeposuit recensuit et adnotationibus illustravit Raymundus Albericius* [Rome: Ex Typographia Komarek, 1759–1770], III, 146).

28. Plantino's comment in a letter dated February 8, 1586 (Albericius, III, 150).

29. In a letter to Baronius dated March 3, 1597 (ibid., p. 203).

30. In a letter to Baronius dated January 31, 1588 (ibid., I, 180).

31. In Seraio's letter of September 28, 1589 (ibid., p. 198), and Masson's letter dated July 1, 1601 (*Vall. Cod.*, Q. 45, p. 1).

32. In the letter dated March 20, 1589 (Albericius, I, 191).

33. Viseur's letter to Baronius dated July 9, 1606 (ibid., III, 332).

34. *Vall. Cod.*, Q. 36.

35. *Acta Sanctorum, Maii, Collecta, Digesta, Illustrata a Godefriedo*

Henschenio et Daniele Paperbrochio e Societate Jesu, II (Antwerp: Apud Michaelem Canobarum, 1680), 359–69.

36. *Venerabilis Caesaris Baronii S.R.E. Card. Bibliothecarii De Vita S. Gregorii Nazianzeni Liber* (Rome: Ex Typographia Komarek, 1760).

37. Baronius expressed his feelings about this matter in a letter to his father, dated January 10, 1582 (*Vall. Cod.*, Q. 46, p. 49).

38. Calenzio, pp. 193–94.

39. Letter dated only by the year 1583 (*Vall. Cod.*, Q. 46, p. 49). An autobiographical note of Baronius, however, reveals that he left Rome for Naples on January 20, 1583, and returned on February 20 of the same year (cf. Calenzio, p. 194).

40. For example, the letter dated November 11, 1583 (*Vall. Cod.*, Q. 46, p. 49).

41. Calenzio, pp. 205–206.

42. Ibid., pp. 217–18.

43. Ibid., pp. 209–10.

44. Pateri's memoirs relates this incident (*Vall. Cod.*, Q. 56, p. 48).

45. For these I follow Ponnelle, p. 245; Calenzio, pp. 219–20; Trevor, pp. 229–32.

46. For example, his letter of June 28, 1583, to his father (*Vall. Cod.*, Q. 46, p. 50).

47. Calenzio cites the documents of the Oratorian congregation (p. 181).

48. Ibid., p. 182.

49. *Vall. Cod.*, N. 88–98.

50. Paolo Aringhi, *Vita del Card. Baronio* (unpublished manuscript), ibid., O. 58, p. 64.

51. As examples, I like to refer to two of the letters Baronius received in this regard. One from Jacobus de Marquais, abbot of Saint Martin's of Tours, dated January 31, 1588, and the other from De Rubeis, dated December 30, 1587 (Albericius, I, 176–80).

52. Baronius mentions these in a letter to Talpa, dated July 9, 1587 (ibid., III, 6).

53. Ibid., pp. 17–26.

54. Baronius refers to this in his letters to Talpa dated February 19, 1588, and to Gian Giovanale Ancina, another co-religionist, dated June 4, 1588 III, ibid., 19, 29).

55. In a letter to Talpa dated July 9, 1588 (ibid., p. 31).

4: THE SUCCESS OF A BOOK AND A MAN

1. For a full treatment of Luther's views on the evolution of the Church, see John M. Headly, *Luther's View of Church History* (New Haven and London: Yale University Press, 1963).

2. James Brodrick, *Saint Peter Canisius* (New York: Sheed and Ward, 1935), p. 676.

3. For this I follow P. Polman, *L'élément historique dans la controverse religieuse du XVIe siècle* (Gembloux, 1932), pp. 213–34.

4. Ibid., pp. 221–23.

5. Angelo Walz, "Baronio 'Pater Annalium Ecclesiasticorum,' " *A Cesare Baronio, Scritti Vari* (Sora, 1963), p. 262.
6. Polman, p. 234.
7. Broderick, p. 683.
8. Ibid., pp. 708ff.
9. Walz, p. 264.
10. Marvin R. O'Connell, *Thomas Stapleton and the Counter Reformation* (New Haven: Yale University Press, 1964), pp. 53ff.
11. Baronius mentions this in his letter to Talpa dated June 26, 1588 (Albericius, III, 30).
12. Calenzio, p. 239; Baronius' letter to Talpa dated August 12, 1589 (Albericius, III, 45). At least three different complete editions were later published from this Antwerp press.
13. Jacobus de Marquais wrote thus to Baronius on November 13, 1589 (ibid., p. 174).
14. Ibid.
15. Ibid., p. 151.
16. Ibid., pp. 159, 165.
17. Francesco Panigarola, *Il Compendio Degli Annali Ecclesiastici del Padre Cesare Baronio. . . .* (Rome: Per gli Heredi di Giovanni Gigliotto, 1590). Preface to the reader.
18. Albericius, III, 35.
19. Angelo Guiseppe Roncalli (Pope John XXIII), *Il Cardinale Cesare Baronio* (Rome: G. de Luca, 1961), pp. 40ff.
20. The famous Jesuit preacher, Antonio Possevino, was among the first to suggest this to Baronius (Baronius' letter to Talpa dated October 22, 1588. [Albericius, III, 35]).
21. Ibid.
22. Baronius mentions this in his letter to Talpa dated August 12, 1589 (ibid., p. 45).
23. Baronius communicates this message to Talpa in the letter of September 23, 1590 (ibid., p. 47).
24. In a letter Baronius wrote to Panigarola, praising his compendium, he said that he "opened the way for it (the *Annales*) to be rendered in other languages" (Caesar Baronius, *Annalium Ecclesiasticorum Apparatus* [Luca: Typographia Leonardi Venturini, 1740], p. 405).
25. Marcus Fugger's letter to Baronius dated December 16, 1589 (ibid., pp. 405-406).
26. Baronius explained the situation to Francesco Maria Tarugi, the rector of the Naples Oratory, in a letter dated May 22, 1589, and implored him that he and the other members of that Oratory may write to Neri in his behalf (Albericius, III, 41-42).
27. P. G. Bacci, *Vita di S. Filippo Neri, con la notizia di alcuni compagni del medesimo Santo aggiunta dal P. Giacomo Ricci* (Rome: Bernabo e Lazzarini, 1745), Part 2, pp. 37-56.
28. Agostino Manni, one of the early Oratorians, reports these in his remembrances about Baronius (*Vall. Cod.*, Q. 56, p. 64).
29. Baronius, *Annalium Apparatus*, pp. 422-24.
30. Memoirs of Baronius' Oratorian colleagues, Pateri and Zazzara (*Vall. Cod.*, Q. 56, pp. 48-57; Calenzio, pp. 258-60).

31. Pompeo Pateri's memoirs (*Vall. Cod.*, Q. 56, p. 48).

32. Paolo Aringhi, *Vita del Cardinale Baronio* (unpublished manuscript). Ibid., O. 58, p. 64.

33. Baronius, *Annalium Apparatus*, p. 410.

34. Letter dated June 9, 1590 (*Vall. Cod.*, Q. 46, p. 84).

35. Calenzio, p. 264.

36. The letter of Gregory XIV to the Vatican librarian, granting him permission to allow Baronius to take home for two months the codex containing the letters of Theodoretus is preserved among the documents of the Vatican Library (I, 29). A reproduction is in Calenzio, p. 922.

37. Baronius described all these in a letter to Talpa, dated July 4, 1592 (Albericius, III, 55–57).

38. Baronius made mention of this in the same letter to Talpa (ibid.).

39. Ibid.

40. Gallonio's unpublished work is kept in manuscript form in the Vallicelliana Library (codices H. 21, 22, and 23). The manuscripts and printed works on the lives of the saints which he collected are also preserved in that library (codices H. 1-20).

41. Pateri's memoirs (*Vall. Cod.*, Q. 56, p. 45).

42. Paolo Aringhi describes Baronius' charitable works during the famine in his unpublished biography (ibid., O. 58, p. 62).

43. Baronius mentions this in his letter to Talpa dated September 2, 1591 (Albericius, III, 52–53).

44. Baronius, *Annalium Apparatus*, p. 432.

45. Ibid., pp. 429–30.

46. Letter dated November 10, 1590 (Albericius, I, 215–17).

47. Letter dated March 31, 1591 (ibid., pp. 217–18).

48. Letter of the University to Baronius dated March 29, 1591 (ibid., pp. 218–19).

49. Faber's letter dated February 22, 1591 (ibid., pp. 222–26).

50. The letter of the president itself could not be traced, but Baronius' reply dated June 1, 1592 is published by Albericius (I, 289).

51. No correspondence from the archbishop could be located. But two of Baronius' letters to the archbishop, thanking him for the gift and at the same time rejecting it, are published by Albericius (letter dated June 1, 1592, in I, 289–90; letter dated August 3, 1592, in I, 290–91).

52. Sottomajor's long letter appreciating the scholarship of Baronius and strongly insisting that he accept the gift of the archbishop is ibid., I, 298–300.

53. Ibid.

54. Baronius' letter to his friend, Cardinal Federico Borromeo, dated October 9, 1592, disclosed this (ibid., III, 58).

55. Calenzio, p. 311.

56. This letter and Baronius' reply were included in the first volume of the *Annales* published from the Oratorian press at Vallicella in 1593 Baronius, *Annalium Apparatus*, p. 407).

57. Ibid., p. 408.

58. Ibid.

59. Letter dedicating the eleventh volume of the *Annales*, dated November 27, 1604 (ibid., pp. 426–27).

60. Riccardo Picchio, *Gli Annali del Baronio—Skarga e la Storia di Paisij*

Hilendarski (Estratto da *Richerche Slavistiche*, N. iii), in memoriam Enrico Domiani (Rome: n.p., 1954), p. 215.

61. For this, I follow Riccardo Picchio (ibid., pp. 213–14).

62. Picchio proves the dependence of Hilendar on the *Annales* through the concordance of the narratives in their texts (ibid., pp. 222–23).

63. Letter dated December 15, 1592 (Albericius, III, 59–60).

64. *Vall. Cod.*, O. 58, p. 97.

65. Pateri in his memoirs (ibid., Q. 56, pp. 48, 65) and Aringhi in his biography of Baronius (ibid., O. 58, pp. 65–66) testify to these.

66. Aringhi (ibid., p. 62).

67. Calenzio cites (pp. 323–26) the official records of the Oratorian Congregation (*Secreti*, Book III, p. 4) and the account by Antonio Gallonio, one of the participants at the election (Antonio Gallonio, *Vita del Beato P. Filippo Neri* [Rome, 1601], pp. 223–24).

68. Letter dated July 30, 1593 (copy in *Vall. Cod.*, Q. 56, p. 67).

69. Several testimonies of contemporary Oratorians about the superiorship of Baronius are found ibid., pp. 64–65.

70. Testimony of Father Pietro Consolino (ibid., p. 65).

71. The letters exchanged between Baronius and the duke regarding this are published by Albericius (I, 374–75).

72. Ibid., III, 65ff.

73. Calenzio, p. 347.

74. Baronius wrote to Talpa on September 18, 1594, about the events that led to his selection as confessor to Clement VIII (letter in Albericius, III, 68).

5: SPLENDID YEARS

1. *Vall. Cod.*, M. 12, 13, 14.

2. Ibid., M. 14, n. vi, p. 50.

3. Vatican Archives, n. 450, Book II.

4. Ibid.

5. Baronius, *Annalium Apparatus*, pp. 415–16.

6. Original manuscript copy in *Vall. Cod.*, Q. 48, pp. 21–26; for a printed version, H. Laemmer, *Analecta Romana*. Kirchengeschichtliche Forschung in romischen Bibliotheken und Archiv (Schaffhausen: Hurter, 1861), pp. 51–52, 65–78.

7. *Vall. Cod.*, Q. 48, pp. 28, 136.

8. A contemporary chronicler recorded this incident. A note to this effect contained ibid., p. 36.

9. Laemmer, *Analecta Romana*, p. 144.

10. Letter in Albericius, III, 272.

11. Ibid., p. 273.

12. Letter dedicating the work to Henry, in Baronius, *Annalium Apparatus*, pp. 424–25.

13. Letter in Albericius, II, 64.

14. Calenzio, pp. 797–98. Baronius transferred this pension to a relative, Leandro Baronio, in 1606, a year before his death. Leandro who had been a captain of the guards in the court of the duke of Urbino had been banished

from Sora and the Spanish territories because of his allegiance to the French.

15. Ibid., p. 354.

16. Ibid., p. 373.

17. Ibid., pp. 371–72.

18. G. Marciano, *Memorie Historiche della Congregatione del' Oratorio* (Napoli: De Bonis, 1693–1702), II, 39.

19. *A Cesare Baronio, Scritti Vari* (Sora, 1963), p. 163.

20. *Libro dei Decreti* of the Oratorian Congregation, Book III, p. 31.

21. This legislation was passed by the general body of the congregation on June 14, 1595 (ibid., p. 34). However, this law was changed in the following year when provisions for indefinite and even lifetime re-election was made by the decree of May 23, 1596 (ibid., p. 46).

22. Legislation passed on November 17, 1595 (ibid., p. 40).

23. Legislation of January, 1596 (ibid., p. 42).

24. The original work was *Trattato degli Instrumenti di Martirio e delle varie maniere di martoriare usate dà gentili contra Christiani descritte et intagliate in rame* (Rome, 1591). The revised Latin edition was *De. SS. Martyrum cruciatibus* (Rome: Tipographia della Congregatione dell' Oratorio, 1594).

25. (2 vols.; Rome, 1591–92).

26. *De robore bellico diuturnis et amplis Catholicorum regnis liber unus adversus Machiavellum* (Rome: Tipographia Bartholomaei Bonfandini, 1593). *De imperio virtutis, sive imperia pendere a veris virtutibus non simulatis, libro duo adversus Machiavellum* (Rome, 1593). *De Ruinis gentium et Regnorum adversus impios politicos libri octo* (Rome: Apud gulielmum Facciottum, 1596). *De antiquo et novo Italiae statu libri quatuor adversus Machiavellum* (Rome: Apud Gulielmum Facciottum, 1596). *De Jure Status, sive de Jure divino et naturali Ecclesiasticae libertatis et potestatis libri sex* (Rome: Bartolomeo Bonfandini, 1600).

27. The most complete version was edited by Francesco Soto himself— famous soprano, director of the Sistine Chapel Choir, and a member of the Oratory—under the title *Laudi Spirituali* (Ferrara: Vittorio Baldini, 1598).

28. Baronius describes the dramatic scene to his friend, Talpa, in a very long letter, dated December 3, 1595 (Albericius, I, 391–95).

29. Baronius discusses these matters in his letter to Talpa (ibid.).

30. Marciano, II, 100.

31. Zazzara's *Memoirs* (Calenzio, p. 449).

32. Barnabeus discusses at great length the frantic efforts of Baronius to escape from this dignity (Hieronimus Barnabeus, *Purpura Sancta Seu Vita . . . Caesaris Baronii . . .* [Vienna: Joh. Jacobum Wolrab, 1718], Book II, chap. iv, pp. 89–98).

33. Zazzara who was eye witness to most of these events recorded in his *Memoirs* (Calenzio, p. 457).

34. Ibid., p. 458.

35. *Vall. Cod.*, Q. 56, pp. 76ff.

36. The letter addressed to the governor of Foligno (his proper name is not given) in ibid., Q. 47, p. 22.

37. Several contemporaries testify to the simple life he led (ibid., Q. 72, p. 158, Barnabeus, Book II, pp. 98–106).

38. His letter of June 21, 1596, contains the above details (*Vall. Cod.*, Q. 46, p. 87).

39. Ibid.

40. Baronius describes in detail all the repairs and decorations made in this church in a letter to Talpa, dated February 22, 1597 (Albericius, III, 79–82).

41. Numerous descriptions of this event in Calenzio, pp. 477–80.

42. Contained in *Vall. Cod.*, Q. 56, Q. 57, Q. 60.

43. Ref. ibid., Q. 74, p. 105.

44. *Libri dei Decreti* of the Oratorians, Book III, p. 74.

45. Letter dated September 11, 1596 (Albericius, III, 182–83).

46. Letter dated September 1, 1596 (ibid., I, 413–14).

47. Baronius, *Annalium Apparatus*, pp. 419–21.

48. Baronius discussed these matters in his letter to Talpa, dated May 16, 1597 (Albericius, III, 86–87).

49. Two of such letters deal directly with this matter and are particularly poignant: the first written on September 14, 1597 (ibid., I, 449), and the other on October 4, 1597 (ibid., III, 90).

50. Calenzio refers to Zazzara's *Memoirs* (Calenzio, p. 637).

51. Ibid., p. 493.

52. Two of Baronius' letters to Talpa deal with the Ferrara affair: the first dated November 8, 1597 (Albericius, I, 456–57), the other dated November 22, 1597 (ibid., III, 91–92).

53. Baronius' letter of November 22, 1597, to Talpa (ibid.).

54. Letter to Talpa, dated May 9, 1598 (ibid., p. 97).

55. E. Sarro, *La vita del ven. Card. Cesare Baronio* (Rome: Aureli, 1862), chap. xxii, p. 131.

56. Baronius wrote to Talpa all these details in a letter dated March 6, 1599, with the stipulation that he should keep them secret for the time being (Albericius, III, 112).

57. Letter dated November 18, 1598 (ibid., III, 106–107).

58. In two of his letters to Talpa he discusses his statements at the Consistory. He also mentions the fact that he may have provoked the ire of the Spanish (letters dated February 6, and February 13, 1599 [ibid., pp. 111–12]).

59. We have record of at least one donation of Baronius at this time in the sum of 1,000 *scudi* on behalf of two nephews (letter to Talpa, October 28, 1598 [ibid., pp. 103–13]).

60. Letter dated October 21, 1598 (ibid., p. 103).

61. Letter dated February 14, 1598 (ibid., p. 94).

62. Letter to Talpa, October 28, 1598 (ibid., p. 104).

63. The above details are contained in a letter to Talpa, dated January 9, 1599 (ibid., pp. 109–11).

64. All this information is from a number of letters Baronius wrote to Talpa (June 24, 1599; January 1, 1600; January 22, 1600; April 8, 1600 [ibid., pp. 114–17, and Marciano, I, 310]).

65. Ibid.

66. Letter in *Vall. Cod.*, Q. 46, p. 76.

67. For a detailed study of Baronius' role as a restorer of historic monuments, see Giovanni Incisa della Rocchetta, "Cesare Baronio Restauratore di Luoghi Sacri," *A Cesare Baronio, Scritti Vari* (Sora, 1963), pp. 323–32.

68. The biographers of Baronius give prominent mention to this fact (Albericius, II, 91; Pateri, p. 54; Aringhi, p. 69).

69. Zazzara's *Memoirs* (Calenzio, pp. 798–99).

70. Baronius, *Annalium Apparatus*, pp. 421–22.

71. Ibid., pp. 422–24.

72. Two of their letters to Baronius, negotiating the matter (dated April 13, 1597, and May 13, 1597) in Albericius, I, 445–46.

73. G. G. Bisciola, *Epitome Annalium Ecclesiasticorum Caesari Baronii,* 2 vols. (Venice: C. Variseus, 1602–1603).

74. Baronius to Talpa, on May 18, 1600 (Albericius, III, 119–20).

75. K. Schulting, *Thesaurus antiquitatis ecclesiasticorum ex VII prioribus tomis Annalium Ecclesiasticorum Baronii ab incunabulis nascentis Ecclesiae usque ad aetatem Gregorii Magni collectus* (2 vols.; Cologne: S. Hemerdem, 1601).

76. F. Bordini, *Summorum Urbis et Orbis Pontificum series et gesta ex Annalibus Caesaris Baronii deprompta* (Paris: A. Angelerius, 1604).

77. Baronius' letter to Talpa on May 18, 1600, gives this information (Albericius, III, 119–20).

78. Ibid.

79. 12 vols. (Moguntiae: Sumptibus Jo. Gymnici et A. Hierati, 1601–1608).

80. 12 vols. (Venice: Apud Haeredem Jo. Scoti, 1601–1612).

81. Baronius, *Annalium Apparatus*, pp. 424–25.

82. For the details of Canisius' works, see James Broderick, *Saint Peter Canisius* (New York: Sheed and Ward, Inc., 1935).

83. Sarro, p. 141. For much of this information, I follow Calenzio, pp. 540–41.

84. C. Schopp, "Epistola ad Caesarem Baronium de editione Ecclesiasticorum Annalium deque sua ad Catholicos Migratione," *Epistola de veritate interpretationis catholicae in ambiguis Scripturarum locis* (Rome: A. Zannetti, 1599).

85. Ibid.

86. Bibliotheca Vallicelliana, Roma, *Mostra per il IV centenario della nascita del Card. Cesare Baronio, 1538–1938* (Rome: La Libreria dello Stato, 1938), n. 191, p. 64.

87. Nicodemo Marco (psyd.), *Cum Nicolae Crasso Juniore civi Veneto Disceptatio de Paroenesi Cardinalis Baronii ad Serenissimam Rempublicam Venetam* (Monachi: Ex Typographio Nicolai Henrici, 1607).

88. Calvin's letter to Baronius (Albericius, II, 72).

89. Several copies of the letters between the two men are preserved in the Vallicelliana Library, a complete set in *Vall. Cod.*, S. 77, pp. 534–49. These letters are also published by Albericius (scattered in Vols. II and III).

90. Letter dated September 15, 1602 (ibid., II, 92).

91. Calenzio, pp. 552–56.

6: THE TRIBULATIONS OF A CURIA CARDINAL

1. This is one of the innumerable contemporary portraits of Baronius. This can be seen in the first volume of R. Albericius, *Venerabilis Caesaris Baronii . . . Epistolae et Opuscula . . .* (Rome, 1759) and in the first volume of the *Annales*, published from Cologne in 1624. For a description of this and many other portraits and statues, see Gaetano Squilla, "Iconografio di Cesare Baronio," *A Cesare Baronio: Scritti Vari* (Sora, 1963), pp. 395–446.

2. H. J. Schroeder, *Canons and Decrees of the Council of Trent* (St. Louis: B. Herder, 1960), p. 255.

3. For a description of the roles played by these two men, see Daniello Bartoli, *Vita del Bellarmino* (Rome, 1678), Book II, p. 166.

4. Calenzio, pp. 469–70.

5. Calenzio cites an entry in the Register of the Congregation of the Index under Clement VIII (p. 155) which recorded the assignment of Baronius and Antoniano for this job on August 2, 1602 (ibid., pp. 570–80).

6. The booklet with the inscription in Baronius' own hand in the Vallicelliana Library (*Vall. Cod.*, G. 90, pp. 154–67).

7. This information comes from a letter which Bellarmine wrote to the superior of the Roman Oratory on May 4, 1612 (letter ibid., K. 9, n. vii).

8. Several of them with the approval of Baronius, ibid., G. 89, n. xvii, pp. 143–227.

9. Ibid., G. 89, G. 90, H. 48, and H. 28 contain many books which Baronius approved.

10. Dante Balboni, "Il Baronio e la riforma liturgica post-tridentina," *A Cesare Baronio, Scritti Vari* (Sora, 1963), pp. 315–22.

11. Ironically, when Jansenism became a strong movement in France in the 1740's, the Oratorians were its early supporters. The involvement was mutual for Jansen, as bishop of Ypres, had helped to found the Oratory in Belgium. Though these Oratories did not have any formal connection with the Roman Oratory, Baronius was in some ways instrumental in founding them, particularly the French Oratory. (For Baronius' role in founding the French Oratory, see Michael Join-Lambert, "Bérulle et le Cardinal Baronius," *A Cesare Baronio*, pp. 347–50. For the involvement of the Oratorians in the Jansenist movement, see H. Daniel-Rops, *The Church in the Seventeenth Century* [Garden City, N.Y.: Doubleday Image Books, 1964], II, 139–40).

12. Published in Lisbon, 1588.

13. Saint Ignatius' seventeenth rule of orthodoxy said that "one must not insist too much upon the all-powerful efficacy of grace, for fear of spreading in men's hearts the error which denies free will."

14. H. Daniel-Rops, *The Catholic Reformation* (Garden City, N.Y.: Doubleday Image Books, 1964), II, 146.

15. Baronius' letter requesting this critique from Lamata cannot be traced. Lamata, however, mentions this request in the desired treatise he sent to Baronius (Albericius, II, 113–20).

16. Ibid., pp. 124–39.

17. For a detailed treatment of Faustus' teachings, see Baronius, *Annales Ecclesiastici* (Luca, 1741), VIII, 523 ff.

18. One of Baronius' letters to his friend, Peter de Villars, archbishop of Vienna, dated March 15, 1603, deals with this topic. The letter also was ac-

companied by a copy of the above-mentioned treatise (Albericius, II, 121–22). A letter to Franciscus Lamata also contains a promise that a copy of the treatise would be soon sent to him (letter dated January 5, 1603 [ibid., III, 342]).

19. Baronius himself mentions his strong admonitions to the Jesuit fathers about this matter in his letter to Archbishop Peter de Villars (letter cited above).

20. With Franciscus Lamata, for example (see n. 18 above).

21. In his critical treatise on Molinism (Albericius, II, 126).

22. This historic memorandum is reprinted ibid., III, 3–12.

23. Ibid., p. 3.

24. Ibid., p. 12.

25. This information comes from one of Baronius' letters to his Oratorian friend, Germanico Fedeli, who at that time was tutoring the young boy at his home in Peruiga (letter dated November 29, 1602 [*Vall. Cod.*, Q. 47, p. 184]).

26. Clement's reply in Albericius, III, 12–14.

27. Ibid., p. 12. The Jesuit biographers of Bellarmine, Bartoli, and Fuligatti do not recognize this. The format of the document itself is like marginal notes relating to each point in the petition. It is not addressed to Bellarmine, and it is not signed by anyone. But throughout the document first person plural is used, as the popes generally do. All these would indicate that probably Pope Clement himself made his response in the form of marginal notes to Bellarmine's petition, as Fuligatti suggests (chap. xx).

28. *Vall. Cod.*, Q. 47, p. 184.

29. Ibid.,

30. Paolo Aringhi, *Vita del Cardinal Baronio* (unpublished manuscript). *Vall. Cod.*, O. 58, p. 70.

31. Carlo Castiglioni, *Il Cardinale Federico Borromeo* (Turin, 1931), p. 53. See also Léonce Celier, *St. Charles Borromée* (Paris, 1912), chap. ii, for a study of Charles Borromeo's career in Rome as a reformer, which was in conformity with Philip Neri's.

32. Cesare Orsenigo, *Life of St. Charles Borromeo*, trans. Rudolph Kraus (London: Herder Book Co., 1943), p. 115.

33. Ibid., p. 314.

34. Federico Borromeo, "Dicta et Facta Sancti Philippi Nerii," In Agostino Saba, *Federico Borromeo e i Mistici del suo Tempo* (Florence, 1933), pp. 261–77. For the influence of Neri on Federico, see Saba's short article, ibid., pp. 34–36.

35. Castiglioni, p. 72.

36. *Vall. Cod.*, Q. 56, pp. 84–94; Q. 46, p. 91; Q. 66, p. 91.

37. Ibid., Q. 56, p. 84.

38. Ibid., p. 85.

39. Ibid.

40. Baronius to Borromeo on October 12, 1602 (ibid., p. 90); Baronius to Borromeo on June 22, 1602 (ibid., p. 88); Baronius to Borromeo on January 4, 1603 (ibid., Q. 46, p. 91); and Baronius to Borromeo on July 27, 1604 (ibid., Q. 56, p. 95).

41. Luzzago's letter is difficult to trace, but we have a copy of the letter Baronius wrote in answer to his (Baronius to Luzzago from Ferrara, on July 2, 1598 [ibid., p. 113]).

42. Baronius to Luzzago on September 29, 1601 (ibid., p. 114), and Baronius to Luzzago on January 19, 1602 (ibid., p. 113).

43. Baronius' letter dated July 6, 1602 (ibid.).

44. The letter, undated, ibid., Q. 46, p. 104.

45. A number of Baronius' letters to the Luccan Fathers are in ibid., Q. 46, p. 70; and in Albericius, II, 150–53.

46. Dated June 20, 1604 (*Vall. Cod.*, Q. 46, p. 70).

47. Albericius, III, 336–37.

48. Letter dated August 5, 1606 (ibid., pp. 334–35).

49. Calenzio, p. 801.

50. Paolo Aringhi, for example, describes the simple way he used to move among the members of the Oratory, discouraging all deferences to him (unpublished manuscript, *Vall. Cod.*, O. 58, p. 67).

51. Ibid.

52. Dated February 8, 1602 (reprinted in Calenzio, pp. 614–15).

53. For a step by step description of the events that led to this separation, see ibid., pp. 584–89.

54. Calenzio gives the details of the measures taken by Baronius and Tarugi for this reunion (ibid., pp. 643–45, 776–91).

55. Ibid., pp. 615–16.

56. Join-Lambert, p. 347.

57. The above information comes from Aringhi's biography of Baronius (*Vall. Cod.*, O. 58, p. 69) and Pateri's memoirs (ibid., Q. 56, p. 58).

58. Pateri's memoirs (ibid.).

59. Letter in Albericius, II, p. 65.

60. Ibid., pp. 68–69.

61. Ibid., pp. 69–70.

62. Ibid., p. 101.

63. Dedicatory letter ibid., pp. 105–10.

64. Casaubon's letter dated May 7, 1603 (ibid., pp. 143–45).

65. Baronius, *Annalium Apparatus*, pp. 425–26.

66. Ibid., p. 67.

7: THE CLAMOROUS CONCLAVES

1. Baronius speaks of these in his letter to Talpa, dated April 12, 1597 (Albericius, III, 83–85).

2. This information from Baronius' letter to Talpa, dated September 15, 1600 (ibid., p. 123).

3. See Calenzio, chap. v, p. 137, n. 1.

4. Albericius, III, 133–34.

5. A list of such abuses in the Vatican Library, Cod. Lat., 5458.

6. A copy of the letter, not dated, and without mention of the confessor's name, in *Vall. Cod.*, Q. 47, p. 85.

7. It is clear from Baronius' letter to Talpa (Albericius, III, 133–34).

8. A copy of the letter in *Vall. Cod.*, N. 2, n. 16, pp. 296–328.

9. A copy of his treatise ibid., pp. 361–69.

10. Ibid., n. 17, pp. 391–419.

11. His treatise, ibid., n. 18, pp. 422–27.

12. Ibid., Q. 48, pp. 61–75.

13. Cardinal Colonna's treatise in Baronius, *Monarchia Siciliae*, pp. 45–50.

14. Ibid., pp. 49–70.

15. Manuscript copy in Vatican Library, Codex, Vat. Lat. 13453.

16. Pietro Strozzi's treatise in *Vall. Cod.*, Q. 38, p. 100; Sismondi's, ibid., p. 111; Rinaldi's, ibid., N. 2, n. 7, pp. 150–57.

17. Calenzio, pp. 717–18.

18. Scotus' letter requesting Baronius to intervene in this matter through the Spanish ambassador in Rome, in *Vall. Cod.*, Q. 46, p. 95.

19. *Tractatus de Monarchia Siciliae*. Accessit Ascanii cardinalis Columnae de eodem tractatu judicium cum ejusdem cardinalis Baronii responsione apologetica et epistola ad Philippum III Regem Hispaniae nunc primum editum (Paris: Hadrianum Beys, 1609).

20. A copy of this letter in Caesar Baronius, *Monarchia Siciliae* (Torino: Bottega d'Erasmo, 1958), pp. 71–74.

21. *Vall. Cod.*, Q. 46, p. 93.

22. A copy ibid., Q. 38, pp. 92–94. For a printed version of this edict in three languages: Spanish, Latin, and French, see Felipe III, rey de España, *Edicto del Rey Don Phelippe d'España contra el Tractado della Monarchia de Sicilia enxerido per Caesar Baronio Cardinal en el tomo undecimo de sus Annales Ecclesiasticos* (Palermo, 1610). The king's edict is dated October 3, 1610, but the date of its promulgation is given as September 17, 1610.

23. Calenzio, pp. 718–19.

24. For example, the Parisian theologian and university professor, L. E. Du Pin, anonymously published his *Defense de la Monarchie de Sicilie contre les enterprises de la Cour de Rome* (Amsterdam: Lucas, 1716).

25. There are two contemporary sources which provide all the details of this dramatic incident. One is the detailed daily report of Cardinal Joyeuse on the activities of the College of Cardinals, prepared for Henry IV of France (A French and Italian copy of it in *Vall. Cod.*, Q. 58, pp. 1–96. A printed version in *Les Ambassades et Negotiations de l'ill. et rev. Cardinal Du Perron* [Paris, 1623], pp. 313 ff). The other is a letter from the Oratorian priest, Severani, to an unidentified co-religionist in Naples (*Vall. Cod.*, Q. 38, p. 239).

26. Francesco Ruffini, *Perchè Cesare Baronio Non Fu Papa* (Perugia: Stab. Tip. Vincenzo Bartelli & C., 1910), p. 26.

27. Calenzio, p. 663.

28. (Anonymous), *Conclavi de' Pontifici romani quali si sono potuti trovare fin a questo giorno* (1667), p. 311.

29. Ruffini, p. 27.

30. Calenzio, p. 690.

31. A letter of Ambassador Scaglia to the duke of Savoy, dated March 11, 1605, reproduced in Ruffini, pp. 27–30. A letter from Cardinal Aldobrandino, after the election, expressing his disappointment about the futility of their efforts, also ibid., p. 31.

32. Ibid., pp. 29–30.

33. The original tally sheet on which Baronius recorded the number of votes each cardinal received, in *Vall. Cod.*, Q. 72, p. 490.

34. *Conclavi de' Pontifici*, p. 328.

35. Nicolo Barozzi, Guglielmo Berchet, eds., *Relazioni degli Stati europei lette al Senato dagli Ambasciaturi veneti nel Secolo XVII*, Serie I, Spagna, Vol. I (Venice, 1856), p. 388.

36. *Conclavi de' Pontifici,* p. 340.
37. Ruffini, p. 35.
38. Ibid.
39. Ibid. Also, Baronius' letter to Talpa, dated April 25, 1605 (Albericius, II, 216). Baronius implies in this letter that he was secretly and tactfully promoting the candidacy of Medici in order to divert the interest of the cardinals from himself. He then expresses his satisfaction about the success of his efforts.

Soon after the elevation of Leo XI, Baronius approached the new pope to recommend to him the cause of Carlo Borromeo's canonization. Not only did Leo accept this recommendation, but he also volunteered to take the necessary steps for the canonization of Philip Neri. Aside from the affection Leo held for Neri, this generosity may be also interpreted as a gesture of gratitude to Baronius for his help in the election (Zazzara's *Memoirs,* p. 112; Calenzio, pp. 680-81).

40. Ibid., pp. 695-97.
41. *Vall. Cod.,* Q. 56, p. 65.
42. Ibid., p. 52.
43. *Conclavi de' Pontifici,* p. 316.
44. Ruffini, p. 36.
45. A copy of Cardinal Joyeuse's letter to Henry IV, dated May 19, 1605, in *Vall. Cod.,* Q. 58, pp. 38-46. Also in *Conclavi de' Pontifici,* pp. 347-57.
46. *Practicarum Conclusionum Juris in omnis foro frequentiarum* (Rome, 1605-1608).
47. Calenzio, p. 682.
48. *Conclavi de' Pontifici,* p. 361.
49. *Vall. Cod.,* Q. 58, pp. 38-46; *Conclavi de' Pontifici,* pp. 347-57.
50. *Conclavi de' Pontifici,* p. 358.
51. Calenzio, p. 937 (he refers to a manuscript of Amideno in the Vatican Library, Codici Ottoboniani, Lat. 3187, pp. 117-18).
52. In *Vall. Cod.,* Q. 56, p. 61.
53. For this I follow Cardinal Joyeuse's report (*Vall. Cod.,* Q. 58, pp. 38-46). Also *Conclavi de' Pontifici,* pp. 362-65.
54. Ruffini, p. 41.
55. *Conclavi de' Pontifici,* p. 371. Also Joyeuse's report (*Vall. Cod.,* Q. 58, pp. 38-46).
56. The official records of the Consistorial Congregation is in conformity with the above documents cited. Calenzio refers to the document C. 3079, p. 121 of the above archives (pp. 688-89). The official records of the acts of Paul V is also in agreement, even though it piously attributes the compromise in favor of Borghese to the work of the Holy Spirit (ibid., Archives of the Consistorial Congregation, C. 3081, p. 1).
57. Ruffini cites (p. 47, n. 2) the authority of Saegmueller, *Lehrbuch des Kath. Kirchner* (Freiburg i B., 1909), pp. 362-63.
58. Ruffini, pp. 44-46. For a detailed study of this matter see Pivano, *Il "Veto" od "Exclusiva" nell' Elezione del Pontifice.* Estratto a Studi in onore di Vittorio Scialoja (Prato, 1904); Vidal, *Le Veto d'exclusion en matière d'élection Pontificale* (Toulouse, 1906); Eisler, *Das Veto der katholischen Staaten bei der Papstwahl seit dem Ende de 16 Jahrhunderts* (Vienna, 1907).
59. Ruffini, p. 44.
60. Ibid., pp. 47-61.

61. Sofia E. Vaccaro, "Perchè il Card. Cesare Baronio non fu papa e non fu santo," *Almanacco dei Bibliotecari Italiani*, 1957, pp. 91–96.

62. Gaetano Catalano, *Il Cardinale Cesare Baronio el a "Regia Monarchia Sicula,"* Estratto da Raccolta di scritti in onore di Arturo Carlo Jemolo, Vol. I, Part I (Milan: Dott A. Giuffae, Editorè, 1962).

63. Calenzio, p. 710.

8: THE FINAL YEARS

1. Calenzio, pp. 735–37.

2. William J. Bouwsma, *Venice and the Defense of Republican Liberty, Renaissance Values in the Age of the Counter-Reformation* (Berkeley and Los Angeles: University of California Press, 1968), p. 372.

3. A manuscript copy of the speech in Vatican Library, Vat. Lat. 6421 (s. XVII), pp. 557–58^V. During the controversy, this speech was reprinted many times and circulated by both sides. The Venetian sympathizers seem to have been especially anxious to publish this together with their rebuttals, for this was a particularly vulnerable document because of the ambiguity of its biblical references. For example, the Venetians published it in Latin, with Giovanni Marsili's refutation (*Duo Vota, hoc est ex animo voto prolatae sententiae, unum Illustrissimi ac Reverendissimi D. Caesaris Baronii Sorani S.R.E. Cardinalis Biblothecarii contra Serenissimam Rempublicam Venetam, alterum Excellentissimi D. Joannis Marsilii Neapolitani Theologi, pro eadem Serenissima Republica.* n.p., 1606). A French version was published together with a rebuttal by an anonymous author (*Avis du Cardinal Baronius Au Pape Paul Cinquiesme, Touchant l'Excommunication des Vénitiens; Response à l'Avis Cardinal Baronius.* . . . n.p., n.d.).

4. A copy in *Vall. Cod.*, Q. 44, pp. 289–91 (letter not dated).

5. Bouwsma, p. 372.

6. *Controversiae Memorabiles inter Paulum V. Pontificem Max. et Venetos, Acta et Scripta Varia.* Summa fide ex Italico in Latinum Sermonem conversa prout Romae et Venet. Excusa prodierunt (in Villa Sanvicentiana, apud Paulum Marcellum: Sumptibus Caldovianae Societatis, 1607), p. 84.

7. This position is at least partially supported by John a Tedeschi in his review of Bouwsma's book in the *Journal of Modern History*, 44 (1972), 259–62. For a more elaborate critique of Bouwsma's central thesis see Renzo Pecchioli's review of the work in *Studi Veneziani*, 13 (1971), 693–708.

8. Bouwsma, pp. 339–352.

9. Ibid., p. 329.

10. Ibid., pp. 247, 333, 334, 338, 343.

11. Ibid., pp. 332–33, 343.

12. Ibid., p. 344.

13. For the details above, I follow Bouwsma, ibid., pp. 339–54.

14. Paul V's bull of excommunication, dated April 17, 1606, in *Controversiae Memorabiles*, pp. 3–13.

15. Bouwsma, pp. 417–482.

16. The letters of the Doge and the Senate to the ecclesiastical authorities

and to the people of Venice, announcing this order, *Controversiae Memorabiles*, pp. 14-21.

17. Antonius Quirinus, *Dissertatio de Jure Serenissimae Reipublicae Venetae in Turbis, quae Illi Movetur a Sanctitate Papae Pauli V*. Auctore Antonio Quirino, Senatore Veneto, ad Patriam suam ac universam ipsius Reipublicae dominum. Impressa Italice Venetiis, Apud Evangelistam Deuchinum, 1606 (ibid., pp. 24-80).

18. Venetiis, Apud Robertum Meietum, 1607 (ibid., pp. 81-168).

19. *Controversiae Memorabiles*, p. 168.

20. *Tractatus de Interdicto Sanctitatis Papae Pauli V*. In quo demonstratur, non esse legitime publicatum, ac multis de causis non obligari Ecclesiasticos illud exsequi, nec illud ab ipsis sine peccato observari. Venice: Apud Robertum Meietum, 1606 (*Controversiae Memorabiles*, pp. 169—).

21. Bouwsma, p. 374.

22. Ibid., pp. 80-81.

23. *Caes. Baronii, S.R.E. Presbyteri Card. Tit. SS. Nerei et Achillei Sedis Apostolicae Bibliothecarii Paraenesis ad Rempublicam Venetam* (Augustae Vindelicorum: Apud Davidem Francum, 1606). This was one of the numerous editions published during the controversy. An Italian translation, prepared by the Florentine writer Francesco Serdonati (Rome: n.p., 1606) was also widely circulated.

24. A copy of this letter and of two official documents granting these concessions, in *Vall. Cod.*, Q. 56, pp. 108-10.

25. For the severe measures dealt against dissenting clergy see Bouwsma, pp. 382-88.

26. *Paraenesis*, p. 76.

27. See note 3 above.

28. *Gerardi Loppersii Antagonistae sententiae Baronii in Sacro Consistorio dictae propugnatio, adversus Joannem Marsilium* (Rome: L. Facius, 1607).

29. *Nicolai Crassi Junioris, Veneti Civis, Philosophi, et J. U. C. Antiparaenesis ad Caesarem Baronium, Cardinalem, pro Seren. Veneta Republica.* (Petavii: Apud Robertum Meietum, 1606).

30. *Nicodemi Macri, Senioris Civis Romani Cum Nicolao Crasso, Juniore Civi Veneto Disceptatio de Paraenesi Cardinalis Baronii ad Sereissimam Remp. Venetam* (Monarchii: Ex Typographio Nicolai Henrici, 1607).

31. Bibliotheca Vallicelliana, Roma, *Mostra per il IV centenario della nascita del Card. Cesare Baronio, 1638-1938* (Rome: La Libreria dello Stato, 1938), n. 191, p. 64.

32. Among them was *Alexandri Lereciae I. C. et Patritii Veronesis ad Illustriss. Caesarem Baronium Presb. Cardinalem epistola de Romanae Curiae rapacitate* (n.p., n.d.).

33. *Discorso Inedito del Ven. Card. Cesare Baronio, Quod Haeretici Sint Habiti Qui Obstinate Jura Ecclesiae Lebefectant* (Rome: n.p., 1861).

34. *Ad Paulum V, Pontificem Maximum, Epistolae Duorum Clarissimorum Italiae Jurisconsultorum* (n.p., 1606). In *Controversiae Memorabiles*, pp. 68-81.

35. *Responsio Doctoris Theologi ad Expistolam Sibi Scriptam a Reverendo quodam Amico Suo de Monitorio Censurarum a Sanctitate Pontificis Pauli V, Promulgatarum Contra Dominos Venetos.* Et de nullitate illarum censurarum e Sacris Litteris, Sanctis Patribus, aliisque Catholicis doctoribus de-

sumpta (Impressa Italicae Venetiis, 1606). In *Controversiae Memorabiles*, pp. 85-105.

36. *Responsio Card. Bellarmini ad Libellum Inscriptum Responsio Doctoris Theologi ad Epistolam Sibi Scriptam, etc.* (Rome: Apud Gulielmum Facciottum, 1606).

37. See the decrees of the Fourth Session of the Council. H. J. Shroeder, *Canons and Decrees of the Council of Trent* (St. Louis, Mo.: B. Herder Book Co., 1960), pp. 18-20.

38. *Defensio Johannis Marsilii in Favorem Responsi Octo Propositiones Continentis: Adversus quod Scripsit Illustriss. ae Reverendiss. Dom. Cardinalis Bellarminus* (Venice: Apud Robertum Meietum, 1606) in (*Controversiae Memorabiles*, pp. 171-422).

39. Bouwsma, pp. 400-401.

40. *Controversiae Memorabiles*, pp. 423-425.

41. For details, see Bouwsma, pp. 400-401.

42. *Tractatus et Rosolutio circa Valorem Excommunicationum.* Joh. Gersonis Theologi et Cancellarii Parisiensis, Doctoris Christianissimi (n.p., n.d.) (ibid., pp. 426-39).

43. Bouwsma, p. 395.

44. *Responsio Card. Bellarmini ad Libellum, Cujus Inscriptio Est: Tractatus et Resolutio Circa Valorem Excommunicationum Joh. Gersonis Theologi et Cancellarii Parisiensis* (Rome: Apud Gulielmum Facciotum, 1606) (ibid., pp. 441-75).

45. *Apologia Adversus Oppositiones Factas ab Illustrissimo ac Reverendiss. Domino Card. Bellarmino, ad Tractatus et Resolutiones Johan. Gersonis Circa Valorem Excommunicationum.* Patris Magistri Pauli Veneti, Ordinis Servorum (Venice: Apud Robertum Meietum, 1606) (ibid., pp. 477-662).

46. One of them ibid., pp. 669-72.

47. Calenzio, p. 750, Bouwsma, pp. 404-407.

48. Bouwsma, pp. 391, 479-482.

49. The archives of the Consistorial Congregation; records for the year 1607, pp. 66-67 (Calenzio reproduces it, pp. 944-45).

50. For details of the above, see Bouwsma, pp. 412-416; Ludwig Freiherr von Pastor, *The History of the Popes*, trans. Dom Ernest Graf (London: Kegan Paul, etc., 1937), XXV, 111-181. For a contemporary report of the diplomatic dealings of Joyeuse, see *Vall. Cod.*, Q. 39, pp. 25-32.

51. For example, Joyeuse wrote to Baronius immediately after he had reached an agreement with the Venetian authorities in which he explained the nature of the settlement. Letter, dated April 21, 1607, in *Vall. Cod.*, Q. 39, p. 42.

52. Calenzio, p. 764.

53. Zazzara's *Memoirs* (ibid., p. 750, 756-757).

54. Hierat's letter to Baronius, dated March 24, 1607 (Albericius, III, 335-36).

55. The letters dated May 1, and June 17, 1606 (ibid., II, 228-31).

56. Letter of Pignorius, dated 1605 (no month, no date) (ibid., pp. 222-23). The book he dedicated to Baronius was *Vetustissimae Tabulae aeneae, scaris Aegyptiorum Simulachris Celatae, accurata explicatio, in qua antiquissimarum superstitionum origines, progressiones, ritus ad Barbaram, Graecam Romanamque historiam illustrandam enarratu, ac multa Scriptorum veterum*

loca qua explanatu qua emendantu (Venice: Apud Joannem Antonium Rampuzettum, 1605). It should be noted that the book was published in Venice but long before the interdict; otherwise, a dedication to Baronius would not have come out of that city.

57. Letter dated August 1, 1605 (Albericius, II, 217–19).

58. *Vall. Cod.*, H. 5, pp. 238–53.

59. Ibid., Q. 69.

60. Calenzio cites a number of them pp. 792–97.

61. De Sales' letter dated November, 1606 (Albericius, II, 234–35).

62. Letter, not dated (ibid., II, 237–38).

63. Letter, dated July 9, 1606 (ibid., III, 332–34).

64. Letter, dated September 9, 1606 (ibid., II, 233–34).

65. Letter, not dated (ibid., II, 66–68).

66. Baronius talks about this in his letter to Talpa, dated June 1, 1606 (ibid., III, 135). Baronius' letter to Sponde, dated August 31, 1606, granting permission to prepare the compendium (ibid., II, 232). Sponde's two-volume compendium of the twelve volumes of the *Annales* came out from Paris in 1612. This was one of the better Latin compendiums, underwent many editions, and was translated into various languages.

67. Baronius, *Annalium Apparatus*, p. 428.

68. *Vall. Cod.*, Q. 74, p. 120.

69. Ibid., Q. 7. The original manuscripts of the previous twelve volumes, written in Baronius' own hand, in the Vatican Library N. 5684–5695.

70. Letter dated February 17, 1607 (ibid., Q. 46, p. 92).

71. Letter dated April 14, 1607 (ibid.).

72. Calenzio, pp. 771–72.

73. Ibid., pp. 803–4.

74. *Vall. Cod.*, Q. 46, p. 96.

75. H. Barnabeus, *Purpura Sancta, seu Vita . . . Caesaris Baronii* (Vienna Austria: Joh. Jocobum Wolrab. 1818), Book II, p. 138.

76. Ibid., Book II, chap ix, pp. 131–47.

77. Ibid.

78. A contemporary report of the ceremonies in *Vall. Cod.*, Q. 74, p. 125. Bucci's oration was immediately published. See M. A. Bucci, *In Funere Caesaris Baronii oratio habita in Ecclesia S. Mariae et Gregorii in Vallicella* (Rome: Zannetti, 1607).

79. Mucanzio's funeral oration in *Vall. Cod.*, Q. 74, pp. 140–54.

80. They are ibid., pp. 176–213.

81. Ibid., pp. 222–44.

82. The provisions of his will drawn up on January 4, 1606, and revised several times subsequently (Calenzio, pp. 816–22).

83. *Libro dei Decreti* of the Oratorians, Book IV, p. 142. (Calenzio, pp. 821–22).

84. These testimonies are scattered in several *Vallicelliana Codices*, namely Q. 56, Q. 58, Q. 59, Q. 72, Q. 74, Q. 75, O. 58. Calenzio summarizes them in pp. 844–62. Barnabei does the same, Book III, chap. xiv, pp. 232–42.

85. Her testimony in *Vall. Cod.*, Q. 72, pp. 447ff., Calenzio, pp. 853–54.

86. Ibid.

87. Ibid.

88. *Vall. Cod.*, Q. 72, p. 499.

89. Baronius' testimony, reprinted in Calenzio, pp. 946–56.

90. Francesco Neri, a Jesuit and a relative of Philip recorded this (*Vall. Cod.*, Q. 56, p. 66).

91. His letter dated May 4, 1610 (ibid., Q. 75, p. 57).

92. Her testimony (ibid., p. 39).

93. Three letters from the bishop of Sora to the Oratorians in Rome, written in 1624, deal with this procedure (ibid., pp. 25-27).

94. Sophia E. Vaccaro, "Perchè il Card. Cesare Baronio non fu papa e non fu santo," *Almanacco dei Bibliotecari Italiani*, 1957, pp. 91-96.

9: BARONIUS THE HISTORIAN

1. Vatican Library, Lat. Cod., N. 3798, Part I, p. 110.

2. Caesar Baronius, *Annalium Ecclesiasticorum Apparatus* (Lucca: Typis Leonardi Venturini, 1740), p. 395.

3. Ibid., pp. 395-99.

4. Ibid.

5. Arnaldo Momigliano, "Pagan and Christian Historiography in the Fourth Century A.D.," *The Conflict Between Paganism and Christianity in the Fourth Century*, ed. A. Momigliano (Oxford-Warburg Studies; Oxford: Clarendon Press, 1953), pp. 91-93.

6. Ibid., pp. 91-92.

7. Ibid., p. 92.

8. For a detailed study of Luther's views in this connection, see John M. Headly, *Luther's View of Church History* (New Haven and London: Yale University Press, 1963). Also, E. Harris Harbison, *A Christian Scholar in the Age of the Reformation* (New York: Charles Scribner's Sons, 1956), pp. 133-35.

9. John T. McNeill, *The History and Character of Calvinism* (New York: Oxford University Press, 1967), p. 123.

10. Herbert Butterfield, *Christianity and History* (London: G. Bell and Sons, Ltd., 1950), pp. 1-2.

11. Hubert Jedin, *A History of the Council of Trent*, trans. Ernest Graf (St. Louis: B. Herder Book Co., n.d.), I, 139-65. Also, Harbison, pp. 35-37, 92-94.

12. G. Billanovich's interesting article shows how Petrarch attempted textual criticism. "Petrarch and the Textual Tradition of Livy," *Journal of the Warburg and Courtauld Institutes* XIV, No. 2 (1951): 137-208.

13. Muretus' commentaries on Terentius and Patullus are especially famous. See his *Opera*, ed. David Ruhnkenius (4 vols.; Lugdunae Batavorum, 1789).

14. Caesar Baronius, *Monarchia Siciliae* (Turin: Bottega d'Erasmo, 1958), p. 3.

15. Caesar Baronius, *Annales Ecclesiastici* (Lucca: Typis Leonardi Venturini, 1739), IV, year 324, n. cxviii, 69; *The Treatise of Lorenzo Valla on the Donation of Constantine*, ed. Christopher B. Coleman (New Haven: Yale University Press, 1922).

16. Beatrice R. Reynolds, "Latin Historiography: A Survey 1400-1600," *Studies in the Renaissance* Vol. II (1955), 17.

17. Aristotle, *Poetics*, 9. 1451 b. 7; 23. 1459 a. 22.

202

18. Polybius, *The Histories*, I. 14; III. 31–32; IX. 2, 6.
19. For example see Saint Philip Neri's exhortation to a group of followers including Baronius, Cardinal Federico Borromeo, Cardinal Agostino Cusano, Cardinal Agostino Valier, Abbot Maffa, and various other prominent figures at the conclusion of a typical evening's discussion at the Oratory, in this particular case on the nature of Christian felicity. Unpublished manuscript, prepared by Cardinal Valier, *Vall. Cod.*, R. 62, pp. 45ff.
20. Cicero, *Brutus*, X. 42.
21. Reynolds, "Latin Historiography. . . ," p. 8.
22. Ibid., p. 9.
23. Beatrice Reynolds, "Shifting Currents in Historical Criticism," *Journal of the History of Ideas*, XIV (1953): 477.
24. Ibid.
25. Ibid., pp. 479–80.
26. Ibid., p. 492. For an extensive analysis of the historiographical principles of these men see ibid., pp. 479–492.
27. Baronius, *Annalium Apparatus*, p. 396.
28. In the "ad lectorem" of Volume X of the *Annales*. Lucca edition (1743), vol. XIV, 285.; *Annalium Apparatus*, pp. 398–99.
29. F. Gilbert, "Barnardo Rucellai and the Orti Oricellari," *Journal of the Warburg and Courtauld Institutes* XII (1949): 127; G. Pellegrini, *L'umanista Bernardo Rucellai e le opere storiche* (Livorno, 1920), p. 19.
30. Reynolds, "Latin Historiography . . . ," p. 9; George Huppert, *The Idea of Perfect History* (Urbana, etc.,: University of Illinois Press, 1970), pp. 15–21, 44–45.
31. Reynolds, ibid., pp. 16, 58.
32. *Annalium Apparatus*, p. 396.; Baronius to Talpa, Dec. 9, 1589 (Albericius, III, 50–51).
33. Baronius to Talpa on December 9, 1589 (Albericius, III, 50–51).
34. Reynolds, "Latin Historiography . . . ," p. 56.
35. Momigliano, "Pagan and Christian Historiography . . . ," pp. 88–89.
36. Ibid.
37. William J. Brandt, *The Shape of Medieval History* (New Haven, Conn., 1966), pp. 76, 73, 51.
38. Reynolds, "Latin Historiography . . . ," p. 9.
39. Donald R. Kelley, "Historia Integra: Francis Baudouin and His Conception of History," *Journal of the History of Ideas* 25 (1964): 35–57; Huppert, *The Idea of Perfect History*, pp. 93–94.
40. Ibid.
41. Baronius, *Annalium Apparatus*, p. 396.
42. Here Baronius' views seem to be similar to Benedetto Croce's in his distinction between chronicler records and history, but Baronius considered the chronicle far better for the discernment of truth while Croce upheld the necessity of synthesis, analysis, and interpretation. (Benedetto Croce, *History: Its Theory and Practice*, trans. Douglas Ainslee, (New York: Harcourt, Brace and Co., Inc., 1921), pp. 11–26).
43. *Vall. Cod.*, Q. 8, n. 1.
44. *Annalium Apparatus*, pp. 398–99.
45. *Annales* (Lucca: Typis Leonardi Venturini, 1743), XIV, 285.
46. In the preface to his edition (*Annalium Apparatus*, p. 254).
47. Momigliano, "Pagan and Christian Historiography," pp. 91–92.
48. Ibid.

49. Lewis Ellis du Pin, *The Universal Library of Historians* (London: R. Bonwicke, etc., 1709), pp. 7–28.

50. Its title is: *Monumenta varia collecta a Caesare Baronio S.R.E. Card. ex auctoribus et codicibus manuscriptis multarum bibliothecarum pro augendis annalibus ecclesiasticis jam scriptis et etiam scribendis sive continuandis* (*Vall. Cod.*, Q. 6).

51. *Index voluminum et operum scriptorum latinorum et graecorum tempore Cardinalis Baronii Romae et alibi in Bibliothecis existentium* (ibid., C. 28).

52. *Photii Patriarchae Constantin. Schismatici Epistolae Graecae-Latinae item aliorum epistolae in causa ejusdem Photii* (ibid., C. 29).

53. Metius' letter dated July 21, 1601, indicates this (ibid.).

54. Ibid., H. 1–H. 20.

55. These two volumes are in three Vallicelliana codices (H. 21–H. 23).

56. See chap. iv, n. 39–40.

57. Elena Pinto, *La Bibliotheca Vallicelliana in Roma*, Miscelanea R. Societa Romana (Rome: n.p., 1930).

58. *Vall. Cod.*, H. 24.

59. Sigonio's letter, dated December 18, 1579, requesting Baronius to examine the work, in R. Albericius, *Epistolae et opuscula . . . Caesaris Baronii* (Rome: Typographia Komarek, 1759–1770), III, 139.

60. Milan, 1734.

61. Caesar Baronius, *Annales Ecclesiastici*, IV (Lucca: Typis Leonardi Venturini, 1739), year 324, n. xiv, 34–35. For a fuller treatment of Fulvio Orsini's collection of historical documents, and their service to historians, see Pierre de Nolhac, *La Bibliotheque de Fulvio Orsini contributions à l'histoire des collectiones d'Italie et à l'étude la renaissance* (Paris, n.p., 1887).

62. His letters (Albericius, I, 292–98).

63. Ibid., II, 145–56.

64. Ibid., pp. 99–101.

65. *Annales*, VII (Lucca: Typis Leonardi Venturini, 1741), year 425, nos. v–vii, 245–47.

66. Faber's letter, dated November 1, 1605 (Albericius, III, 326–29).

67. His letter (ibid., I, 303–305).

68. Baronius' letter (n.d.) to Lollinus, requesting this favor (ibid., pp. 451–52); Lollinus' two letters (n.d.) which accompanied the above documents (ibid., pp. 451–56).

69. His letter, dated January 28, 1603 (ibid., II, 111–12).

70. Copy of Baronius' letter to Petavius, dated November 4, 1604 (*Vall. Cod.*, Q. 44, p. 242).

71. Chap. III, pp. 60–61.

72. Flavio Biondo, *Historiarum ab inclinatione Romanorum imperii decades* III (Basel, 1531); Pius II (Aeneus Sylvius Piccolomini), *Cosmographia* (Basel, 1571). For more information of archaeology and historiography of the time please see Arnaldo Momigliano, "Ancient History and the Antiquarian," *Journal of the Warburg and Courtauld Institutes*, XIII, (1950): 291.

73. For an excellent account of the historical data uncovered in the catacombs, see Cavaliere di Rossi, *Roma Sotteranea*, (2 vols; n.p., 1879); I. B. de Rossi, *Inscriptiones Christianae urbis Romae, Septimo Saeculo antiquiores* (2 vols.; n.p., 1861 and 1888).

74. *Annales,* I (Lucca: Typis Leonardi Venturini, 1738), year 57, n. cxiv, 456–57.
75. Ibid., II, year 130, n. ii, 117–18.
76. Ibid., year 226, nos. vii–x, pp. 474–75.
77. Ibid., IV, year 324, nos. lx–lxii, 50–52.
78. Ibid., II, year 119, n. ii, 83–85.
79. Ibid., year 120, nos. i–iii, pp. 87–88.
80. Ibid., IV, year 324, nos. xiii–xvii, 34–35.
81. Ibid., VII, year 425, nos. iv–v, 244–46.
82. *Annalium Apparatus,* n. cxvii, pp. 473–80; *Annales,* I, year 44, n. xxv, 296.
83. Fossati, "Il metodo degli Annali ecclesiastici del card. Baronio," *Scuola Cattolica,* LVI (1938): 542.
84. Ibid.
85. Isaacus Casaubonus, *De Rebus Sacris et Ecclesiasticis Exercitationes* XVI. Ad Cardinalis Baronii Prologomena in *Annales* et primum eorum partem, de D. M. Jesu Christi Nativitate, Vita, Passione, Assumptione. Cum prolegomenis auctoris, in quibus de Baronianis Annalibus candide disputatus (Geneva: Sumptibus Joannis Antonii et Samulis De Tournes, 1665), Prolegomena, pp. 4–5.
86. Pius II (Aeneus Sylvius Piccolomini) *De liberorum educatione,* ed. J. S. Nelson (Washington, 1940), p. 187.
87. Pius II (Aeneas Sylvius Piccolomini), *Historia Bohemica* (Basel, 1575).
88. Reynolds, "Latin Historiography . . . ," p. 12.
89. G. Saitta, *Il pensiero italiano nell' umenesimo e nel Rinascimento.* (Bologna, 1949). 1, 188.
90. *Annalium Apparatus,* p. 398.
91. *Annales,* XI (Lucca: Typis Leonardi Venturini, 1742), year 604, n. xxxix, 62.
92. *Annalium Apparatus,* p. 398.
93. *Annales,* III (Lucca: Typis Leonardi Venturini, 1738), year 218, n. xc–xcvi, 660–63; *Annales,* IV, year 326, nos. xviii–xxii, 167–69. For a detailed study of Baronius' disagreements with Eusebius, see Banjamino Santoro, "Eusebio Giudicato dal Baronio," *Per Cesare Baronio Scritti Vari.* Nel Terzo centenario della sua Morte. (Rome: Athenaeum, 1911), pp. 331–54. Also, I. Daniele, *I documenti Constantiniani della "Vita Constantini" di Eusebio Cesarea* (Rome: n.p., 1938).
94. Angelo Walz, "Baronio, 'Pater Annalium Ecclesiasticorum,' " *A Cesare Baronio, Scritti Vari* (Sora: n.p. 1963), p. 271; *Annales,* XI, year 604, n. xl, 62.
95. *Annalium Apparatus,* p. 396.
96. *Annales,* I, year 44, n. i, 388.
97. P. Polman, *L'élément historique dans la controverse religieuse du XVIe siècle* (Gemblous, n.p., 1932), p. 530; Antonius Pagius, "In criticam Baronii, praefatio ad lectorem," *Annalium Apparatus,* pp. 260–61.
98. Ibid.
99. Calenzio, p. 242.
100. *Annales,* XIV (Lucca: Typis Leonardi Venturini, 1743), 285.
101. Letter dated December 9, 1589 (Albericius, III, 50–51).
102. *Annales,* IV, year 324, n. cxviii, 69.
103. Ibid.

104. Letter to Talpa, dated December, 1590. See, M. Borelli, ed., "Memorie Baroniane dell'Oratorio de Napoli," *A Cesare Baronio*, Scritti Vari (Sora, n.p., 1963). pp. 110–11.

105. *Vall. Cod.*, Q. 47, p. 20.

106. Hieronymus Fuscus, *De donatione Constantini Magni Ecclesiae Romanae plura et praecipua, adversus jam defunctum Cardinalem Baronium.* The unpublished manuscript in Bibliotheca Casanatense, Roma. ms. 1030.

107. *Annales*, IV, year 324, nos. i–lx, 30–50.

108. Walz, p. 273.

109. Caesar Baronius, *Tractatus de Monarchia Siciliae* (Leyden: Sumptibus Petri Vander Aa., n.d.; reproduced by Bottega d'Erasmo [Turin: n.p., 1958]; G. De Libero, *Cesare Baronio Padre della storia ecclesiastica* (Rome: Tipographia Moderna Pia Societa San Paolo, 1939), p. 190.

110. *Annales*, XVI (Lucca: Leonardi Venturini, 1744), year 996, n.l., 361–62.

111. Angelo Walz, *Studi storiografici* (Rome: n.p., 1940) p. 16; E. A. Rayan, *The Historical Scholarship of Saint Robert Bellarmine* (New York: n.p., 1946), pp. 157ff; Walz, "Baronio 'Pater Annalium Ecclesiasticorum,' " p. 274.

112. Rayan, Ibid.

113. *Annalium Apparatus*, p. 395.

114. *Annales*, XV (Lucca: Typis Leonardi Venturini, 1744), year 867, n. xcvi, 116.

115. Ibid.

116. Letter dated August 5, 1589 (Albericius, III, 44).

117. Letter dated July 20, 1591 (ibid., pp. 51–52).

118. Marcantonio Sabellico, *Rapsodiae historiarum enneadum* (Paris, 1527); Platina (Bartolommeo Sacchi), *Vitae Summorum Pontificorum ad Sixtum IV* (Venice, 1479).

119. Huppert, *The Idea of Perfect History*, pp. 118–150.

120. *Annalium Apparatus*, p. 396.

121. *Annales*, XV (Lucca: Typis Leonardi Venturini, 1744), year 900, n.i, 500.

122. Ibid., year 867, n. cxvi, p. 116.

123. Reynolds, "Latin Historiography . . . ," p. 21.

124. For a fuller discussion of this, see Herbert Butterfield, *Christianity and History* (London: G. Bell and Sons, Ltd., 1950), Introduction, pp. 1–8.

125. *Annales*, IX, year 518, ns. i–lxxxvii, 209–31.

126. Ibid., XV, year 867, n. lxxv, 108–109.

127. Arnold J. Toynbee, *A Study of History*, ed. D. C. Somervell (New York: Dell Publishing Co., Inc., 1965); William H. McNeill, *The Rise of the West* (New York and Toronto: New American Library, A Mentor Book, 1965).

128. For a discussion of Vico's concept of history, see Karl Lowith, *Meaning in History* (Chicago: University of Chicago Press, 1962), pp. 115–35.

129. For a detailed discussion on historical determinism, see Sir Isaiah Berlin, *Historical Inevitability* (New York: Oxford University Press, 1954), Sections III and IV, pp. 30–54.

130. Nicolò Machiavelli, *The Prince, and the Discourses*, ed. Max Lerner (New York: Modern Library, 1950), pp. 91–94.

131. See Jacob Burckhardt's treatment of the roles of fortune and misfortune in history in his *Force and Freedom*, ed. James H. Nichols (New York:

Pantheon Books, Inc., 1943), chap. vi; R. G. Collingwood, *The Idea of History* (New York: Oxford University Press, 1946), p. 214; also see his *An Essay on Metaphysics* (New York: Oxford University Press, 1940), pp. 290–95.

132. G. M. Trevelyan, "Bias in History," *History* XXXII, No. 115 (March, 1947): 1–15.

133. Ernest Nagel, "The Logic of Historical Analysis," *Philosophy of History in Our Time*, ed. Hans Meyerhoff (Garden City: Doubleday and Co., Inc., 1959), p. 213.

Bibliography

Baronius scholars are very fortunate in having the whole collection of his papers and memorabilia preserved in his own library, the Vallicelliana Library of Rome. The following codices of the Vallicelliana collection containing his correspondence (some, original and others, copies) and many manuscripts he collected and notes he took are particularly valuable.

C. 28 Index Voluminum et Operum Scriptorum Latinorum et Graecorum quae Tempore Caesaris Card. Baronii Manuscripta Romae, et alibi in variis Bibliothecis Servabantur.

C. 29 Photii Patriarchae Constantin. Schismatici Epistolae Graecae—Latinae, item Aliorum Epistolae in causa ejusdem Photii.

H. 1 Index vetus Nominum Sanctorum et Aliorum Monumentorum quae sunt in Codicibus Manuscriptis Collectis ab Antonio Gallonio, Congr. Orat. Rom. Presbytero.

H. 2 Officium et Vitae Sanctorum Collectae ab Antonio Gallonio.

H. 5 Vitae Sanctorum et alia Monumenta Collecta et etiam ex Graecis Codicibus Mss. Latinate donata a Viro Cl. Metio (Federico) Galatino, deinde Episcopo Termulensi, a Cardinale Baronio pluries in Annalibus Ecclesiasticis Laudato.

M. 13 Scritture Spettanti alla Francia. Tomo III: Concernénte L'Assoluzione del Ré Arrigo IV. Fatta da Papa Clemente VIII. Et una Miscellanea di varie Materia e Tempi diversi.

M. 14 Scritture Spettanti alla Francia. Tomo IV: Concernénte la Riconciliazione d'Enrico IV, Re di Francia, e di Navarra con la S. Sede Apost. Gl'Aftari della Regalia, et altri cosé diversé.

N. 2 Raccolta di varii Trattati utilissimi e rari sopra la Monarchia di Sicilia.

O. 7 De Vita, Virtutibus et Gestis B. Philippi Nerii et Instituto Congregationis Oratorii. Libri VIII. Scripti ab Auctore Coaevo et ejus discipulo. Opus authographum, multis in locis correctum et auctum a Caesare Card. Baronio et aliis.

O. 58 Vitae et Sententiae, Gestae et Dicta Patrum Congregationis Oratorii de Urbe, a S. Philippo Nereo Fundata, hic a Paulo Aringho Congregationis ejusdem Presbytero diligenter in unum collecta.

Q. 7   Annalium Ecclesiasticorum Caesaris Baronii—Initium Tomi XIII. Cui
         Praemittitur Ordo qui servandus proponitur in Historia Ecclesiastica
         pervestiganda, ab Adventu Jesu Christi usque ad XV ejusdem saeculum.

Q. 34   Caesaris Baronii—De Vita et Actis S. Gregorii Nazianzeni Episc. Com-
         mentarium propria manuscripta.

Q. 38   Scritture Spettanti alla Monarchia Sicilia et all'Interdetto di Venezia.
         Molte delle quali sono scritti di mano del Card. Baronio ò dal medesimo
         corrette et emendate.

Q. 39   Monumenta Historica Spectantia ad Interdictum Venetiarum sub
         Paulo V. Pont. Max.

Q. 43   Epistolae Illustrium ac Doctorum Hominum ex variis orbis partibus
         missae ad Caesarem Baronium—et Responsiones Cardinalis Baronii ad
         eosdem.

Q. 44   Epistolae Caesaris Card. Baronii ad diversos et diversorum ad Cardi-
         nalem Baronium.

Q. 45   Virorum Illustrium Epistolae Authographae ad Caesarem Card. Baro-
         nium et Card. Baronii ad eosdem et alios.

Q. 46   Epistolae Italicae Caesaris Baronii—ad Patrem, Matrem, Patrum et
         Alios itemque Aliorum ad Caesarem Baronium.

Q. 47   Lettere Scritte dal Card. Baronio a Diverse Persone e da questa al
         medesimo Cardinale delle quali Lettere alcune sono originale et altre
         copie.

Q. 48   Opuscula varia Caesaris Card. Baronii item apologetica pro ipso vel
         ab aliis pro Baronio scripta, quibus accedunt Epistola Danielis Ray-
         mundi ad Baronium—et monumenta historica conclavis Leonis Papae XI
         et Pauli Papae V.

Q. 56   Collectanea de Rebus et Actis Caesaris Baronii—Tomus I.

Q. 57   Collectanea de Rebus et Actis Caesaris Baronii—Tomus II.

Q. 58   Conclavi doppo la morte de sommi Pontifici Clemente VIII et Leone
         XI, né quali fu trattato di elegger Papa il Cardinale Baronio . . .

Q. 73   Vita Caesaris Baronii . . . auctore Michaele Angelo Buccio . . .

Q. 74   Monumenta spectantia ad patriam, genus, vitam, Baronii Sorani,
         Congr. Orat. Romani Presbyteri, deinde Sanctae Rom. Eccl. Cardinalis
         Bibliothecarii.

Q. 75   Monumenta historica et Encomia illustrium et doctorum virorum
         spectantia ad Caesarem Baronium S.R.E. Cardinalem Biblioth.

Q. 76   Epigrammata Graeca et Latina Joannis Soromini in laudem Ss. Mar-
         tyrum Nerei et Achilei, item in laudem Caesaris Cardinalis Baronii.

         The following manuscripts in the Vatican Library also contain some infor-
mation on Baronius' life and work.

Vat. Lat. 10447 (s. XVII), ff. 166–167 (aut)
    Elci, Scipione d'
    "Asserisce il Baronio anno 146 e lo conferma com l'autorita di S. Giro-

lamo Nullam prope fuisse haeresim quae non habuerit feminam auctricem
vel adjutricem. . . ." (degli Annali Eccl. di Caesare Baronio).
Vat. Lat. 13453 (s. XVIII), ff. 253-262.

(Voti dei Cardinali Maffeo Barberini, Cardinale di Nazareth, Giangarzia
Millini e Girolamo Berneri intorno all' edito publicato in Sicilia contro il
tomo XI degli Annali del Baronio concèrnénte la Storia del Regno di
Sicilia).
Vat. Lat. 6421 (s. XVII), ff. 557-558 v.

Voto (dato nel concistotio del 17 Aprile 1606, contra la republica veneta).
Vat. Lat. 6183, ff. 319; 352 v.

Farnese, Vittoria—duchesa d'Urbini (1547-1574).
"Lettera quattro a Gulielmo Sirleto, Urbino, 30 Aprile 1565—Gradoli, 26
Febraio, 1565. Nella prima . . . nella terza parla di Cesare Baronio."

For the numerous letters Baronius wrote to the Naples Oratory, some dealing with matters of the Oratorian Congregation and others concerning the
correction and proof-reading of the *Annales*, see Mario Borelli, "Memorie
Baroniane Dell' Oratorio di Napoli," *A Cesare Baronio, Scritti Vari* (Sora:
n.p., 1963), pp. 97-222.

The earliest published biography of Baronius was Hieronimus Barnabeus'
Vita Caesaris Baronii (Rome: V. Mascardus, 1651). The next biography appeared in Raymundus Albericius' *Venerabilis Caesaris Baronii—Epistolae et
Opuscula* (3 vols.; Rome: Tipographia Komarek, 1759-1770). These volumes
contain an extremely valuable collection of Baronius' correspondence. A more
recent biography is Generoso Calenzio's *La Vita e Gli Scritti del Cardinale
Cesare Baronio* (Rome: Tipographia Vaticana, 1907). This is by far the most
erudite yet to be published, though most unreadable; but it has unlimited use
as a source book for Baronius' students. The latest biography is Giuseppe de
Libero's *Cesare Baronio Padre della Storia Ecclesiastica* (Rome: Pia Societa
San Paolo, 1939) which is a popularized and summarized version of Calenzio's
work. The only English biography is A. Kerr's *The Life of Caesar Cardinal
Baronius* (London: British Art and Book Co., 1898), which is nothing more
than a pious hagiography.

Among the works of Baronius, the most important, of course, is the *Annales*. It underwent numerous editions, the latest of which is *Caesaris Baronii
Annales Ecclesiastici* (37 vols.; Bar-le-Duc: L. Guerin, 1864-1887). These
volumes include also the continuations of Odoricus Raynaldus, Jacobus La-
derchi, and Augustinus Theiner. I have used, however, the Lucca edition in
38 volumes (Lucca: Typis Leonardi Venturini, 1738-1759) which contains the
critical comments of Antonius Pagius and the continuation of Raynaldus. The
Baronian edition of the *Martyrologium Romanum* was reprinted numerous
times but the earliest (Rome: Typographia Dominici Basae, 1586) is available
in the Vatican Library. As for the minor works of Baronius, *Tractatus de
Monarchia Siciliae* has been recently reprinted from an undated Leyden edition by Bottega d'Erasmo (Turin, 1958); *Paraenesis ad Rempublicam Venetam* is available in several languages but I used one of the earliest Latin edi-

tions (Augsburg: Apud Davidum Francum, 1606); *Vita S. Gregorii Nazianzeni* is included in Albericius' *Epistolae et opuscula;* and *Vita Sancti Ambrosii* is contained in Vol. VI of *Sancti Ambrossi . . . operibus adjunctus* (Rome: Typographia Vaticana, 1587). For a fairly complete list of the numerous continuations, translations, and compendia of the *Annales* as well as a list of the editions of other works of Baronius, see *A Cesare Baronio* (pp. 57–66). The same work also gives (ibid.) a list of the existing manuscript copies of Baronius' works.

The *Annales* provoked a historical controversy which lasted for two centuries. Numerous scholars took sides either with Baronius or against him. The following are the more important of the polemical works dealing directly with the contents of the *Annales.*

Basnage de Flottemanville, Samuel. *Annales politico ecclesiastici annorum DCXLV a Caesare Augusto ad Phocum usque.* Rotterdam: R. Leers, 1706.
_____. *De rebus sacris et ecclesiasticis exercitationes historico-criticae in quibus card. Baronii Annales ab Anno Christi XXXV in quo Casaubonus desiit expenduntur.* Utrecht: G. van der Water, 1692.
Belloti, Constantino. *Gregorius Magnus instituto Sanctiss. Patris Benedicti restitutus.* Brescia: P. Tureinus, 1603.
Beni, Paolo. *De ecclesiasticis Baronii cardinalis annalibus disputatio.* Rome: Apud Impressores Camerales, 1596.
Blondel, David. *Traité historique de la primauté en l'Eglise auquel les Annales Ecclesiastiques du Cardinal Baronius, les Controverses du Cardinal Bellarmin . . . sont confrontées avec la response du Roy de la Grand Bretagne.* Geneva: J. Chouet, 1641.
Boulanger, Jules Cesar. *Diatribae ad Isaaci Casauboni Exercitationes adversus Ill. Cardinalem Baronium.* Lyons: Haeredes G. Rovilli, 1617.
Cappel, Jacques. *Vindiciae pro Isaaco Casaubono adversus Heribertum Rosweydum recognitae et assertae cum ejusdem notis in Rosweydi librum de fide haereticis servanda.* Sedan: n.p., 1616.
Casaubon, Isaac. *De rebus sacris et ecclesiasticis exercitationes XVI ad Card. Baronii Prolegomena in Annales.* Frankfurt: J. Bring, 1615.
Casaubon, Meric. *Pietas contra maledictos patri nominis et religionis hostes.* London: ex Officina Bibliopolorum, 1621.
Comber, Thomas. *The Church History Cleared from the Roman Forgeries and Corruptions Found in the Councils and Baronius: From the Year 400 Till the End of the Fifth General Council, An. Dom. 553. Being the Third and Fourth Parts of the Roman Forgeries.* London: Printed by S. Roycroft for R. Clavell, 1695.
_____. *Roman Forgeries in the Councils During the First Four Centuries. Together with an Appendix Concerning the Forgeries and Errors in the Annals of Baronius.* London: Printed by S. Roycroft for R. Clavell, 1689.
Contelori, F. *Concordiae inter Alexandrum III et Fridericum I Imp. Venetiis*

confirmatae narratio ad veritatem scriptum stabilita . . . Caesaris Baronii auctoritas a calumniis vindicata. Paris: D. de la Noue, 1632.

Cooke, Alexander. *Pope Joan: A Dialogue between a Protestant and a Papist; Manifestly Proving That a Woman, Called Joan was Pope of Rome; Against the Surmises and Objections Made to the Contrary by Robert Bellarmine and Caesar Baronius, Cardinals; Florimondus Raemondus and Other Papist Writers, Impudently Denying the Same.* London, 1625. Reprinted in *The Harleian Miscellany.* London: White and Co., 1809.

Crakanthorp, Richard. *Virgilius Dormitans: Romes Seer Overseene. Or a Treatise of the Fifth General Council Held at Constantinople, Anno 553, Under Justinian the Emperour in the Time of Pope Virgilius.* London: Printed by M. F. for Robert Mylbourne, 1631.

D'Artis, Jean. *In Annales Ecclesiasticos Caesaris Baronii et Is. Casauboni Exercitationes. Animadversiones . . . in quibus Baronius quidem tanquam ab Aristarcho arguitur, sed a Casauboni tanquam Phalaridis sagittis liberatur.* Paris: D. Langlaeus, 1616.

Du Moulin, Louis. *A Short and True Account of the Several Advances the Church of England Made Towards Rome. Or a Model of the Grounds upon which the Papists for These Hundred Years Have Built Their Hopes and Expectations that England Would Ere Long Return to Popery.* London: n.p., 1680.

Eudaemon-Johannes, Andreas. *Defensio Annalium Ecclesiasticorum Caesaris Baronii adversus falsas calumnias, errores ac mendacia Isaaci Casauboni.* Cologne: J. Kinchius, 1617.

_____. *Responsio ad Epistolam Isaaci Casauboni.* Cologne, n.p., 1612.

Fuscus, Hieronymus. *De Donatione Constantini Magni Ecclesiae Romanae, plura et praecipue Fuscus Hieronymus adversus jam Defunctum Card. Baronium pro eadem Donatione et Laurentii Vallae Opusculum de Falsa Donatione Constantini.* Unpublished manuscript in Biblioteca Casanatense, Rome. Mss. No. 1030.

Gallonio, Antonio. *Apologeticus liber pro assertis in Annalibus Ecclesiasticis de monachatu S. Gregorii Papae adversus D. Constantinum Bellotum.* Rome: Typographia Vaticana, 1604.

Goldast von Haimensfeld, Melchior. *Reverendissimorum et illustrissimorum S. Rom. Imperii Principum Apologiae pro Henrico IV adversus Gregorii VII impias ac malignas criminationes.* Hanover: T. Villerianus, 1611.

_____. *Replicatio pro Caesarea et Regia Francorum Majestate adversus Jacobi Gresteri crimina lesae majestatis.* Hanover: T. Villerianus, 1611.

Grester, Jacob. *Commentarius Pauli Bernriedensis Antiqui Scriptoris de Vita Gregorii VII Pont. Max. Nunc Primum in Lucem Editus cum Notis per Jacobum Gresterum Societatis Jesu Theologum. Ejusdem Gresteri Caesar Baronius S.R.E. Card. Amplissimus a Melchioris Goldasti Calvinistae Inscitia ac Calumniis Vindicatus.* Ingolstadt: Ex Typographeo Adami Sartorii, 1610.

_____. Gemina Adversus Melchiorem Guldinastum Calvinianum Rep-

212   BIBLIOGRAPHY

licatorem, vel potius Quadruplatorem Defensio. . . . Ingolstadt: Andreas Angermarius, 1612.

Kortholt, Christian. *Disquisitiones anti-Baronianae . . . una cum Adami Tribechovii exercitationibus ad Baronii Annales.* Leipsige and Hamburg: Sumptibus Reumannianis, 1708.

Magendie, A. *Antibaronianus Magenelis seu Animadversiones in Annales Cardinalis Baronii . . . Quibus accesserunt quaedam ad Baronium animadversiones Davidis Blondelli.* Leyden: A. Mestrezatius, 1679.

Montaigu, Richard. *Analecta Ecclesiasticarum Exercitationum.* London: Pro Societate Bibliopolarum, 1622.

_____. *Antidiatribae ad Priorem Partem Diatribarum J. C. Bulengeri adversus Exercitationes Casauboni.* N.p., Officina Hulsiana, 1625.

Otte, Johann Heinrich. *Examinis Perpetui in Annales Caes. Baronii, Centuria I–III.* Tiguri: D. Gessnerus, 1676.

Reding, Augustine. *Vindex Veritatis Annalium Ecclesiasticorum Caesaris Baronii adversus Arrogatum Joh. Henrici Ottij Tigurini. Examen Perpetuum.* Typis Monasterii Einsidlensis, Jo. Reymann, 1680.

Rosweyde, H. *Lex Talionis XII Tabularum Cardinali Baronio ab Isaaco Casaubono Dicta; Retaliante Heriberto Rosweydo.* Antwerp: Officina Plantiniana, 1614.

Tribbekow, A. *Exercitationes ad Annales ubi desiit Isaacus Casaubonus in Academia Kiloniensi ad Disputationem Propositae.* Kiel: J. Reumannus, n.d.

The following secondary sources also have valuable information about the life and times of Baronius. Some of them also include critiques of his historiographical methods by modern commentators.

A Cesare Baronio, Scritti Vari. Sora: n.p., 1963.

Appolis, Emile. *Le "Tiers Parti" Catholique au XVIIIe Siècle.* Paris: Editions A. et J. Picard, 1960.

Bacci, P. G. *Vita di S. Filippo Neri. Con la Notizia di Alcuni Compagni del Medesimo Santo Aggiunta dal P. Giacomo Ricci.* Rome: Bernabò e Lazzarini, 1745.

Batiffol, P. *Histoire du Bréviaire Romain.* Paris: Picard, 1911.

Bouwsma, William J. *Venice and the Defense of Republican Liberty.* Berkeley and Los Angeles: University of California Press, 1968.

Brezzi, P. "Ritratto del Baronio." *Studium*, LIV (1958), 380–93.

Brodrick, James. *Saint Peter Canisius.* New York; Sheed and Ward, 1935.

Bucci, M. A. *In Funere Caesaris Baronii Oratio Habita in Ecclesia S. Mariae et Gregorii in Vallicella.* Rome: Zannetti, 1607.

Bugnini, A. "De Methodo Historico Caesaris Baronii." *Pastor Bonus*, III (1939), 473–81.

Calosi, Giovanni Battista. *Il Baronio e i Suoi Annali.* Florence: Tipographia Bodoniana di E. Morandi, n.d.

Castiglioni, Carlo. *Il Cardinale Federico Borromeo.* Turin: Tipographia della Societa Editrice Internazionale, 1931.

Catalano, Gaetano. *Il Cardinale Cesare Baronio e la "Regia Monarchia Sicula."* Estratto da Raccolta di scritti in onore di Arturo Carlo Jemolo (Volumo primo, tomo primo). Milan: Dott. A. Giuffre-Editore, 1962.

Coleman, Christopher B., ed. *The Treatise of Lorenzo Valla on the Donation of Constantine.* Text and translation into English. New Haven: Yale University Press, 1922.

Conclavi de' Pontifici Romani quali si sono potuti trovare fino a questo giorno. (Anonymous). (No place, no publisher), 1667.

Controversiae Memorabiles inter Paulum V. Pontificem Max. et Venetos. Acta et Scripta Varia. Summa Fide ex Italico in Latinum Sermonem Conversa prout Romae et Venet. excusa Prodierunt. In Villa Sanvincentiana: Apud Paulum Marcellum, Sumptibus Caldovianae Societatis, 1607.

Croce, Benedetto. *Storia del Regno di Napoli.* Bari: Gius. Laterza e Figli, 1925.

Cuthbert, Father. *The Capuchins: A Contribution to the History of the Counter-Reformation.* London: Sheed and Ward, 1928.

De Libero, Giuseppe. *Vita di S. Filippo Neri* . Rome: Oratorio di Roma, 1960.

_____. *L'Opera Polemica ed Apologetica di Cesare Baronio.* Estratto dalla Revista Roma. Rome: Instituto di Studi Romani-Editore, 1938.

Delumeau, Jean. *Vie Economique et Sociale de Rome dans la Seconde Moitié du XVIe Siècle.* 2 vols. Paris: E. De Boccard, 1957-59.

Discours d'un Religieux Professor en Théologie sur le sui et d'un voyage qu'il a esté oblige de faire à Paris à l'occasion de la doctrine de la Grâce. Avec une lettre important du Cardinal Baronius . . . Paris: n.p., 1652.

Douglas, Richard Mateer. *Jacopo Sadoleto, 1477-1547: Humanist and Reformer.* Cambridge, Mass.: Harvard University Press, 1959.

Dowling, J. G. *An Introduction to the Critical Study of Ecclesiastical History.* London: n.p., 1838.

Dragonetti de Torres, A. *Lettere Inedite dei Cardinali de Richelieu, de Joyeuse, Bentivoglio, Baronio* . . . Aquila: Vecchioni, 1929.

Du Moulin, Louis. *Declaratory Considerations upon the Present State of the Affairs of England: By Way of Supplement.* London: n.p., 1679.

Duo Vota, hoc est ex animo voto prolatae sententiae: unum D. Caesaris Baronii . . . contra serenissimam rempublicam venetam. Alterum . . . D. Joannis Marsilii . . . pro eadem serenissima republica. N.p., n.p., 1606.

Du Pin, Louis Ellis. *The Universal Library of Historians.* London: Printed for R. Bonewicke, etc., 1709.

Felipe III, Rey de España. *Edicto del Rey Don Phelippe d'España contra el Tractado della Monarchia de Sicilia enxerido per Caesar Baronio Cardenal en el tomo undécimo de sus Annales Ecclesiásticos.* 3 ottobre 1610. N.p., n.d.

Forti, G. *Vita del Venerabile Servo di Dio Cesare Baronio.* Macerata: C. Zenobi, 1672.

Fossati, Louigi. *Gli Annali Ecclesiastici del Card. Cesare Baronio.* Rome: Casa Editrice "La Scuola Cattolica," 1938.

Fossati, Louigi. "Il methodo degli Annali Ecclesiastici del card. Cesare Baronio," *Scuola Cattolica*, LXVI (1938), 538–62.

_____. "Il valore degli Annali Ecclesiastici del Baronio," *Scuola Cat-
tolica*, LXVI (1938), 682–706.

Fremotti, C. *La Riforma Cattolica del Sec. XVI e gli Studi di Archeologia
Cristiana.* Rome: Pustet, 1925.

Frugoni, Arsenio. *Incontri nel Rinascimento; Pagine di Erudizione e di Critica.*
Brescia: La Scuola, 1954.

Fueter, E. *Storia della Storiografia Moderna.* Traduzione Italiana di A. Spinelli. 2 vols. Naples: R. Ricciardi, 1943–44.

Huppert, George. *The Idea of Perfect History.* Urbana: University of Illinois
Press, 1970.

Illyricus, Flacius Matthias. *Catalogus Testium Veritatis, quin ante nostram
aetatem Pontifici Romano atque Papisimi erroribus reclamarunt.* 2 vols.
Lyons: Ex Typographia Antonii Candidi, 1597.

_____. *Ecclesiastica Historia, Integram Ecclesiae Christi Ideam, quantum
ad Locum, Propagationem, Persecutionem, Tranquillitatem, Doctrinam,
Haereses, Ceremonias, Gubernationem, Schismata, Synodos, Personas,
Miracula, Martyria, Religiones extra Ecclesiam, ac statum Imperii politicum attinet, secundum singulas Centurias, perspicuo ordine complectens:
singulari diligentia ac fide ex vetustissimis ac optimis historicis, patribus,
ac aliis scriptoribus congesta: Per aliquot studiosos ac pios viros in urbe
Magdeburgica.* Basel: Per Joannem Oporinum, 1560.

Jedin, Hubert. *Papal Legate at the Council of Trent, Cardinal Seripando.*
Translated by Frederic C. Eckhoff. St. Louis: B. Herder Book Co., 1947.

Joannes XXIII, Pope (Angelo Giuseppe Roncalli). *Il Cardinale Cesare Baronio.
Conferenza tenuta il 4 dicembre 1907 nel Seminario di Bergamo, ricor-
rendo il terzo centenario dalla morte.* Rome: Edizioni di Storia e Lettera-
ture, 1961.

Jouhandeau, Marcel. *St. Philip Neri.* Translated by George Lamb. London:
Longmans, Green and Co., Ltd., 1960.

Kelley, Donald. *The Foundations of Modern Historical Scholarship.* New
York: Columbia University Press, 1968.

Laemmer, H. *De Caesaris Baronii Literarum Commercio Diatriba.* Freiburg i.
B: Herder, 1903.

Lolli, Mario. *Cesare Baronio e gli Annali della Chiesa.* Rome: Rip. San Filippo
Neri, 1931.

Loppers, Gerard. *Antagonistae Sententiae Baronii in Sacro Concistorio Dictae
Propugnatio, adversus Joannem Marsilium.* Rome: L. Facius, 1607.

Macro, N. (Pseud.). *Cum Nicolao Crasso Juniore Disceptatio de Paraenesi
Cardinalis Baronii ad Ser. Rempublicam Venetam.* Monachi: N. Henricus,
1607.

Magendi, Andre. *Antibaronianus Magenelis seu Animadversiones in Annales
Cardinalis Baronii . . . Quibus accesserunt quaedam ad Baronium animadversiones Davidis Blondelli.* Leyden: A. Mestrezatius, 1679.

Marciano, Giovanni. *Memorie Historiche della Congregazione dell'Oratorio.*
5 vols. Naples: De Bonis, 1693–1702.

Marsilio, G. (Pseud. Nicholaus Crassus). *Antiparaenesis ad Caesarem Baronium Cardinalem pro Ser. Veneta Republica.* Padua: R. Meiettus, 1606.

Mayer, J. F. *De Fide Baronii et Bellarmini ipsis Pontificis Ambigua Ecologae.* Amsterdam, 1697.

Mercati, Giovanni. *Per la Storia della Biblioteca Apostolica Bibliotecario Cesare Baronio.* Perugia: n.p., 1910.

Momigliano, Arnaldo, ed. *The Conflict Between Paganism and Christianity in the Fourth Century.* London: Oxford University Press, 1963.

O'Connell, Marvin R. *Thomas Stapleton and the Counter-Reformation.* New Haven and London: Yale University Press, 1964.

Orsenigo, Cesare. *Life of Charles Borromeo.* Translated by Rudolph Kraus. St. Louis: B. Herder Book Co., 1943.

Paschini, Pio. *La Riforma Gregoriana del Martyrologio Romano.* Monza: n.p., 1923.

_____. *Roma nel Rinascimento.* Vol. XII: *Storia di Roma.* Bologna: L. Cappelli, 1940.

Pattison, M. *Isaac Casaubon, 1559-1614.* Oxford: Clarendon Press, 1892.

Pecchiai, Pio. *Roma nel Cinquocento.* Vol. XIII: *Storia di Roma.* Bologna: L. Cappelli, 1948.

Pecchioli, Renzo, A review of William J. Bouwsma, *Venice and the Defense of Republican Liberty. Renaissance Values in the Age of the Counter Reformation.* In *Studi Veneziani,* 13 (1971), 693-708.

Per Cesare Baronio, Scritti Vari nel Centenario della Morte. Rome: Athenaeum, 1911.

Picchio, Riccardo. *Gli Annali del Baronio-Skarga e la storia di Paisij Hilendarski.* In Memoriam Enrico Damiani. Rome: n.p., 1954.

Pirri, P. *L'Interdetto di Venezia del 1606 e i Gesuiti. Silloge di documenti con introduzione.* Vol. XIV: *Biblioteca Instituti Historici S.J.* Rome: Institutum Historicum, S.J., 1959.

Polman, Pontien. *L'élément historique dans la controverse religieuse du XVIe siècle.* Gemblous: n.p., 1932.

Ponnelle, Louis and Louis Bordet. *Saint Philippe Néri et la Société Romaine de son Temps, 1515-1595.* Paris: La Colombe, 1958.

Pontano, Giovanni Gioviano. *Le Guerre di Napoli.* Venice: n.p., 1544.

Reynolds, Beatrice. "Shifting Currents in Historical Criticism," *Journal of the History of Ideas,* XIV (1953), 471-480.

_____. "Latin Historiography: A Survey 1400-1600," *Studies in the Renaissance,* II (1955), 5-66.

Ridolfi, Roberto. *The Life of Girolamo Savonarola.* Translated by Cecil Grayson. New York: Knopf, 1959.

Ritter, Saverio. *Un Umanista Teologo: Jacopo Sadoleto, 1477-1547.* Rome: Francesco Ferrari, 1912.

Ronzy, P. "Le relations de Baronius et de Papire Masson d'après leur correspondence inédite, 1591-1607." *Annales de l'Université de Grenoble,* XXXIV (1923), 265-306.

Rossi, Filippo De. *Descrizione di Roma . . . formata nuovamente, con la auttorita di . . . celebri scrittori.* Rome: n.p., 1719.

Ruffini, Francesco. *Perchè Cesare Baronio Non Fu Papa. Contributo alla storia della 'Monarchia Sicula' e del 'Jus Exclusivae'.* Perugia: Tip. Vincenzo Bartelli & Co., 1910.

Sarra, E. *La Vita del Ven. Card. Cesare Baronio.* Roma: Aureli, 1862.

Spini, Giorgio. 'I trattatisti dell'arte storica nella Controriforma italiana", in *Contributti alla storia del Concilio di Trento e della Contrariforma.* Florence, 1948, 109–136.

Trevor, Meriol. *Apostle of Rome: A Life of Philip Neri, 1515–1595.* London: Macmillan and Co., Ltd., 1966.

Vannutelli, P. *La Vita del Card. Cesare Baronio.* Rome: A.V.E., 1938.

Walz, C. A., "La Storiografia del Baronio e la Storiografia di Oggi." *Anglicum,* XVII (1940), 88–110.

Zaccaria, F. A. *Preliminare del Roccoglitore sugli Annali del Card. Baronio.* Vol. I: *Raccolta di Dissertazioni di Storia Ecclesiastica.* Rome: Barbiellini, 1792.

Index

217